*Praise for*

# States of Race

With theoretical sophistication and analytical brilliance, this collection is essential reading that provides readers with critical tools to understand the relation between Canadian (and North American) racisms, neoliberalism, and the "War on Terror." These eight essays incisively reveal the multiple, interconnected, and transnational projects of racism through a critical race feminism that is an exemplary practice of solidarity, coalition, and critique.

> – **Inderpal Grewal**, Women's, Gender and
> Sexuality Studies, Yale University

A refreshing and thoughtful collection that explores a range of realities faced by women and feminists of colour. . . . The editors and contributors have interwoven critical race and transnational feminism, post-structuralist feminist theory, and philosophy to offer incisive analyses on a range of current topics of interest to all critical thinkers across the globe. This volume – subtle, illuminating and accessible – should be required reading for students and faculty in critical race theory, women's studies, and political and feminist philosophy courses.

> – **Falguni A. Sheth**, Philosophy and Political Theory,
> Hampshire College, Amherst, Mass.

# States of Race

## Critical Race Feminism
## for the 21st Century

edited by
Sherene Razack, Malinda Smith,
and Sunera Thobani

Between the Lines
Toronto

**States of Race: Critical Race Feminism for the 21st Century**

First published in 2010 by
Between the Lines
720 Bathurst Street, Suite #404
Toronto, Ontario
M5S 2R4

1-800-718-7201

www.btlbooks.com

**Library and Archives Canada Cataloguing in Publication**

    States of race : critical race feminism for the 21st century / edited by Sunera Thobani, Sherene H. Razack, and Malinda S. Smith.
Includes bibliographical references.
ISBN 978–1–897071–59–5

1. Race relations – History – 21st century.  2. Feminist theory.  I. Thobani, Sunera, 1957-  II. Razack, Sherene  III. Smith, Malinda Sharon, 1962-
HT1521.S73 20         305.8009'051         C2010–901689–0

Cover design by Jennifer Tiberio
Text design and page preparation by Steve Izma
Printed in Canada

**Mixed Sources**
Product group from well-managed forests, controlled sources and recycled wood or fiber
www.fsc.org  Cert no. SW-COC-000952
© 1996 Forest Stewardship Council
FSC

Between the Lines gratefully acknowledges assistance for its publishing activities from the Canada Council for the Arts, the Ontario Arts Council, the Government of Ontario through the Ontario Book Publishers Tax Credit program and through the Ontario Book Initiative, and the Government of Canada through the Canada Book Fund.

Canada Council
for the Arts
Conseil des Arts
du Canada

Canadä

ONTARIO ARTS COUNCIL
CONSEIL DES ARTS DE L'ONTARIO

*To all those who have helped to build and sustain
Researchers and Academics of Colour for Equality/Equity
(RACE)*


*All royalties from this book will be donated to RACE.*

# Contents

· · · · · · · · · · · · · · · · · · · · · · · · · · · · · · · · · · · · · ·

# Preface: A decade of critical race studies

. . . . . . . . . . . . . . . . . . . . . . . . . . . . . . . . . . . . . .

"IF YOU LOOK AROUND THE WORLD you will see that the Aryan races will not wholesomely amalgamate with Africans or the Asiatics," Canada's first prime minister, Sir John A. Macdonald, stated in the House of Commons in May 1885. Macdonald went on to conclude, "It is not desired that they come; that we should have a mongrel race; that the Aryan character of the future of British America should be destroyed."[1] Over a half-century later, another Canadian prime minister, Mackenzie King, likewise argued that if the "lower races" were permitted into Canada they would "debase" Anglo-Saxon civilization just as surely as "the baser metals tended to drive the finer metal out of circulation."[2] Reinforcing the consensus among political elites of the day, and perhaps anticipating Samuel Huntington's "clash of civilizations,"[3] Leader of the Official Opposition Arthur Meighen added that the temperaments, habits, and natures of Orientals made coexistence with them an "impossibility" and, thus, it was essential "that we maintain here our racial purity" in Canada.[4] In the early twenty-first century, Stephen Harper's Conservative government issued a new *Citizenship Guide*, which stated, "Canada's openness and generosity do not extend to barbaric cultural practices."[5] The new *Citizenship Guide* defends Anglo-Saxon civilizational practices against what it calls the "barbaric cultural practices" of the Others. What is notable about this suspect gesture, nominally in support of women's rights, is that it is blind to the persistence of violence against women in Canada, including the hundreds of murdered and disappeared Aboriginal women. It suggests, instead, that such violence lies within the *barbaric cultures* of non-Western – Asian, African, and Middle Eastern – societies. It is a contemporary expression of earlier representations of the impossibility that Others cannot "wholesomely amalgamate" with the dominant Canadian culture.

Despite over a century of discourse in which race, culture, and civilization have been inextricably linked with nation-building in Canada, the dominant imaginary of the country is a tolerant, multicultural society, one that has apologized for and moved beyond its racialized origins in the dispossession of its Indigenous peoples – First Nations, Inuit, and Métis – and the exclusion and subjugation of what Mackenzie King called its "lower races." The stubborn persistence of this imaginary presents a particularly powerful challenge to critical social theorists engaged in contesting dominant narratives of race, nation, and the racial state. This anthology draws upon the interdisciplinary research areas of Researchers and Academics of Colour for Equality/Equity (RACE) to examine the current state of critical race and anti-colonial feminist scholarship. It analyzes contemporary theoretical and political issues within the framework of the historically racialized and gendered power structures of a white settler society, and the ongoing colonial practices to demonstrate that race and gender are constitutive of the structures and subjectivities that shape the nation and the global order.

We, the editors, are three women of colour currently on the RACE coordinating committee. The book's eight chapters examine different aspects of the racialized discursive practices and socio-political institutions that shape globalization and imperialism, media representations, academic debates, solidarity initiatives between Indigenous peoples and people of colour, and transnational activism for social justice. As editors, we sought to bring together essays that would illustrate many dimensions of a Canadian feminist anti-racist theorizing. By no means exhaustive, this collection nevertheless intends to highlight themes that have helped to shape a Canadian feminist anti-racist politics, and that distinguish Canadian scholarship from critical race feminist debates elsewhere. The anthology features the work of women who are associated with the organization RACE. The first cross-Canada network of Indigenous faculty and faculty of colour, RACE was founded in 2001 with a commitment to promoting critical anti-racist and anti-colonial feminist scholarship and praxis. Over the decade, we have built an enduring national network, in dialogue and collaboration with leading international critical race scholars from the United States and Europe, who have participated in the nine RACE conferences and other events across Canada between 2001 and 2010.

The RACE network of scholars, activists, and practitioners have promoted critical race feminist scholarship and praxis in several ways, including organizing the only annual critical race conferences in Canada; building stronger research and mentoring networks among faculty of colour and Indigenous scholars at the local, national, and regional levels; and fostering stronger links between academics, community-based researchers, and social justice practitioners. RACE has organized nine annual conferences to date in almost every region of Canada. Past conferences were held at the University of British Columbia in 2001 and 2003; the Ontario Institute for Studies in Education (OISE) at the University of Toronto in 2002 and 2007; York University in 2004; Dalhousie University in 2005; the University of Regina in 2006; Ryerson University in 2008; and jointly at Concordia and McGill in 2009.

The Vancouver-based Race and Gender Teaching and Advocacy Group

(RAGTAG) was founded by Sunera Thobani in 1998 and the moment became a formative one for the RACE network. RAGTAG was a group of anti-racist scholars and activists from various academic institutions and community organizations who were committed to contesting dominant race and gender relations in teaching, learning, and service delivery. Members included Barbara Binns, Nogha Gayle, and Yasmin Jiwani. They organized a national conference and consultation on furthering race and gender studies in Canada on May 1, 2001. This first conference and national consultation was held at the University of British Columbia in Vancouver, and a seven-member steering committee was elected that included Agnes Calliste (Atlantic Canada), Yasmin Jiwani (Quebec), Sherene Razack (Ontario), Patricia Monture (Saskatchewan), Aruna Srivastava (Alberta), Sunera Thobani (British Columbia), and Vanaja Dhruvarajan (Manitoba). The conference was attended by some two hundred academics and community activists. They adopted three recommendations, which continue to shape RACE ten years on: first, to organize annual national conferences on critical race and gender issues; second, to develop a national association to enable collaboration between Indigenous peoples, people of colour and their allies, and researchers to promote critical race scholarship; and third, to build networks at the regional level.

Since then, RACE conferences have asked the thorny questions and grappled with the major issues that impact Indigenous peoples and people of colour in Canada and around the world. The second RACE conference in 2002 was organized by Sherene Razack and co-sponsored by the Centre for Integrative Anti-Racism Studies, part of the Ontario Institute for Studies in Education (OISE) at the University of Toronto. The conference brought together over eighty presenters, all of whom were scholars of colour working on critical race and feminist issues. The call for papers set the agenda, stating, "Study of racial hierarchies demands nothing less than the tools of history, sociology, anthropology, literary studies, geography, law and education, among other scholarly domains." In this multidisciplinary spirit it brought together Indigenous and Canadian scholars from across disciplines to reflect on the state of Canadian critical race scholarship and the condition of knowledge production on race issues in universities. The goals of the conference were threefold: first, to profile and critically reflect on contemporary Canadian critical race scholarship; second, to examine the structures and conditions of knowledge production on race issues in Canadian universities; and third, to examine university partnerships with communities of colour in order to explore the connections between scholarship and social change. More than 350 scholars and community activists attended the conference, and their papers covered a broad spectrum of local and global issues, including a critical analysis of the dehumanizing violence resulting from the ongoing Israeli occupation of Palestine.[6] In such contexts, what is the responsibility of intellectuals and academic-activists? This question recognized that in the post–9/11 environment, intellectuals increasingly speak the truth to power about the workings of power, but they do so in academic environments characterized by fear and censorship. How should critical race scholars in Canada face these challenges of the criminalization of dissent in universities that claim a commitment to academic freedom?[7]

In May 2003, the 3rd Annual Critical Race Conference was initiated by Sunera Thobani, co-hosted by Begum Verjee, and organized by a coalition of scholars and activists at the University of British Columbia. The conference focused on pedagogy and practice in the changed political climate of the "War on Terror." It brought together critical race educators, theorists, and community activists to critically reflect upon the structures, knowledges, and sites of action in multiple dimensions of oppression and various mediums, including the arts. The focus of the conference emphasized institutional partnerships with Indigenous communities and communities of colour, along with the creation of international citizenship linkages with Indigenous peoples and people of colour. The event was held at the First Nations Longhouse, and drew approximately four hundred participants, who helped to expand the RACE Network. The opening ceremony and keynote addresses by Jeanette Armstrong and Graham Hingangaroa Smith examined the marginalization of Indigenous scholars and students at universities built on stolen Aboriginal lands, and highlighted the necessity of developing pedagogical practices drawing upon the histories and traditions of Indigenous peoples, along with their ongoing acts of resistance. In two other keynote addresses, Nahla Abdo critically examined Israeli aggression against the Palestinian population in the aftermath of 9/11, while Sherene Razack explored the impact of the new security certificates on the citizenship rights of Muslims. Wayson Choy's address outlined the challenges faced by writers of colour in Canada. The corporatization of the university, the resistance of universities to "walking the talk" of equity practices, and the role of knowledge production in international conflict also emerged as major themes of the conference.

In the spring of 2004, the Centre for Feminist Studies at York University hosted the 4th Annual Critical Race Conference. The 2004 conference theme and resulting discussions led to a seminal publication, "Race, Racism, and Empire: Reflections on Canada," a collection of ten essays in a special issue of the journal *Social Justice* edited by Enakshi Dua, Narda Razack, and Jody Nyasha.[8] The volume was divided into three sections. The first section focused on situating the debates on race, racism, and empire in the geopolitical order, and included an introduction by the editors and essays by Sherene Razack, Sedef Arat-Koç, and Yasmin Jiwani. The second section, "Transnational Processes and the Articulation of Race and Gender," included three essays by Andil Gosine, Narda Razack, and Kiran Mirchandani. The final section, "Theorizing Anti-Racism and Racial Knowledge," included four essays by Bonita Laurence and Enakshi Dua, Himani Bannerji, Gordon Pon, and Jody Nyasha Warner. These critical race feminist essays focused attention on the unique manner in which race, racism, and empire are articulated in the Canadian context. The authors argued for the importance of Canadian critical race scholarship, "theorizing the relationship between race, racism, anti-racism and empire; exploring transnational processes in the construction of race and racism; and reflecting on the re-articulation of race and racism in Canada in the post–September 11 period as it has been shaped by local and transnational forces." Collectively, the articles pointed to the ways in which Canada was implicated in post–September 11 militarization, and global discourses which framed difference in terms of a "clash of civilizations." The essays also explored the way in which the construction of Canada as a national space has been tied to a transnational discourse of whiteness, and the ways in which such processes shape diasporic identities.

Over the next five years, the critical race and anti-colonial conference themes explored some of the major issues of the day, including racial violence; the race/culture debates within social justice theory; the question of rights and who has them in the aftermath of 9/11 and the War on Terror; and the global dimensions of race in the face of neo-liberal orthodoxy, a new imperialism, and the paradoxes of "doing good" abroad. On April 1 and 2, 2005, the James R. Johnston Chair in Black Studies, David Divine, co-hosted the fourth conference in Halifax, Nova Scotia, on the theme "Racial Violence and the Colour Line of the New World Order."[9] The conference drew attention to themes that remain salient today, including the number of Indigenous women who have been murdered and disappeared across Canadian cities, the racial profiling of Indigenous men and men of colour, and the plight of Palestinians, Iraqis, and Afghanis living under foreign occupation. The conference and its keynote speakers – Beverley Jacobs Gowehgyuseh, Anthony Farley, Isaac Saney, and Wanda Thomas Bernard – also helped focus critical race scholarship on three questions: How do we understand the tremendous racial violence in the lives of First Nations peoples and people of colour? How do we organize to end it? What are the roles and responsibilities of community activists, academics, lawyers, social workers, teachers, and other professionals in ending violence within communities and against communities of colour?

The following year, the conference moved across the country and between May 4 and 6, 2006, the Canada Research Chair in Social Justice and Aboriginal Education at the University of Regina, Carol Schick, co-hosted the 5th Annual Critical Race and Anti-Colonial Studies Conference, entitled "Race/Culture Divide in Education, Law and the Helping Professions."[10] This conference drew attention to the ways in which culture-talk elided discussions of race and racism in Canada. It asked the following question: What does it mean to employ cultural and/or anti-racist strategies for liberation? The conference keynote speakers and presenters critically interrogated the ways in which racism is organized in contemporary society through a language of culture. While racialized groups are less often portrayed as biologically inferior, as was the case in much nineteenth-century scientific racism, dominant groups – most often, although not exclusively, European and white – frequently perceive subordinate groups – most often non-whites – as possessing cultures that are inferior and overly patriarchal. Marginalized groups are marked in ways in which their cultural difference and culture-talk function to keep them confined to a secondary status. In the context of culture-talk, the rights of Indigenous peoples and people of colour are routinely infringed upon when education, legal, and health care professionals evaluate their claims, often on the basis of a superficial and racist understanding of cultural difference. Conference attendees explored what analytical frameworks would enable professionals to assess the meaning and relevance of cultural differences and, at the same time, help them avoid ranking cultures and inadvertently devalorize non-white cultural practices when making educational, legal, and medical decisions. The ensuing debates highlighted important questions about the implications of culture-talk, and whether it displaces critical thinking and theorizing about the effects of continuing settler colonialism. The conference also highlighted the need for critical race feminist scholars to raise questions and to think through critical and cultural strategies that do not reinforce racism or rationalize colonial violence.

The next three conferences were hosted in central Canada. From May 3 to 4, 2007, Sherene Razack from Sociology and Equity Studies at OISE/University of Toronto, co-hosted the 7th Annual Critical Race and Anti-Colonial Studies Conference, entitled "Transnational Racism: 'The Right to Have Rights.'" From First Nations, migrants and refugees, Muslims and Arabs detained as terror suspects, to Palestinians, Haitians, Iraqis, Afghanis, homeless groups, youth of colour, among others – many groups are abandoned and excluded from humanity. Such groups are also evicted from the political community and law. As Hannah Arendt noted in *The Origins of Totalitarianism*, "The conception of human rights, based upon the assumed existence of a human being as such, broke down at the very moment when those who professed to believe in it were for the first time confronted with people who had indeed lost all other qualities and specific relationships – except that they were still human. The world found nothing sacred in the abstract nakedness of being human."[11] These groups become communities of people without "the right to have rights"[12] and live in areas where violence may be directed at them with impunity. All such excluded groups are racialized, that is, understood as being a lower form of humanity than people of European origin. The conference focused attention on abandoned populations and groups evicted from the law, as well as the contradictions and the involvement of the liberal state, which David Theo Goldberg and Charles W. Mills, among others, theorize as "racial liberalism."[13]

In November 2008, Sedef Arat-Koç of the Department of Political Science and Public Administration at Ryerson University in Toronto organized the 8th annual conference under the theme "Race-ing Hegemonies, Resurging Imperialisms: Building Anti-Racist and Anti-Colonial Theory and Practice for Our Times."[14] The conference called for papers exploring the context of racial liberalism and the growing contradictions of illiberal democracy in an age of intensified neo-liberal globalization:

> We are subject daily to revelations about the violence and hypocrisy behind the claims to democracy and human rights in the discourses of the new imperialism. Likewise, there is mounting evidence of the ravages wreaked by globalized capitalism on most of humanity. Despite this, imperialist wars and neo-liberal, globalized capitalism continue to enjoy hegemonic status in economic, political, social, and cultural realms. Underpinning these hegemonies and central to the very possibility and acceptability of the forms of violence, destruction, injustices, and inequalities are race and colonial logics whose force of destruction is borne by colonized and racialized groups, especially those who also face class and gender subordination.

The conference's three goals were, first, to build knowledge of the raced, classed, and gendered nature of the hegemonies of imperialism and neo-liberal globalization; second, to provide a more specific focus on how Canada and Canadians are implicated in these processes within their country and abroad; and third, to help build communities and practices of resistance against racism, colonialism, imperialism, and neo-liberal globalized capitalism. With this in mind, the conference brought together academics and activists in order to critically explore the nature of these hegemonies and to build anti-racist and anti-colonial alliances.

The 9th Critical Race and Anti-Colonialism Conference, "Compassion, Complicity and Conciliation: The Politics, Cultures and Economies of Doing Good," was jointly organized by Yasmin Jiwani and Gada Mahrouse at

Concordia University, and Aziz Choudry at McGill University from June 5 to 7, 2009. The call for papers noted,

> Global political activism, official apologies, charity, advocacy and solidarity campaigns, "rescue" missions, truth and reconciliation hearings, private philanthropy, "humanitarian" interventions. . . . The politics, cultures, and economies of doing good seem to have gained a redemptive, sanctioned, and empowering status, which has elevated actions and actors above critical scrutiny.

In light of this, the conference aimed to interrogate the politics and practice(s) of "doing good." Conference keynote speakers and participants in the plenary sessions turned a critical gaze on a number of important questions: What is defined as "doing good" and how is it tied to constructions of benevolent Others? Who is positioned and empowered to "do good"? What are the relations between humanitarianism and imperialism? The conference also employed an anti-racist and anti-colonial lens to reveal past and present humanitarian actions and interventions, and how such a lens may inform present and future anti-racist and anti-colonial feminist practices.

This volume has been compiled to coincide with the 10th Annual Anti-Racism and Critical Race Studies Conference, "Race-Making and the State: Between Post-racial Neo-liberalism and Racialized Terrorism,"[15] being organized by Malinda S. Smith at the University of Alberta in Edmonton for November 2010. The aim of this tenth anniversary conference is to draw attention to the "wilfull forgetting" in the majority of Canadian and international studies scholarship, of racial thinking, race-making and racial imaginaries, which have long served the imperial and colonial designs of empires and states alike. The racial idea was a fundamental element of the modern state.[16] For Voegelin, it was irrelevant whether race was a biological or genetic fiction, a distinction upon which many social constructivists have been fixated. The fiction of race, however, has not belied its power or its real life political, material, or social salience. As Hannah Arendt persuasively argued, race thinking has been widespread across the West since at least the eighteenth century, and has functioned as a political device to differentiate the "primitive," "savage," and "barbarian" from the "civilized"[17] – precisely the kind of thinking we see reproduced in Canada's new *Citizenship Guide*.

Racism was a powerful ideological weapon in imperialist policies, including the "scramble for Africa," and in the dispossession of Indigenous lands here in Canada. In *Society Must Be Defended*,[18] the French social theorist Michel Foucault advanced the notion of "state racism" as one expression of the biopower of the modern state, a power that unleashed governing technologies to "make live" some groups and abandon or "let die" others. Other important works on "states of race" and the "racial state," which the tenth conference will take up, include the works of two of RACE's founding members – Sherene Razack's *Casting Out*[19] and Sunera Thobani's *Exalted Subjects*.[20] These works, like those of other critical race scholars across North America have linked imperial and colonial racisms to the conceits of modern liberal states, which purport to be race neutral, colour-blind,[21] and even post-racial, while masking, reproducing, and even reinforcing historical inequities.

The eight essays in this volume argue that a critical race feminism for the twenty-first century must be attentive to two dominant logics: on the one hand, neo-liberalism's imaginaries of an individualized, atomized person who can leave behind her or his racial, ethnic, and gendered self and, on the other hand, the collective imaginaries of 9/11 and the War on Terror, which make clear that "outsider groups" and the "barbarians" are always shaped by racial and gendered markers. Arguably, neo-liberalism has depoliticized structural inequalities.[22] This paradox disdains the historical memory of institutional and structural racism and sexism and "forgets" that these practices have shifted over time, space, and regimes with effects which are sometimes devastating. This anthology draws on our collective experience in promoting critical race feminist scholarship. The eight chapters are written with a view to identifying future directions for such research and scholarship.

## Notes

1 Sir John A. Macdonald, *Hansard*, May 5, 1885, quoted in Malinda S. Smith, "Race Matters and Race Manners," in *Reinventing Canada: Politics of the Twenty-First Century*, ed. J. Brodie and L. Trimble (Toronto: Prentice Hall, 2003), 112.

2 MacKenzie King, *Hansard*, May 8, 1922, quoted in Smith, "Race Matters and Race Manners," 112.

3 Samuel P. Huntington, *The Clash of Civilizations and the Remaking of the World Order* (New York: Simon and Schuster, 1996); and Samuel P. Huntington, ed., *The Clash of Civilization? The Debate* (New York: Foreign Affairs, 1996).

4 Arthur Meighen, *Hansard*, May 8, 1922, quoted in Smith, "Race Matters and Race Manners," 113.

5 See Kathryn Blaze Carlson, "The Citizenship Guide Says No to 'Barbaric' Practices," *National Post*, November 12, 2009, ⟨http://www.nationalpost.com/news/story.html ?id=2216251⟩, accessed February 23, 2010; and Radha Jhappan, "No Barbarians Please, We're Canadian," Rabble.ca (December 3, 2009), ⟨http://www.rabble.ca/ news/2009/12/no-barbarians-please-were-canadian⟩, accessed February 23, 2010.

6 James L. Turk and Allan Manson, eds., *Free Speech in Fearful Times: After 9/11 in Canada, the U.S., Australia and Europe* (Halifax: Lorimer, 2007).

7 Malinda S. Smith, "Post–9/11: Thinking Critically, Thinking Dangerously," preface

to *Securing Africa: Post-9/11 Discourses on Terrorism*, ed. Malinda S. Smith (Ashgate: Aldershot, 2010), xi–xvii.

8 *Social Justice: A Journal of Crime, Conflict and World Order*, Special Issue: Race, Racism, and Empire: Reflections on Canada, 32,4 (2005).

9 The 4th Annual Critical Race and Anti-Colonial Studies Conference, Dalhousie University, Halifax, April 1–2, 2005, ⟨http://jamesrjohnstonchair.dal.ca/Racial_Violence_and_.php⟩, accessed February 23, 2010.

10 Call for Papers, the 5th Annual Critical Race and Anti-Colonial Studies Conference, University of Regina, May 4–6, 2006, ⟨http://www.csse.ca/News/2005/Sept05/RACEConferenceCall.pdf⟩, accessed February 23, 2010.

11 Hannah Arendt, *The Origins of Totalitarianism* (New York: Harcourt, 1973), 299.

12 See Peg Birmingham, *Hannah Arendt and Human Rights* (Indianapolis: Indiana University Press, 2006); and Seyla Benhabib, *The Rights of Others* (Cambridge: Cambridge University Press, 2004).

13 Charles W. Mills, "Racial Liberalism," *PMLA* 123,5 (October 2008), 1380–97; Jodi Melamed, "The Spirit of Neoliberalism: From Racial Liberalism to Neoliberal Multiculturalism," *Social Text* 24,4 89 (2006), 1–24; and David Theo Goldberg, *The Racial State* (Cambridge: Blackwell, 2002).

14 The 8th Annual Critical Race and Anti-Colonial Conference, November 14–16, 2008, ⟨http://www.arts.ryerson.ca/raceconf/program/index.html⟩, accessed February 23, 2010.

15 The 10th Annual Critical Race and Anti-Colonial Studies conference, University of Alberta, November 8–10, 2010, ⟨http://www.criticalraceconference.arts.ualberta.ca/Critical_Race_Conference/Call_for_Proposals.html⟩, accessed February 23, 2010.

16 Eric Voegelin, *Race and the State*, ed. Klaus Vondung, trans. Ruth Hein (Baton Rouge: Louisiana State University Press, 2002).

17 Hannah Arendt, "Race Thinking before Racism," *The Review of Politics* 6,1 (January 1944), 36–73.

18 Michel Foucault, *Society Must Be Defended: Lectures at the Collège de France, 1975–76* (New York: Picador, 2003).

19 Sherene H. Razack, *Casting Out: The Eviction of Muslims from Western Law and Politics* (Toronto: University of Toronto Press, 2008).

20 Sunera Thobani, *Exalted Subjects: Studies in the Making of Race and Nation in Canada* (Toronto: University of Toronto Press, 2007).

21 Patricia J. Williams, *Seeing a Color-Blind Future: The Paradox of Race (Reith Lectures, 1997)* (New York: Farrar, Straus and Giroux, 1998).

22 Janine Brodie, "From Social Security to Public Safety: Security Discourses and Canadian Citizenship," *University of Toronto Quarterly* 78,3, (2009), 687–708.

# Introduction
# States of race: Critical race feminism for the 21st century

. . . . . . . . . . . . . . . . . . . . . . . . . . . . . . . . . . . . . . . .

Sherene Razack, Malinda Smith, and Sunera Thobani

THE FEMINIST, ANTI-RACIST INTELLECTUAL TRADITION of which the contributors to this anthology are a part emerges out of a long Canadian history. Indigenous women were the first to powerfully critique Canada as a white settler society and to analyze its ongoing colonial practices. For some of the first feminist scholars of colour, most of whom entered the academy in the 1980s and 1990s, Maria Campbell's *Halfbreed*, published in 1973, was a significant starting point for developing a feminist anti-colonial critique. *Halfbreed* gave non-Indigenous readers their first close-up view of Canadian settler colonialism, lived through the experiences of an Indigenous woman. In an interview with a German journalist, Maria Campbell offered this comparison:

> We were busy in the 1940s hearing about the horrible things Germany was doing. Nobody ever would believe that in Saskatchewan at the same time people were loaded into cattle cars, not having bathrooms or facilities, and were carted off, hauled some place, and dumped off in the middle of the snow – and some of those people dying. We never hear about things like that. We need to write those stories ourselves.[1]

Janice Acoose notes in the path-breaking collection *Looking at the Words of Our People: First Nations Analysis of Literature*,[2] that Campbell's fictionalized autobiography is an important legacy for Indigenous women because it represents them "as survivors of the oppressive colonial regime, and abusive relationships, as well as systemic racism and sexism."[3] Campbell analyzed how settler colonialism operates through the church and schools, wrecking families and leaving drug and alcohol addiction, self-hatred, internalized racism, and a pervasive racial *and* sexual violence in its wake. But she also showed that Indigenous and Métis women survive these harsh realities, recalling her great-grandmother, who successfully resisted both the violence of her Scottish immigrant husband and the eviction from her home when it was designated as a national park. Beatrice Culleton's *In Search of April Raintree*,[4] a novel written ten years after *Halfbreed*, reminded us in fiction, as so many Indigenous and Métis women writers did for the next thirty years, of both the brutalities of ongoing settler colonialism and the fierce resistance to it.

Colonialism has always operated *through* gender. Lee Maracle wrote, "Whereas Native men have been victims of the age-old racist remark 'lazy drunken Indian,' about Native women white folks ask, 'Do they have feelings?' "[5] Native women are neither people nor women; "No one makes the mistake of referring to us as ordinary women."[6] Thus, a person without feelings can be violated with impunity. Maracle put it this way:

> We are a conquered people. Spiritually dead people, warmed up and forced to behave as though we were alive. I am certain it is because we have been raped. Our men know that we have been raped. They watched it happen. Some of the rape we have been subjected to was inflicted by them. Some of them were our fathers and our brothers. We are like a bunch of soft knots in dead trees, chopped down by white men, the refuse left for our own menfolk.[7]

Today, with hundreds of "missing" Indigenous women, women who are presumed murdered, we confront daily what Indigenous scholars mean when they write that sexual violence is how you "do" colonialism.[8]

When we women of colour and immigrant women examine the contours of our own oppression, we do so with the words of Campbell, Culleton, Maracle, and others, such as Métis scholar Emma Larocque, ringing in our ears. "My Hometown Northern Canada South Africa," Larocque's powerful poem, presses us to remember that the colonial histories and histories of enslavement and colonialism out of which we ourselves came, and the realities of racism we now confront in Canada, must be linked to the white settler colonial project in which we find ourselves.[9] For some, this has been a hard connection to sustain; it is so much easier to forget that this is stolen land, and that Indigenous men, women, and children continue to bear the ongoing violence of dispossession on their bodies. How can we theorize our "place," when the place itself is stolen? This challenge remains the pre-eminent one for anti-racist feminists as we struggle to understand our own oppression as well as our relatively increased access to social power. Whereas Indigenous women are constructed as women without feelings, to use Maracle's words, women of colour are often imagined as women who have *only* feelings. As Himani Bannerji wrote in the anthology *Returning the Gaze*, people think of women of colour as non-intellectual, emotional, "mindless nurturers."[10] They publish our poetry, Bannerji observed wryly, but not our theory, echoing Trinh T. Minh-ha's point that "we are the voice of difference they long to hear."[11] We are often the nation's fetish object. For Bannerji, this meant that we had to stop the practice of conceptualizing oppression in terms of unitary categories of gender, race, or class. She called for an integrative analysis, and situated herself as an anti-racist, feminist Marxist scholar. Eschew romantic notions of voice and agency, Bannerji advised. Resist the specialness invoked for fetishes. Instead, apply Marx's concept of mediation, and track how social relations come into production in and through each other.[12]

Indeed, many Black and Asian feminist scholars relied on Marx's thinking to theorize how race, class, and gender operated simultaneously in the oppression of racialized women. In 1989, Makeda Silvera published *Silenced*, a compelling exploration of the lives of Black women who could only enter Canada as domestic workers. *Silenced* was a powerful description of both the racial state and the everyday racism that Black domestic workers encountered.[13] Around the same time, Agnes Calliste began her research on Black sleeping car porters, domestic workers, and nurses. What these studies showed was that the labour market was both gendered and raced. Nevertheless, these effects could not be understood as discrete systems of oppression but rather as interlocking ones. Using race as the entry point, these feminist scholars explored the limitations of segmented labour theory and argued that, from an anti-racist viewpoint, it was possible to track the racialization of gender and class. Calliste concluded that "racially specific notions of femininity and masculinity played an important role in justifying the restriction of Black women and men to menial and backbreaking jobs, such as domestic work, chronic care nursing and portering, as well as conditioning managerial strategies of control."[14] White nurses often collaborated with management to harass Black nurses, Calliste reported, as clear an indicator as any that gender could not be theorized outside of race or class. On the ground, the implications of an interlocking analysis for feminist/anti-racist organizing were clear: Black nurses, for example, found themselves confronting the state, their employers, *and* their own unions. Roxana Ng showed how immigrant women were made (produced, that is) as a labour market category and as commodities which could be bought by employers in a process in which community agencies that operated on their behalf played a salient role.[15]

The work produced by the women who founded Researchers and Academics of Colour for Equality/Equity (RACE) was an important part of the theorizing of interlocking systems of oppression. Patricia Monture, an Indigenous scholar, anchored her feminism in an anti-colonial analysis. Provocatively stating that "equality is not a high standard in my way of thinking,"[16] Monture explained why a white feminist analysis where violence against Aboriginal women was an issue of what men did to women remained impossible for her. Violence "is not just a mere incident in the lives of Aboriginal women. Violence does not just span a given number of years. It *is* our lives. And it is in our histories. For most Aboriginal women, violence has not been escapable."[17] "A cyclone of pain," violence had to be understood as colonization itself. From residential schools, to dispossession and sexual violence within their communities, Aboriginal women encounter a legally sanctioned violence that they do not share with other women. A feminism that failed to recognize the impact of settler colonialism, one that focused on equality without addressing issues of sovereignty, for example, was not a useful solution. Indeed, Monture concluded, "Canadian laws are not an Aboriginal answer."[18] She went on to argue, "For me they [solutions] are located in the collective memory of my people and our ancestors, and not in constitutional reform. Our survival as a people has always depended on our creativity and not on a political power-sharing relationship with the federal government."[19]

In a bid to examine how race, class, and gender operate through each other in the white settler colonial project, Sherene Razack considered the "gendered racial violence" enacted on Pamela George, an Aboriginal woman who was brutally murdered by two white men during an encounter in prostitution. Insisting that we understand the encounter as fully colonial, Razack proposed that what brought Pamela George to prostitution the night of her death, and what brought the two men to enact violence against her, must be seen as a central aspect of an ongoing colonialism. The men knew themselves as men and as colonizers through practices of violence; Pamela George came to the encounter dispossessed and unable to survive except through prostitution. In her book *Exalted Subjects*,[20] Sunera Thobani proposed that we consider the constitution of the Canadian national subject through a genealogy of colonial forms of power. White citizens, exalted as the rightful owners of the land, draw on their entitlement as colonizers of Indigenous peoples to manage all racial Others. Offering a finely detailed analysis of the gendered basis of this project, Thobani maintained that we cannot begin to unpack the category of "the citizen" in all its racial and gendered dimensions unless we begin with colonization. It is the insight that colonization is ongoing, and that it is a project sustained by interlocking systems of oppression, that has most distinguished the Canadian feminist antiracist project.

## The political context: 9/11 and the War on Terror

Indigenous women and women of colour have historically been differently, and unequally, located within the Canadian state, both in relation to "Canadians" and to each other. The racial and gendered politics of the state were organized through a complex triangulation of relations, with Indigenous peoples marked for physical and cultural extinction, European settlers for integration, and people of colour for perpetual outsider status as "immigrants" and "newcomers."[21] This pattern of racial politics has continued to shape processes of racialization within the settler society, with the consequence that not only are the experiences and interests of Indigenous women and women of colour quite different but they are also conflictual. While women of colour have struggled for equal access to citizenship and its rights and entitlements,[22] citizenship has been defined as the "final solution" for Indigenous peoples, marking the end of their claims to sovereignty and land.[23]

The launch of the War on Terror at the beginning of the twenty-first century led to a profound shift in the national and international political landscape. The restructuring of the global economy had picked up considerable speed during the last decade of the twentieth century, and the remaking of the Canadian welfare state was likewise accelerated, with particular racialized consequences. Social programs were being massively defunded and dismantled, and the deregulation of the economy was increasing corporate power at the expense of the poor and working-class populations. Although the dispossession of Indigenous peoples and their struggles for sovereignty had remained a central feature of Canadian politico-legal life, racialized constructs of Indigenous peoples during the era of the "welfare" state legitimized this dispossession in a particular kind of way. The construction of Aboriginal women as "bad mothers," for example, and of Aboriginal leaders as fiscally irresponsible, helped channel public anger against funding for Aboriginal programs.[24] Also criminalized in numerous other ways, Aboriginal women were engaged in struggles at the front lines of the nation's key political and socio-economic institutions, including the child welfare system and the prison system, which instantiated coloniality in everyday life.[25]

Struggles for access to education and employment shaped Aboriginal women's activism, as did the revival of languages and reinterpretation of "cultural" and "traditional" practices.[26] Surviving the violence of daily life, especially the sexualized violence, heightened these challenges, as hundreds of Aboriginal women were "disappeared" around the country. The high level of "disappearances" and murders of Aboriginal women, including those residing near the Vancouver Downtown Eastside and along the Highway of Tears, compelled the Native Women's Association of Canada (NWAC) to launch a national campaign to prompt state action. The NWAC report, "Voices of Our Sisters in Spirit," documented the cases of 520 Aboriginal women and girls who had gone "missing," or were found murdered.[27] Lack of mainstream interest and police inaction had led to a mounting toll in these cases, and NWAC and Amnesty International launched an international campaign to end this violence.[28] Aboriginal men also faced the brunt of police brutality, and a number of cases came to light during this decade of Aboriginal men dying while in police custody or as a result of being driven out of Canadian towns by the police and left unsheltered on the cold winter nights of the prairies. Indeed, Canada faced condemnation at the United Nations for failing to protect Aboriginal men from police violence.

Access to citizenship and its entitlements for women of colour, constituted as perpetual outsiders ("immigrants") in the national imaginary was organized through the policies and politics of immigration during the last three decades of the twentieth century. Immigrant women, primarily designated as the "family class" and relegated mainly to the bottom rungs of the labour market, were used to restructure the workforce into a low-wage economy. Even the organizations set up by immigrant women to further their economic and political advancement became integrated into state structures through the politics of multiculturalism and state funding.[29] The liberalization of immigration and citizenship policies during the 1960s and 1970s allowed them greater access to education, employment, and social services, but the restructuring of the welfare state that began with the ascendency of neo-liberalism ensured that such gains would remain tenuous and limited at best. The adoption of multiculturalism as official state policy led to the "culturalization" of "immigrant" communities as incommensurable with the nation, giving rise to what Bannerji described as a form of "ethnic" citizenship.[30]

The experience of domestic workers from the Philippines through the Live-in Caregiver Program (LCP) provided a stark demonstration of the vital link between the restructuring of the welfare state, restriction of access to citizenship, and the increased vulnerability of migrant women's labour. In 1992, the Live-in Caregiver Program was introduced by the federal government. Like the previous Foreign Domestic Movement Program introduced in 1981, the LCP organized the provision of cheap child care to middle- and upper-class families in lieu of a state-funded, universally available child care program. However, by forcing domestic workers to live in their place of employment, the LCP introduced a form of indentureship in its reorganization of this labour. Moreover, the LCP has enabled middle- and upper-class women (a disproportionate number of whom are white) to climb up the professional and employment ladder on the basis of their increased access to this cheap, exploitative labour.[31]

In the climate of a rising neo-conservative politics in the last decade of the twentieth century, and an increasingly overt hostility towards the "burden" placed by immigrants and refugees on "national" resources, the decision of the Canadian government to participate in the War on Terror presented significant new challenges to the work of Indigenous and critical race feminists. The historically racialized and gendered anti-immigrant and anti-refugee animosities now coalesced in the figure of the "Muslim," targeting the black and brown bodies of those who "look like Muslims" for surveillance, expulsion, and abandonment.[32] The construct of the irrational and fanatic "terrorist" intent upon the destruction of "the West" that became pervasive globally through the war legitimized public assertions of the civilizational superiority of the West. As Razack found in her book *Casting Out: The Eviction of Muslims from Western Law and Politics*, the citizenship rights and legal protections previously afforded to Muslims were rapidly stripped away by the security certificates, racial profiling, and rendition to torture that became part of the "new" anti-terrorism measures adopted by the state.

Revealing just how tenuous the inclusion of people of colour into citizenship has been since the liberalization of the global economy in the 1960s, the post–9/11 anti-terrorism measures have made the protection of their citizenship rights a major concern of Muslim populations. Other states around the world have followed suit, adopting similar measures and using them to increase their own surveillance and marginalization of these populations within their borders.[33] In the meantime, the notion of a "clash" of civilizations which frames the War on Terror has strengthened the transnational alliances between the Canadian state and other Western states as they have come together to defend their "universal" cultural values in relation to the Muslim world. This resurgent discourse of a civilizationally and culturally superior "West" has shifted the language of race from that of cultural "difference" and "tolerance" that had reigned since the 1970s multicultural era to one in which culture and civilization increasingly were conflated with whiteness.

As a number of scholars have noted, gender became a major justification for the war: "saving" Muslim women from the alleged violence of Islam and misogyny of Muslim men became a major ideological plank.[34] This newfound interest in Muslim women's lives was a key feature in the mobilization of public support for the invasion of Afghanistan. The desire to "free" Afghan women and girls continues to be celebrated in the Canadian media and shores up political support for the Canadian participation in the war.

What then, are some of the major issues that are being identified by Indigenous and critical race scholars in this changed geopolitical climate? The neo-liberal state's increasingly overt resort to violence in national and global contexts remains a major focus of attention. Razack drew attention to the underlying violence that underpinned the Canadian state's construct as a "peacekeeper" at the international level.[35] With the War on Terror, the robust participation of Canada as a major partner in the occupation of Afghanistan has clearly transformed how the Canadian state seeks to position itself on the global stage. Canadians may well subscribe to the myth of "peacekeeping" that prevails in their imaginations, a myth upheld by the official and media designation of the occupation as the "Afghan Mission." Nevertheless, the violence of the Afghan occupation cannot but help prompt comparisons to the violence waged against the Aboriginal populations within the confines of the "national" territory.

A rich discussion has emerged in Aboriginal women's theorization of their experience and activism, and its relation to feminism. By drawing on Indigenous histories, philosophies, and values, as Patricia Monture and Patricia McGuire discuss in *First Voices: An Aboriginal Women's Reader*, Aboriginal women are "questioning the way things are in Canada."[36] The revival of Indigenous knowledge systems and the rejection of Eurocentric discourses and values have been identified by many of the Aboriginal women in the collection as key to their activism and scholarship. In *Making Space for Indigenous Feminism*, Joyce Green described a symposium organized to discuss Indigenous women's relationship to feminism, noting that although Aboriginal women's activism was clearly "feminist" in form, few among them identified as feminists. Indeed, many of the women rejected this designation, not least because of concerns that feminism was an alien ideology that would undermine Aboriginal culture. Verna St. Denis, however, noted that Aboriginal people have been through some level of "socialization into Christianity and as well as incorporation into the patriarchal capitalist political economy and education system, and are therefore subject to western ideologies of gender identities and relations."[37] These multiple perspectives can only strengthen the work of Aboriginal scholars, because despite the varied ways in which they theorize Aboriginal "feminism" and women's activism, they all approach the reproduction of coloniality and the workings of the state as central to the subjugation of Aboriginal women and men.

The ease with which the discourse of "saving" Muslim women, with its attendant racial logic in support of Western intervention in the Middle East and Central Asia, most particularly in Afghanistan, has deepened the cleavages among women of colour especially with respect to the ways in which we articulate our relationship to "feminism."[38] Although "feminism" in its white incantation has a long history of furthering colonial and imperial projects of the state, the scholarship of anti-racist feminists and Third World women had some impact in mitigating its imperial reach. With the War on Terror, Western "feminism" became deeply implicated in a colonial and imperialist overextension, and made for strange bedfellows with a neo-conservative ideology and politics.[39]

The materiality of our experiences has ensured that Indigenous and critical race feminist scholars have never been "at home" in the nation or the academy, albeit in different and often conflicting ways. The asymmetrical relations between and among us have important consequences for the possibility of creating alliances. Unlike our white colleagues, Indigenous women have yet to experience the "benevolent" face of the Canadian state, and women of colour have only very reluctantly been included in the social safety nets and security of the nation. Indeed, what our scholarship reveals is that our different relations to the central institutions of the state, the nation, and the institutional structures of the academy have changed little, and that our unequal locations within these are not shifting in any fundamental manner, even though the contradictions and paradoxes of these locations within the era of a global War on Terror are growing stronger.

## The outline of this book

Within Canada, critical race feminism, that is, a Canadian feminist anti-racism, has been inextricably linked to debates within the women's movement and feminist scholarship. It has also been influenced by critical legal theory and critical race theory, which first emerged as defining bodies of scholarship in law and later in the social sciences and humanities, with a self-conscious effort to make sense of race, class, and gendered constructs and their implications.[40] As the eight essays in this volume suggest, rather than one perspective or approach, critical race feminism in Canada has become part of a movement and a constellation of theoretical standpoints in North America and around the world that include, among others, tribal critical theory, Asian CritLit, and Latina/o critical theory.[41] While early critical race feminist theorizing, particularly in the United States,[42] framed its interventions around the historical and contemporary experiences of women of colour, in Canada, the critical race feminist interventions have more explicitly engaged the experiences of Indigenous people within the Canadian settler state and Indigenous women within feminism; the challenges posed by the settler state for women of colour and Indigenous women; and the possibilities and limits of an anti-colonial praxis within a settler state. Within this constellation, race, like gender, is understood as a social construction that "orders and constrains,"[43] as well as interlocks with other vectors of power and oppression. Critical race feminism, like critical race theory, more broadly interrogates questions about race and gender through a critical-emancipatory lens, posing fundamental questions about the persistence, if not magnification, of race and the "colour line" in the twenty-first century; about racialized, gendered relations in an ostensibly race- and gender-neutral liberal state; and about the ways in which these interlink with continuing coloniality and Indigenous dispossession in the settler state.

The chapters in this book do not offer one perspective on critical race feminism. Rather, they interrogate various critical perspectives on race, gender, and class and, specifically, how ideas about them have been defined, produced, and performed across time and space. The essays tease out the intimate connection between race, racism, and the modern state form,[44] the *longue durée* of "racial thinking" within liberal states,[45] and the ongoing challenges posed by racial liberalism,[46] which promises liberty, equity, and social justice but comfortably coexists with deep economic and social inequalities and social exclusion. The historical and contemporary mediations on gender, race, and class have been saturated by dynamics of power, privilege, and social and cultural capital in Canada. These, in turn, have shaped state, media, and popular discourses on, for example, Indigenous dispossession, immigration and policies of assimilation, and the role of the state in practices of internment and abandonment of specific populations. Race and gender also shape the political economy of life chances, particularly in areas of access to education, employment and income, and housing. Yet despite the salience of race, mainstream scholars within many disciplines fail to account for the ways in which race-making is political and a central project of the modern liberal state.[47] With few exceptions, the disciplinary literatures evidence a kind of amnesia, containment of the "race question,"[48] or systematic forgetting.[49] The scholarly silence, oversights, and erasures are, in fact, determining ones, complicit in the maintenance of the racial state and its racial projects through silences, absences, and evasions which shape what counts as knowable, worthy of knowing, and political knowledge itself. This book's chapters offer critical mediations on critical race feminist approaches to these questions in Canada. Such knowledge, it argues, is important for making sense of the ambiguities and contradictions of the modern liberal state which is, fundamentally, a racial state, a white settler state whose very amnesic conception rests on racialization constructs and relations with Canada's Indigenous peoples.

The book's chapters also take up emerging critical whiteness studies,[50] with several essays exploring the constitution of whiteness and its relation to critical race theorizing. Whiteness is inextricably connected to the constitution of the Other. In the War on Terror, for example, it interrogates the constitution of the West as the white Self who is endangered by the hatred and violence of its Islamist Other. This Manichean construct reconfigures the practices that constitute whiteness. Critical race feminist theorists have long defined "whiteness" as a form of subjectivity that is socially constructed, historically contextual, and inherently unstable. The equation of whiteness as a social identity with the socio-political category of the West has been defined as particularly problematic for its furthering of colonial and imperialist projects. Critical race theorists have also noted that the economic and political power of the West has enabled white subjects to exalt themselves even as they have sought to define the nature of the Other.

The book is divided into two parts, each with four chapters. In Part One, the first chapter by Patricia Monture, "Race, Gender and the University: Strategies for Survival," examines how, commencing in the 1970s, feminist calls for gender equity started to be heard across university campuses in Canada. Women's studies departments began to be recognized. At some universities, Native studies departments were also being established. If inclusion can be measured by these structural accomplishments, then progress was made. At the University of Saskatchewan, as was the case in many other universities, gender became a question that university administrators addressed, often in response to women's calls for action towards engendering the academy. In the early 1990s, the University of Saskatchewan released the president's report on gender equality. Almost two decades later, the report is rarely referred to, and many of the issues identified are still issues for women on campus today. This is more pronounced for Indigenous women and women who are racialized. This chapter offers a retrospective on the impact of the politics of the 1970s and 1980s on university campuses, and considers the progress we have made on issues of inclusion of Indigenous women and racialized women. In this chapter, Monture also integrates the traditions of her own people, the Mohawk, into the work as she reflects on her personal experiences of the academy.

Chapter 2, "Gender, Whiteness and the 'Other Others' in the Academy" by Malinda S. Smith, troubles the growing divide between "gender equity" and "the other equity groups" in the academy by drawing on Sara Ahmed's productive distinction between "this Other and Other Others."[51] It offers a genealogy of how the social category "equity" has come to be associated with and often reduced to "gender equity" and further, how the category "woman" has come to privilege white women. Through disruptive storytelling, the chapter explores the discursive moves whereby white women are placed in an oppositional relationship to the "Other Others" (non-white women, Indigenous women, women with disabilities) and are privileged as the group for whom justice can be achieved in the here and now, while justice for the Other Others is perpetually deferred. What does this say about the prevailing understanding of justice and the nature of social inequality? Monture suggests this discursive privileging of women is reinforced in the dominant critical theories drawn upon by feminists, including psychoanalysis and deconstruction, in which "woman" is constructed as *the* Other, and has come to signify the difference that makes a difference to transforming the academy. Drawing on Michel Foucault,[52] the author shows how these constructs and corresponding equity practices have engendered a dividing practice: first, they privilege women as "the Other" and further marginalize non-white women and Indigenous women who, in turn, are produced as the "Other Others." Second, they reinforce the increasingly racialized divide between gender equity signifying white women and the "Other Others" signifying non-whites, primarily men. Foucault's notion of governmentality[53] helps to trace the ways in which neo-liberal orthodoxy and the corporatization of the academy have reinforced this divide, with gender equity or "gender diversity" increasingly pitted against "diversity," which increasingly signifies non-whites. At the same time, there is a determining silence about the invisibility and inequitable experiences of non-white and Indigenous scholars. The chapter concludes with an examination of the fundamental challenge this dividing practice poses for a feminist ethics of alterity, one which recognizes the need for collective activism, embodied encounters, and a willingness to engage in the hard work of dialogue and solidarity that includes a politics of engagement and speaking *to* and not simply speaking *about* non-white women and Indigenous women.

Chapter 3, "Doubling Discourses and the Veiled Other: Mediations of Race and Gender in Canadian Media" by Yasmin Jiwani shifts the focus from the academy to the media. Jiwani examines the different ways in which race is understood and portrayed in Canadian national media. Exploring local coverage in Montreal's English-language daily newspaper *The Gazette,* as well as national newspapers such as *The Globe and Mail,* and surveying some popular Canadian television shows such as the Canadian Broadcasting Corporation's (CBC's) *The Border* and *Little Mosque on the Prairie,* Jiwani interrogates the discursive strategies that are utilized to represent racialized groups and issues concerning race and racism. She pays particular attention to the backdrop of normality that is produced and reinforced through the Manichean representations that contrasts "the normal" or the "mainstream" with representations of the Other. Jiwani argues that just as the euphemisms of "diversity," "multiculturalism," and "culture" are often used as signposts to connote race in popular talk and thought, this is also true in the dominant media, where similar discursive devices are used to obscure racism, to culturalize race, to deny its significance in shaping the lives and realities of racialized Others, and to deflect attention from its root causes. In this manner, the racialized economy of representations serves to maintain the myth of a tolerant, benevolent national imaginary. Gender, she suggests, plays a critical role in buttressing this national mythos, both in the play of imperial feminism that particular topical issues invoke as well as in the reigning tropes of victimization that are used to corral popular representations of Indigenous women and women of colour.

In the final chapter of Part One, "Abandonment and the Dance of Race and Bureaucracy in Spaces of Exception," Sherene H. Razack seeks to understand the phenomenon of abandonment (states of exception), where people of colour are routinely evicted to spaces in law where law has ceased to operate. She explores the cases of refugees who have been granted asylum but who are refused full citizenship rights on the grounds that they pose a security threat to Canada. Not permitted to know what is held against them, and kept for years in a state of limbo, "security delayed" individuals live in a Kafkaesque world of non-rights. Zones of non-law, Razack argues, are legal and bureaucratic places where racism and irrationality have full reign. Violence is authorized against people in spaces of non-law, a violence clothed in bureaucratic rituals that have the outer appearance of rationality. Race, she argues, is not only necessary in order for legal abandonment to occur but it also provides its modus operandi. Security and immigration officials need not be competent and logical when the subject is racialized, a situation that both produces and is produced by the state of exception.

Part Two of the book opens with chapter 5, "Indigenous Women, Nationalism, and Feminism" by Isabel Altamirano-Jiménez, an Indigenous Zapotec from southern Mexico who teaches Indigenous studies and political science at the University of Alberta. Altamirano-Jiménez argues that post-colonial feminists have challenged us to think critically about how race, nationality, class, ethnicity, and sexuality inform axes of gender difference among women as a social group. However, post-colonial interventions have not been extensively used to explore the experiences of Indigenous women. Altamirano-Jiménez problematizes the common assumption that Indigenous women should avoid using "foreign" feminist analyses and defend Indigenous nationalism, even if it is embedded in sexism. These assumptions, she argues, call into question the relationship between Indigenous women, feminism, and nationalism. She further argues that race, gender, and nationalism are not hierarchical but relational categories of analysis in understanding the breadth and depth of Indigenous women's experiences. Specifically, this chapter argues that Indigenous feminism is in tension with Indigenous nationalist discourses and the construction of a political identity mimicking rigid definitions of Indigeneity, which constrain and enable Indigenous peoples. Using an Indigenous feminist analysis, this chapter critically analyzes various sources of Indigenous women's oppression. It formulates some working arguments on how Indigenous women have appropriated feminism and ground it to their own experiences, spaces, and circumstances.

In chapter 6, "White Innocence, Western Supremacy: The Role of

Western Feminism in the 'War on Terror,'" Sunera Thobani examines Western feminist responses to the "War on Terror." Noting the different political positions taken by feminists who opposed the war and those who supported it, her reading of a number of key feminist texts demonstrates significant similarities in their theoretical assumptions about the nature and causes of the war. Thobani argues that these assumptions and the analytic perspectives they give rise to have buttressed, rather than eroded, hegemonic constructs of the "West" and its Islamic "Other." Further, she argues that because these feminists define themselves as endangered by violence and terror, they have helped revitalize "Western" feminism through a focus on the global that constitutes the West's gendered subject as the mark of the "universal," and the world of Muslims as one of death, violence, and misogyny.

In chapter 7 "New Whiteness(es), Beyond the Colour Line? Assessing the Contradictions and Complexities of 'Whiteness' in the (Geo)Political Economy of Capitalist Globalism," Sedef Arat-Koç argues that we need to complicate, historicize, and contextualize race in an era of neo-liberal globalism and new imperialism. There is a long but sometimes neglected tradition in anti-racism theory and practice, from W.E.B. Du Bois to the later writings of Martin Luther King, Jr. and many other anti-colonial theorists, which links race to class, global political economy, and geopolitics, and defines anti-racism as part of a larger politics of social justice. Mainstream discourses on race have become increasingly sophisticated. The self-proclaimed non-racism of liberal "colour-blindness" and neo-liberal multiculturalism portray a post-racial world of freedom and opportunity. However, it is not changing the presence – in fact, it is denying the salience – of race and racism in the present world. Mainstream race discourse in the United States seduces racialized people into an imagined belonging as "Americans" and as universal subjects. Yet as race and class inequalities increase worldwide and class formations change through neo-liberal globalization, there is a "whitening" of sections of non-European peoples as they are welcomed into a transnational bourgeoisie. While this phenomenon is not new, as we have witnessed with critical whiteness studies such as *How the Irish Became White*,[54] Arat-Koç argues for an increased urgency to identify and theorize race – and the new whiteness – in the context of global capitalism and imperialism. Race is explored as a technology of power which goes beyond skin colour and identity, to one which involves the "historic repertoires and cultural, spatial, and signifying systems that stigmatize and depreciate one form of humanity for the purposes of another's health, development, safety, profit and pleasure."[55] This chapter draws on anti-Indigenous secessionism in Bolivia and some responses to protests of Indigenous peoples in Peru in order to explore one dimension of the contemporary relationship between race, neo-liberal globalism, and the new imperialism: the response to resistance by racialized subjects. Arat-Koç argues that resistance to globalism and imperialism increasingly are represented in racialized terms. Resisters from the Third World, racialized groups, and Indigenous peoples are depicted as ignorant, irrational, backward and primitive who are "impeding progress" with a culturally innate inability to adapt to the realities and imperatives of the modern world.

In the final chapter of this volume, "Questioning Efforts that Seek to 'Do Good': Insights from Transnational Solidarity Activism and Socially Responsible Tourism," Gada Mahrouse examines various well-meaning initiatives to consider how the liberal paradigm impedes social change. With a specific emphasis on Charles Mills's idea of "racial liberalism" the chapter is guided by the following question: How do we analyze racialized power in social justice interventions? In determining the chapter's primary concern as questions of racialized power, Mahrouse sets a twofold objective: first, to illustrate that social justice initiatives and efforts are rich sites for exploring racialized privilege and whiteness; second, to reflect upon the pedagogical challenges that emerge in anti-racism education. Drawing upon specific examples of sites that range from transnational direct action activism to socially responsible tourism, Mahrouse reveals that such interventions are fraught with contradictions and paradoxes with respect to race and power. By mapping out a path of inquiry for studying racialized power, privilege, and social injustice within an increasingly globalized world, Mahrouse considers not only how various well-meaning initiatives may inadvertently fail to disrupt relations of racialized power, but also how they may become implicated in reproducing them. Mahrouse offers critical reflections that inform how those of us with Western privilege might avoid being seduced by the sense of innocence that comes with well-meaning but often misguided efforts to "do the right thing." She argues that when various well-meaning efforts are explored through a critical race theoretical lens, one can begin to see the extent to which the white hegemony of the liberal paradigm impedes social change.

The eight essays and introduction in this book contribute to a growing body of critical race feminist literature in Canada and beyond. They engage with many of the core themes in critical race studies and explore the varied experiences and perspectives of Indigenous women and women of colour in Canada. Importantly, the authors map out many of the complex dynamics, possibilities, and limits of solidarity and resistance for an anti-racist and anti-colonial feminism. In so doing, they remind us of the necessity of continuously engaging with shifting discourses and processes of subject formation, changing forms of power relations both locally and globally, and the persistence of violence in all its forms. Above all, the contributors to this book identify many of the necessary struggles in the contemporary era and an agenda for a critical race feminist politics of transformation in the twenty-first century.

## Notes

1 Maria Campbell quoted in Janice Pelletier Acoose, "A Revisiting of Maria Campbell's *Halfbreed*," in *Looking at the Words of Our People: First Nations Analysis of Literature*, ed. Jeannette C. Armstrong (Penticton: Theytus Press, 1993), 148.
2 Acoose, "A Revisiting of Maria Campbell's *Halfbreed*," 138–50.
3 Ibid., 140.
4 Beatrice Culleton, *In Search of April Raintree* (Winnipeg: Pemmican Publications, 1983).
5 Lee Maracle, *I Am Woman* (Vancouver: Press Gang Publishers, 1996), 17.
6 Ibid., 18.
7 Ibid., 56.
8 Andrea Smith, "Heteropatriarchy and the Three Pillars of White Supremacy: Rethinking Women of Color Organizing," in *The Color of Violence: The Incite! Anthology*, ed. Incite! Women of Color Against Violence (Cambridge, MA: South End Press, 2006), 63–73.
9 Emma Larocque, "My Hometown Northern Canada South Africa," *Native Poetry in Canada: A Contemporary Anthology*, ed. Jeannette Armstrong and Lally Grauer (Peterborough, ON: Broadview Press, 2001), 154.
10 Himani Bannerji, *Returning the Gaze: Essays on Racism, Feminism and Politics* (Toronto: Sister Vision Press, 1993).
11 Trinh T. Minh-ha, *Woman, Native, Other* (Bloomington: Indiana University Press, 1989).
12 Bannerji, *Returning the Gaze*; and Malinda S. Smith, "Race Matters and Race Manners," in *Reinventing Canada: Politics of the Twenty-first Century*, ed. Janine Brodie and Linda Trimble (Toronto: Prentice Hall, 2003).
13 Makeda Silvera, *Silenced: Caribbean Domestic Workers Talk with Makeda Silvera*, 2nd ed. (Toronto: Sister Vision Press, 1989).
14 Agnes Calliste and George Dei, eds., *Anti-Racist Feminism* (Halifax: Fernwood, 2000), 149. See also Sarah-Jane (Saje) Mathieu, "North of the Colour Line: Sleeping Car Porters and the Battle Against Jim Crow on Canadian Rails, 1880–1920," *Labour/Le Travail* 47(2001), ⟨http://www.historycooperative.org/journals/llt/47/02mathie.html⟩, accessed March 10, 2010.
15 Roxana Ng, *The Politics of Community Services: Immigrant Women, Class and State*, 2nd ed. (Halifax: Fernwood, 1996).
16 Patricia Monture-Angus, *Thunder in My Soul: A Mohawk Woman Speaks* (Halifax: Fernwood, 1995), 179.

17 Ibid., 170.

18 Ibid., 185.

19 Ibid.

20 Sunera Thobani, *Exalted Subjects: Studies in the Making of Race and Nation in Canada* (Toronto: University of Toronto Press, 2007).

21 Ibid. See also Maracle, *I Am Woman.*

22 Himani Bannerji, *The Dark Side of the Nation: Essays on Multiculturalism, Nationalism and Gender* (Toronto: Canadian Scholars' Press, 2000); Sherene H. Razack, *Looking White People in the Eye: Gender, Race, and Culture in Courtrooms and Classrooms* (Toronto: University of Toronto Press, 1998); Thobani, *Exalted Subjects.*

23 Val Napolean, "Extinction by Number: Colonialism Made Easy," *Canadian Journal of Law and Society* 16,1 (2001), 113–45.

24 Sharon MacIvor, "A Social Policy Agenda for First Nations Women," in *Critical Choices, Turbulent Times,* ed. Frank Tester, Chris McNiven, and Robert Case (Vancouver: UBC School of Social Work, 1996); Marlee Kline, "Complicating the Ideology of Motherhood: Child Welfare Law and First Nations Women," in *Open Boundaries: A Canadian Women's Studies Reader,* ed. B. Crow and L. Gotell (Toronto: Prentice Hall, 2005), 189–99; Monture-Angus, *Thunder in My Soul.*

25 Monture-Angus, *Thunder in My Soul.*

26 Joyce Green, ed., *Making Space for Indigenous Feminism* (Halifax: Fernwood, 2007); and Monture-Angus, *Thunder in My Soul.*

27 Native Women's Association of Canada, "Voices of Our Sisters in Spirit," ⟨http://www.nwac-hq.org/en/documents/VoicesofOurSistersInSpirit2ndEditionMarch2009.pdf⟩, accessed March 10, 2010. See also, Amnesty International, "Stolen Sisters: Discrimination and Violence Against Indigenous Women in Canada" (2004), ⟨http://www.amnesty.ca/campaigns/sisters_overview.php⟩, accessed March 10, 2010.

28 Amnesty International, "Stop Violence Against Indigenous Women," ⟨http://www.amnesty.ca/campaigns/svaw_indigenous_women.php⟩, accessed March 10, 2010.

29 Roxana Ng, Joyce Scane, and Pat Staton, *Anti-Racism, Feminism, and Critical Approaches to Education* (Westport, CT: Bergin and Garvey, 1995); Himani Bannerji, *Thinking Through: Essays on Feminism, Marxism and Antiracism* (Toronto: Women's Press, 1995); Dionne Brand, *Bread Out of Stone: Recollection, Sex, Recognitions, Race, Dreaming, Politics* (Toronto: Vintage Canada, 1998); Smith, "Race Matters and Race Manners"; and Linda Carty and Dionne Brand, "Visible Minority Women: A Creation of the Colonial State," in *Returning the Gaze: Essays on Racism, Feminism and Politics,* ed. Himani Bannerji (Toronto: Sister Vision Press, 1993).

30 Bannerji, *Dark Side of the Nation.*

31 Sedef Arat-Koç, "Gender and Race in 'Non-Discriminatory' Immigration Policies in Canada 1960s to the Present," in *Scratching the Surface: Canadian Anti-Racist Feminist Thought,* ed. E. Dua and A. Robertson(Toronto: Women's Press, 1999), 207–33; and Sedef Arat-Koç and Fely Villasin, "Caregivers Break the Silence: Report on the Preliminary Findings of a Participatory Action Research on Violence, Abuse and Family Disintegration Experienced by Live-in Caregivers on the Live-in Caregiver Program (LCP)," prepared for Status of Women Canada, June 2000.

32 Reem Bahdi, "No Exit: Racial Profiling and Canada's War Against Terrorism," *Osgoode Hall Law Journal* 41,2/3 (2003), 293–317.

33 See Malinda S. Smith, ed., *Securing Africa: Post-9/11 Discourses on Terrorism* (Aldershot, UK: Ashgate, 2010).

34 Sunera Thobani, "Gender and Empire: Veilomentaries and the War on Terror," in *Global Communications: Toward a Transcultural Political Economy*, ed. P. Chakravartty and Y. Zhao (Lanham, MD: Rowan and Littlefield, 2008), 219–42; Miriam Cooke, "Saving Brown Women," *Signs: Journal of Women in Culture and Society* 28,1 (2002), 468–70; Lila Abu-Lughod, "Do Muslim Women Really Need Saving? Anthropological Reflections on Cultural Relativism and Its Others," *American Anthropologist* 104,3 (2002), 783–90; Usha Zacharias, "Legitimizing Empire: Racial and Gender Politics of the War on Terrorism," *Social Justice* 30,2 (2003), 123–32.

35 Sherene H. Razack, *Dark Threats and White Knights: The Somali Affair, Peacekeeping, and the New Imperialism* (Toronto: University of Toronto Press, 2004).

36 Patricia Monture and Patricia McGuire, eds., *First Voices: An Aboriginal Women's Reader* (Toronto: Inanna Publications, 2009), 520.

37 Verna St. Denis, "Feminism Is for Everybody: Aboriginal Women, Feminism and Diversity," in *Making Space for Indigenous Feminism*, ed. J. Green (Halifax: Fernwood, 2007), 41.

38 See Sunera Thobani, "White Innocence, Western Supremacy: The Role of Western Feminism in the 'War on Terror,'" in this volume.

39 See Robin L. Riley, Chandra Talpade Mohanty, and Minnie Bruce Pratt, eds., *Feminism and War: Confronting U.S. Imperialism* (London: Zed Books, 2008).

40 Ng, Scane, and Staton, *Anti-Racism, Feminism, and Critical Approaches to Education*; Carol A. Aylward, *Canadian Critical Race Theory: Racism and the Law* (Halifax: Fernwood, 1999); Calliste and Dei, eds., *Anti-Racist Feminism*; and Adrien Katherine Wing, ed., *Critical Race Feminism: A Reader*, 2nd ed. (New York: New York University Press, 2003).

41 Kimberlé Crenshaw, Neil Gotanda, Gary Peller, and Kendall Thomas, eds., *Critical Race Theory: The Key Writings that Formed the Movement* (New York: New Press, 1995); Richard Delgado, ed., *Critical Race Theory: The Cutting Edge* (Philadelphia: Temple University Press, 1995); Richard Delgado and Jean Stefancic, *Critical Race Theory: An Introduction* (New York: New York University Press, 2001).

42 Wing, ed., *Critical Race Feminism*.

43 A. Javier Treviño, Michelle Harris, and Derron Wallace, "What's So Critical About Critical Race Theory?" *Contemporary Justice Review* 11,1 (2008), 7–10.

44 Emmanuel Chukwudi Eze, *Achieving Our Humanity: The Idea of the Postracial Future* (New York: Routledge, 2001).

45 Hannah Arendt, "Race Thinking before Racism," *The Review of Politics* 6,1 (January 1944), 36–73.

46 See Charles W. Mills, "Racial Liberalism," *PMLA*, 123, 5 (October 2008), 1380–97; Jodi Melamed, "The Spirit of Neoliberalism: From Racial Liberalism to Neoliberal Multiculturalism," *Social Text* 24,4 89 (2006), 1–24.

47 Thobani, *Exalted Subjects*; Jennifer Henderson, ed., *Settler Feminism and Race Making in Canada* (Toronto: University of Toronto Press, 2003); Anthony Marx,

"Race Making and the Nation-State," *World Politics* 48,2 (1996), 180–208; David Theo Goldberg, *Racial State* (Cambridge, MA: Blackwell, 2002).

48 See John MacLean, *Canadian Savage Folk: The Native Tribes of Canada* (Toronto: William Briggs, 1896); André Siegfried, *The Race Question in Canada* (London: Eveleigh Nash, 1907); Eric Voegelin, *Race and State*, ed. Klaus Vondung, trans. Ruth Hein (Baton Rouge: Louisiana State University Press, 1933); and Michel Foucault, *Society Must Be Defended: Lectures at the Collège de France, 1975–76* (New York: Picador, 2003).

49 Sankaran Krishna, "Race, Amnesia and the Education of International Relations," *Alternatives: Global, Local, Political* 26,4 (2001), 401–24.

50 Richard Delgado and Jean Stefanic, *Critical Whiteness Studies: Looking Behind the Mirror* (Philadelphia: Temple University Press, 1997); Ruth Frankenberg, ed., *Displacing Whiteness: Essays in Social and Cultural Criticism* (Durham, NC: Duke University Press, 1997); P. Carr and D.E. Lund, eds., *The Great White North? Exploring Whiteness, Privilege and Identity in Education* (Rotterdam, NLD: Sense Publishers, 2007); Bruce Baum, *The Rise and Fall of the Caucasian Race: A Political History of Racial Identity* (New York: New York University Press, 2006).

51 See Sara Ahmed, "This Other and Other Others," *Economy and Society* 31,4 (2002), 558–72.

52 Michel Foucault, "The Subject and Power," in *Michel Foucault: Beyond Structuralism and Hermeneutics*, ed. Hubert Dreyfus and Paul Rabinow (Chicago: University of Chicago Press, 1983), 208–26.

53 Michel Foucault, "Governmentality," *Ideology and Consciousness* 6 (1986), 5–21.

54 Noel Ignatiev, *How the Irish Became White* (New York: Routledge, 1996).

55 Nikhil Pal Singh, *Black Is a Country: Race and the Unfinished Struggle for Democracy* (Cambridge, MA: Harvard University Press, 2004), 223.

Part One

· · · · · · · · · · · · · · · · · · · · · · · · · ·

# Race, gender, and class in the Canadian state

# 1 : Race, gender, and the university: Strategies for survival

Patricia Monture

## Prologue

As I TURNED OVER THE WRITING of this chapter in my mind, I found myself sitting and reflecting on the history of the RACE (Researchers and Academics of Colour for Equality/Equity) organization. While reminiscing, I remembered the Race and Gender Teaching and Advocacy Group (RAGTAG) conference that Dr. Sunera Thobani and others had organized at the University of British Columbia in 2001. Chatting before the conference, my friend Dr. Sherene Razack commented that we would be the "grandmothers" at the gathering. I didn't say much to her then because I just couldn't imagine that this would be so. When I arrived at the gathering and glanced around the room, I was shocked to see that she was right. I knew that there were no Aboriginal women who I could look to as role models in this country, but I had never noticed before among my feminist colleagues, that I had so few racialized mentors who were teaching at Canadian universities. A review of the literature on racialization and gender in the academy also demonstrates the gap that Dr. Razack had pointed out to me. Before us, I am sure there were other scholars of colour, and perhaps even an Aboriginal person or two. The gap that I am identifying is about the commitment to centre both race and gender in one's work. As Professors George Dei and Agnes Calliste note:

> Our schools, colleges and universities continue to be powerful discursive sites through which race knowledge is produced, organized and regulated. Marginalized bodies are continually silenced and rendered invisible not simply through the failure to take issues of race and social oppression seriously but through the constant negotiation of multiple lived experiences with alternative knowledges.[1]

The way race knowledge is organized in Canadian educational systems makes us realize that the right race knowledge is white and white is "normal." It is scholars who are studying the process of racialization and who are challenging the presumptions about knowledges portrayed as neutral and natural but are really raced (and e-raced). These are the scholars who understand the importance of space and the way that it is racialized and also sexualized.[2]

Unlike many other conferences I went to, I had prepared a written paper for the RAGTAG meeting, but did not publish it after presenting it. Recently, I thought I should look for the paper to see if it was something I should polish up and publish. Rereading it nearly a decade later, I was struck by the unhappy realization that I could have written it yesterday. Elsewhere, I have written about my own lived experiences of the university and thought that, as an academic "grandmother," the issue of survival was something that would be meaningful to address. It was difficult to discuss this issue in a written form, as I struggled with the feeling that I was being patronizing, and clearly this is not my intent. The words I shared at UBC in 2001 have formed the basis for this chapter.

---

AFTER SEVERAL YEARS OF WORK, the Task Force on Federally Sentenced Women released its report, entitled *Creating Choices,* in 1990.[3] As a document on the lives of women who are federally incarcerated, it has been viewed as groundbreaking. Even so, scant attention has been paid to the report itself, which crosses lines of race/culture and gender. More specifically, it has not been understood as a government document in which activists attempted to address the racialization Aboriginal women experience in the criminal justice system. In some aspects of its discussion, the document recognizes decolonization as an important context for understanding the experience of Aboriginal women both before prison and during their sentences. In its presentation, the report creates space for Aboriginal women in a separate chapter, acknowledging the history and context which underlies their imprisonment. It also includes integrated information about Aboriginal women when their needs and concerns surface in particular ways in the broader discussion. This approach, integrated yet equally separate, illustrates an important standard when working in racialized, gendered, and sexualized spaces. The degree to which this was actually recognized by the individual Task Force members is not known. But claiming a space for a racialized gender analysis in that report was a struggle. As a member of the working group of the Task Force on Federally Sentenced Women, I wish to capitalize on the energy already expended and the accomplishment that was made.

The mandate of the Task Force was described in chapter 2 by the Aboriginal authors in this way:

Women must have choices. This is as true for Aboriginal women as it is for all women. Historically, the criminal justice system in general and the federal prison system specifically, have clearly failed to provide options for women. The mandate of this Task Force was to review federal policies about sentenced women *as women*: a task that previously has not been undertaken in the numerous reports completed on the Prison for Women. Previously, women were mere add-ons to a male system of federal incarceration. In the 1980's, this has been recognized as both unrealistic and paternalistic. Control over women's futures, over women's choices, must rest within women's own experience. Likewise, adding-on Aboriginal women to the review of women serving federal sentences amounts to the same mistake as tacking women onto the tails of a system designed by, for and about men.[4]

It is not the examination of the prison system that I wish to focus on here. What I wish to note is the way in which the preliminary conclusions of the Task Force are equally applicable to the university. Taking the same quote, I changed a few words and added emphasis:

Women must have choices. This is as true for Aboriginal women as it is for all women. Historically, the *education* system in general and the *university* specifically, have clearly failed to provide options for women. The mandate of this Task Force was to review *educational* policies about women *as women*: a task that previously has not been undertaken in the numerous reports completed on the *education system in Canada*. Previously, women were mere add-ons to a male system of *education*.

My point is simple (and intended to shock people into action). More consideration has been given to the experiences of Aboriginal women in the Canadian prison system than to the experiences of Aboriginal women in Canadian universities. This is not to say that the experiences of women in prison should be ignored. After all, it is uncanny how their experiences of exclusion parallel the exclusion of women in broader society. This, in fact, was one of the starting premises of the Task Force.

There is a second reason why the comparison of the prison and the education system in Canada is important. Much of the colonial oppression that Aboriginal people survived is embedded in the institutions Canada has created. Some of those institutions, such as residential schools, were created solely for that purpose. When people wonder why Aboriginal people just can't let the past be the past, they don't understand the present-day impacts of institutional oppression, including the continued suppression of our own ways and social systems that we have survived. A few years ago, a student sat in my office and said to me of the university: "This is the same as the residential school, except now we come here willingly." It is notable, that as the prominence of the residential schools began to decline, the child welfare system began to scoop more and more Aboriginal children. There is also the overrepresentation of Aboriginal persons in the Canadian criminal justice system, first noted in the report of the Canadian Corrections Association in 1967.[5] From the position of Aboriginal peoples, the difference between these institutions and the damage they have done appears minimal.[6]

It is not clear to me that we can confidently say there has been a recognition that the Canadian education system has been widely acknowledged as "unrealistic and paternalistic," or as racist and colonial. The experiences of Aboriginal women in institutions of higher education remain largely invisible. If the experiences remain personal and are told only anecdotally among ourselves (when we have the opportunity), then the hope that things will change is built on utter foolishness. It has been suggested to me that speaking about issues of racialization in the academy is risky. Although I have indeed experienced the sharp edge of backlash, I speak to these issues because it is the only way to unmask and destabilize the power held over so many of us. And if I cannot hang on to the hope of transformative change, then I cannot continue to engage the university.

My stories are not meant to diminish the work of many Aboriginal scholars and scholars of colour, for whom I have a great deal of respect. My point is simply (and there is a sensitive irony in the middle of this) that in our institutions of "higher learning," we have failed to consistently recognize that knowledge is always gendered and raced (although the race is often e-raced). It is not neutral, and there is no single form of it. We have failed to acknowledge this, and the universities have failed to act on it when it has been brought to their attention that their ways are exclusionary, silencing, and perhaps even violent. It is important to continue to work on ways of forcing the universities to acknowledge the gendered, raced, classed, abled, and homophobic spaces in which we work, but that is not my purpose here. Rather, I wish to turn my attention to an analysis of my own experiences, to explore ways in which survival in the university is possible. Granted, I do not believe that survival is a very lofty goal. I do believe that we are entitled to expect much more of institutions of higher learning. But if we cannot survive the university, then the transformation of that space will remain illusive. Not all of the scholars who experience racialized and sexualized violence (and making someone invisible is indeed violence, even though no physical blows are dealt) in that institution will speak about it.

Surviving the university must be understood as a cluster of strategies. These strategies are both individual and collective in nature. Not all of them will work for all individuals. We have to pick and choose our courses of action, depending on who we are and what we do well. Our choices also depend on where our tolerance levels lie. Together, however, we must remember to support each and every person who is engaged in the struggle, even though we may sometimes make different choices. Our safety in the university is tied to the strength of other racialized individuals. As a Kanien'kehaka (Mohawk) woman, I draw on the categories found within our Indigenous knowledge systems to discuss these ideas. These categories are knowing yourself, understanding the space (or territory) you are in, and respecting what you have learned from experience as knowledge. This then brings me to a conclusion that highlights the need to recognize the isolation in which we continue to work.

## Understand who you are

Perhaps this is an Aboriginal-specific strategy, based on understanding theories of decolonization. It is also an individualized strategy. As a Kanien'kehaka woman, living and working in Cree territory, it is essential for me to maintain connections with the people, community, ceremonies, and teachings of both the territory in which I live as well as those of my nation, as these things affirm who I am. In sharing these thoughts, I recognize that not every racialized person in the academy has the ability to access their own communities the way I do. It is my relationships with community that affirm why I am where I am (that is, teaching at a university). The affirmations that I receive about my identity and my struggles allow me to confront the constant desire to leave a space where I do not always feel welcomed or included. Although many people believe, with reason, that the university will affirm their choices and successes, this is not equally the experience of racialized women. The failure of the university to affirm our choices and our successes must be seen as its failure, and not our own.

As an academic, I have had an unusual career. I have taught in three distinct disciplines: law, sociology, and Native studies. I was academically trained in only two of those disciplines, law and sociology. Interestingly enough, the most marginalized space that I occupied was in Native studies, both at an individual level as well as a result of the place of the department in the university structure. Obviously, then, one of the survival strategies I have engaged in is changing my location within the academy. My last change of disciplinary places was a move to the Department of Sociology at the University of Saskatchewan in 2004. Perhaps it is because of the structure of the discipline that I felt more comfortable there. Sociology has many recognized subfields (compared to Native studies), and a number of sociologists work in interdisciplinary ways that have always made this discipline feel like a comfortable place for me as both a student and a professor. I am fortunate that many of my current colleagues take equality, equity, and oppression seriously in their work. The strategy of moving around in disciplines and places, however, also has its drawbacks. Disciplinary moves require you to retool all of your courses since the theoretical position of the discipline must be reflected in what you do. It takes a lot more energy and work than what is required to move your office.

Considering this affirming experience also means I must acknowledge that the more successful I become at the university and the more "status" I carry (from student to tenured full professor), the more of a threat I become to the university structure and the people within it. As an undergraduate student, I was able to loudly challenge structures and opinions (note: not knowledge) that I found offensive as an Aboriginal person. In analyzing the thirty years I have spent in the university, it has become clear that my "power" is often inversely related to the position I hold. Now if I express my rage too loudly, I am censored, ignored, or marginalized. This made little sense to me, at first. As a professor, I expected to receive a certain degree of respect for my accomplishments. In my youth, I believed that at some point in my life I would earn enough degrees to demonstrate that I was "equal" and as knowledgeable as "white folk." This has not consistently been the case. If there is anything that has been particularly painful about my university experience, it is the tenacity of this inverse relationship. It is the next step that I believe is most important, and that is learning to not feel personally responsible for the shortcomings of an institution that is only willing to recognize a single model of knowledge and knowledge-sharing.

## Understand where you are

The work of scholars who have examined the concept of space has been most helpful in my analysis of the university and my relationship with it. In Sherene Razack's article on the brutal murder of Pamela George in Regina in 1995, she establishes the connection between racialized spaces as degenerate (the "stroll" or the "reserve") and white spaces as respectable (such as the university, sports fields, and government offices). Dr. Razack notes:

> Primarily, I claim that because Pamela George was considered to belong to a space . . . in which violence routinely occurs, while her killers were presumed to be far removed from this zone, the enormity of what was done to her remained largely unacknowledged.[7]

There are two reasons why I raise Dr. Razack's work as an example. First, I teach at the University of Saskatchewan in the city of Saskatoon. It is two and a half hours north of Regina. There is little to distinguish the prairie ambiance of Regina and Saskatoon. In Saskatoon, we have the deaths of Calinda Waterhen, Eva Taysup, and Shelley Napope, all murdered by the serial killer John Crawford.[8] This was a man who stalked "Indian" women on the "stroll." We also have unresolved trauma after the disclosure of "starlight tours" which were conducted by the Saskatoon police, and the deaths resulting from that practice. It is within this environment of frontier justice that I teach my classes. Where I am matters very much to what and how I teach.

Second, and perhaps more importantly, we need to more clearly understand the consequences of the bodies that cross from "degenerate" space into "respectable" space. In Razack's analysis, she demonstrates how easily white men can legitimately occupy either space and cross between them with ease. This needs to be understood as a paramount privilege. Just as the violence that took Pamela George's life was predictable, perhaps not in the specific but in general, brown bodies crossing into the hallowed halls of academia are often preyed upon in ways that are also predictable – from the student or colleague who never meets your gaze, the criticism of your writing style and the venues in which you choose to publish, the accusations that you are not good enough because you must be an "equity hire" or, worse, that some qualified white man is not here because you have taken his rightful place. Then there are the career-ending decisions made in tenure cases, or the decisions with significant financial implications, such as merit pay or promotion.

The resistance we face to our mere presence in the university is often an experience of multiple and overlapping acts of oppression and hate. Frequently, others suggest that colonialism is a thing of the past, without understanding that the historic losses continue to have present-day consequences. Patterns of colonialism, along with raced and/or gendered hate are continuous occurrences, sometimes even our daily experience. It is important that we continue to decode our experiences of "respectable spaces" and our journeys through the racialized and gendered hate we experience in them. It is only through sharing our experiences that there is any hope that the patterns of systemic and individualized violence against racialized scholars will end. Sharing our stories is the only way to create an opportunity to transform these spaces into ones that respect all people.

The opposite of the ability to cause transformation of the spaces we work in is the creation of resentment. A resentment I carry is the fact that I have developed an academic (and personal) expertise in the area of "equity." This was never one of my goals when I returned to university. My aims were singularly focused on the forced application of criminal law sanctions against Aboriginal people and the resulting consequences, such as our over-representation in the prison population. This realization causes recurring resentment for me, because it was never my ambition to be an equity object or expert (and one is related to the other). Dealing with that resentment can be an emotional and destabilizing experience. It means acknowledging the way in which racialized social arrangements (including educational spaces) can force us to perpetually react and resist.

Despite the resentment we sometimes carry, it is important to understand what we have learned about the university as white space, about surviving the racialized, gendered violence as not just experience but as knowledge. We are equity experts, despite the lack of choice we have in the matter. It is important to remember our knowledge is not mere emotion, although our courage to speak may often come through emotion rather than reason. In times of trauma we sometimes shed tears, but I understand in my people's way that water is both women's responsibility and their medicine. It is a strength, not a weakness. In fact, each of us came into the world on the water. Think of it as power. That is woman power. And never apologize for your strength.

## Understand our experience is knowledge

Universities are isolating places by nature, and any individual who is othered experiences multiples of the base isolation. Consider the tasks we complete – reading, writing, teaching (including class preparation), and researching. Most often, these are individualized tasks. This is why it is so essential that we look to our experiences and allow the knowledge that we have gained through our suffering and struggle with marginalization to inform the way we challenge the institution. This means different things for different people, and it is important to recognize that fact. Through sharing our experiences, even the difficult ones, we can start to build communities of racialized scholars. At the same time, we must recognize the vulnerability of non-tenured colleagues, who carry a larger burden than our own. Those of us with the security of tenure must speak loudly to the injustices we experience. Nothing is going to change if we keep quiet.

It is very important for us to negate the isolation, where we often feel crazy, difficult, or alone, by creating affirming spaces. These spaces need to be both intellectual and physical. We can accomplish these things only through investment, and I know we are already tired. It is important that we take steps to challenge our isolation both individually and structurally.

We must also provide a welcoming environment (even if it is just a corner) for new faculty and students. Those of us who have learned to manage institutional environments have done so by creating networks and knowledges. We need to share these opportunities with racialized graduate students, especially the women. Much of what happens in the university, the way in which many opportunities are shared, occurs within "the old (white) boys club." When asked to give keynote lectures at other universities, insist that the organizers create a private space for you to meet with students who also experience othering (and if food is provided, then the students are most likely to come!). Make this a part of the process of accepting such invitations. The "old (white) boys clubs" have not been dismantled despite women challenging their existence, so we need to replicate these networks for those who are othered, but have secured seniority in the institution. We need to create space in academic journals, creating new ones to ensure the important work of "minority" scholars is published. But most importantly, we need to share our opportunities in a way that affirms gender and race. Finally, we need to carefully consider where we spend our energies, as workloads for racialized scholars tend to become unmanageable. This is because of the time we spend supporting students, decoding the institution, and searching for course materials that don't entrench whiteness as the neutral and natural foundation of all knowledge. Recent research shows that women have benefited much more from equity policies and practices in universities than have scholars of colour or Indigenous faculty. Ena Dua questions if the policies were, in fact, created to address racism.[9] Summarizing the interviews she conducted with equity and human rights officers in Canadian universities, Dua wrote:

Some felt they spoke about the pressure they felt to be silent about the racism within the university. Some of those interviewed were ostracized as a result of their efforts to implement anti-racist policies. Importantly, some of the interviewees tied the resistance of senior administrators to the way in which whiteness dominated their world-views. Simply put, members of senior administration denied that racism existed in their institutions, and would respond defensively to cases of racism.[10]

Committing ourselves to the equity mandate or serving on equity committees may not be the best use of our energies if we are working in an institution where senior administrators are closed to the idea that racism surrounds us in the university.

We must acknowledge the importance of discovering the unwritten rules that drive many university decision-making processes. For example, the creation of new peer-reviewed journal opportunities may not fully solve the difficulties we face in securing tenure.[11] In the institution where I work, tenure decisions do not focus only on publishing in peer-reviewed journals, but consider whether or not those journals are "the" journal in the field. In a recent case where the scholar being considered chose to publish in new international journals, they were judged to be substandard (I believe that means not Western). Tenure was denied. In my experience on the committee that reviews tenure decisions for the college, no consideration was given to the kind of scholarship being published, or whether there were systemic barriers to publishing in "the" journal of a particular field. Does a scholar who is conducting research on homophobia necessarily have access to the top journals in any field, or are those journals and their editors perhaps homophobic? We need to take the time to share our survival strategies, especially when dealing with the issues of tenure and promotion (because these are at the core of surviving the institution). Do not assume others know what needs to be done to prepare for tenure. We need to make it clear to new professors that there is a good chance they will have to appeal decisions and they should not personalize this process. Despite the time it involves, we need to sit on university- and college-level committees where the decisions about tenure, merit pay, and promotion are made. Most of all, we must remember that the negative decisions are not really about us but about the institutions we work in. And when our racialized colleagues are challenged, we must stand with them in solidarity.

It is important to understand how our jobs are different from the non-Aboriginal or non-racialized, non-female colleague in the office next door. This simply means we must always take account of race and gender (as well as class, ablism, and sexual orientation). This difference impacts on our quality of life, tenure, and opportunities for promotion and hiring. It is important to keep track of the courses we have developed. The difficulty of finding good course materials, and the time spent encouraging others to write specific things to fill those gaps must be documented. The many hours spent supporting students, scholars, and other professionals who are similarly situated must be recorded. Doing so will make it easier to be kind to ourselves when we acknowledge these things and recognize there is good reason why we feel so tired.

When I speak of the energy we devote to decoding the university, this includes the structural obstacles we confront. A few racialized scholars have documented the difficulties they have had with peer-review processes. There is no doubt in my mind that every racialized scholar in the institution who is conscious of their situation has received peer-review comments that have left them seething. I know I have had this experience on more than one occasion. Although I understand the rhetoric behind the "blind" peer-review process, I also view it as a structural barrier. In my busy schedule, I try to make time to peer review articles with the hope that they will be written by Indigenous authors if the topic is an Indigenous one. I really do not want to read any more bad scholarship submitted for publication by non-Indigenous scholars who have not even considered the privilege that comes from their whiteness. But because the process is blind, I am not met with a friendly response if I ask whether the author is Indigenous. I must first agree to review the paper, and then determine if it is something that is penned by an Indigenous person. This is just one example of a process at the university that must be reviewed to respect the needs of racialized and Indigenous scholars, as well as the different workloads we carry.

We need to continue to find ways to "brown" the spaces that we work in. On several occasions, I have brought drummers to conferences I have organized in "mainstream" spaces on campus. For years after, every time I walk through that space, I conjure up the way it looked when it was browned. I can remember the sounds of the drums, and the beauty of the brown faces that surrounded me. I recall the feeling of being in a space that was full of peace and safety, in which I felt proud to be an Indigenous person. I take those few opportunities where we have browned the university space as landmarks that remind me of what could be if our knowledges and ways were fully respected in the institutions we work in. I hold that dream in my heart and mind and pray that it will be a reality for my children.

The next piece of advice is my favourite. Entertain creative, even crazy ideas. Change comes out of creating flux. It comes from finding ways to challenge existing power structures. To accomplish this task, we need to carefully critique the spaces we are working in. Although I recognize the importance of creating spaces such as departments of Indigenous, women's, or Black studies, their existence does not necessarily create a revolution. Often, they create only marginalized spaces and organizations that are chronically underfunded, and sometimes even massage the guilt of white administrators. We need to question why knowledges other than Western knowledge do not form the core of what we are teaching. After all, it is not just racialized students and female students who benefit from this inclusion. All students benefit when they are exposed to different ways of knowing the world. For example, Aboriginal knowledges focus on the connections that we have in the world. We do not fragment knowledge. We must dare to cross the boundaries that disciplines and professions tend to bind us in. Consider the environmental knowledges of Aboriginal peoples, which have always been based both on sustainability and respect for the land. If more of these teachings were understood or there was space to share them, we would be in less trouble than we are now with the damage we have done to our natural environments.

## Conclusion

Power is complex. We must begin empowering ourselves, which might sound a little crazy since most university professors are educated and privileged. But our educational experiences are often akin to battering. We must nourish our own well-being, which depends on our intellectual, spiritual, emotional, and physical strength. This is a simple reminder to take care of ourselves. Get away when you are not okay.

Power in the university is also complex. It comes from multiple sites and sources. Most often, in my experience, administrators deny they have any power at all. What we often lack as members of university communities is the simple courage to do things differently. And things do need to be done differently. The exclusion of women (and racialized persons, queers, the differently abled, and economically challenged) from higher education up until the recent past tells me what I need to know – that knowledge in the university is not complete, nor will it be, until all of the voices that have been silenced, marginalized, or excluded are heard and respected.

## Notes

1 Frances Henry and Carol Tator, eds., *Racism in the Canadian University: Demanding Social Justice, Inclusion, and Equity* (Toronto: University of Toronto Press, 2009), 3.

2 Sherene H. Razack, *Looking White People in the Eye: Gender, Race, and Culture in Courtrooms and Classrooms* (Toronto: University of Toronto Press, 1998); Sherene H. Razack, ed., *Race, Space, and the Law: Unmapping White Settler Society* (Toronto: Between the Lines, 2002); as well as Tracey Lindberg, "What Do You Call an Indian Woman with a Law Degree? Nine Aboriginal Women at the University of Saskatchewan College of Law Speak Out," *Canadian Journal of Women and the Law* 9,2 (1996), 301–35.

3 Task Force on Federally Sentenced Women, *Creating Choices: The Report of the Task Force on Federally Sentenced Women* (Ottawa: Correctional Service of Canada, 1990).

4 Ibid., 17–18.

5 Canadian Corrections Association, *Indians and the Law* (Ottawa: Department of Indian Affairs, 1967).

6 There is another personal connection behind my willingness to compare the university to the prison. I began volunteering with the Correctional Service of Canada when I started attend Queen's University (first in sociology and then in law) in 1983. In prison, the relationships of power are clear – there are bars, guards, guns, and locked doors. It is through the overt power displayed in a prison that I began to see the embedded relationships of power in both the law and law schools. I don't remember the exact moment or cause of the excruciating pain I was feeling, but I

remember telling a faculty member at Queen's law that I thought the prison was a more honest institution than the law school was. Prison was honest about who had power and who did not.

7 Sherene H. Razack, "Gendered Racial Violence and Spatialized Justice: The Murder of Pamela George," *Canadian Journal of Law and Society* 15,2 (2000), 93.

8 For a full discussion, see Warren Goulding, *Just Another Indian: A Serial Killer and Canada's Indifference* (Calgary: Fifth House Publishers, 2001).

9 Ena Dua, "On the Effectiveness of Anti-Racist Policies in Canadian Universities: Issues of Implementation of Policies by Senior Administration," in *Racism in the Canadian University*, ed. Henry and Tator, 162n1.

10 Ibid., 164.

11 See the discussion of my tenure battles in Patricia Monture, " 'Doing Academia Differently': Confronting 'Whiteness' in the University," in *Racism in the Canadian University*, ed. Henry and Tator, 76–105.

# 2 : Gender, whiteness, and "other Others" in the academy

Malinda S. Smith

ENGENDERING HEGEMONIC WHITENESS and the myth of colour-blindness in the academy requires us "to counsel against the facile innocence of those three notorious monkeys, Hear No Evil, See No Evil, and Speak No Evil. Theirs is a purity achieved through ignorance. Ours must be a world in which we know each other better."[1] Despite the risk of being called a "tattle-tale," a disciplinary technique often employed to silence potentially subversive stories,[2] I want to trouble the growing divide between "gender equity" and "the other equity groups" by drawing on what Sara Ahmed productively distinguishes as between "this Other and other Others."[3] In particular, I am concerned with how the social category "woman" and, particularly, the sexual difference between women and men has come to occupy a privileged status in equity praxis in the academy.[4] In feminist theory, psychoanalysis, and deconstruction, "woman" is constructed as *the* Other, and has come to signify the difference that makes a difference to institutional transformation. Building on Ahmed and Michel Foucault, I suggest these constructs and corresponding equity practices have engendered a dividing practice: first, they privilege (white) women as "the Other" and further marginalize non-whites (visible minorities),[5] Aboriginal peoples, and persons with disabilities as the undifferentiated "other Others;" and, second, this dividing practice produces "other Others" as a second order category for whom justice can be deferred into the future.

This chapter suggests that as white women have gained a critical mass in the academy, everyday embodied experiences, implementation of policies, and empirical data within the academy have supported the shift from broadly conceived equity to gender equity. Early equity policies within the academy assumed that white women would be the early, if not the exclusive beneficiaries of the institutional quest for equity, and "women first" would become something of a self-fulfilling prophecy. This certainly was the case of the 1993 report – *Developing and Implementing Departmental Employment Equity Plans in the Faculty of Arts* – produced by the University of Alberta's

Faculty of Arts' Employment Equity Task Force on which I served. This historic report's explicit observations paradoxically foreshadowed the current dividing practices between gender equity and the "other Others" and so it offers a productive segue into this chapter's analysis. Our faculty was leading the way within the university on equity but there was also recognition that we could learn lessons from elsewhere, as other Canadian universities were undergoing similar processes. Despite this lead, the report also captured the limits of social justice thinking in that moment. The report's claim, which lies at the centre of this chapter's analysis, was made as a caveat which, at the time, worried a few non-white faculty members, not the least because the assumptions behind the caveat seemed to play into the anti-equity opponents' views of unqualified or, at best, not-yet-qualified "other Others."

The report made the following claim: "Despite our expanded focus on four designated groups . . . it is clear from experiences in other universities that *the greatest immediate equity gains will be seen in the recruitment and retention of women in academic positions.*"[6] Non-white and Aboriginal women were not expected to make immediate gains: neither were non-white males. As the report clarifies, "achieving equity goals for visible minorities, the disabled and native persons are [not] any less urgent than for women. Rather, we are *merely* acknowledging that the progress toward equity for the three *other designated groups*, although they are cross-cut by gender, will be a greater challenge for faculty."[7] This moment in the quest for equity in the academy was a salutary one. Almost twenty years later, it is clear that this decision, which seemed reasonable and compelling for many, although less so for non-whites and Aboriginal peoples, set a course which engendered a dividing practice among women and the "other Others." In this dividing practice, the "other equity groups" were divided from hegemonic whiteness and, further, the latter was reinforced through a second-stage dividing practice in which gender came to stand in for whiteness. This critical decision effectively forced a fork in the road and the university was content to go down one road – "women first." This path, in turn, narrowed the options available for future decision-making. Achieving broad-based equity that included the "other Others" was envisioned as a "challenge," whereas equity for white women was seen as an immediately achievable goal. The expectation was that a critical mass of white women would create an environment that "is more conducive to achieving employment equity in the broadest sense, although at first it may primarily affect [white] women academics."[8] Fifteen years later, a report by the Canadian Association of University Teachers (CAUT) made the following astonishing claim: "Unfortunately, despite its importance, a complete and reliable picture of the status of equity-seeking groups in Canada's universities and colleges is not available. With the exception of gender, Statistics Canada collects virtually no national-level data on equity in the academy. While we know anecdotally that many equity-seeking groups remain seriously under-represented in Canadian colleges and universities, the lack of consistent and reliable data makes it very difficult to determine the full extent of this problem."[9] What was produced as a "challenge" in 1997 was reproduced as "unfortunate" in 2007 and, arguably, reinforced the increasingly racialized divide between gender equity signifying white women and the "other Others" signifying non-whites, primarily men.

How did it come to be that the term "women" was necessarily understood to include primarily, if not exclusively, white women – since it is placed in opposition to the other three equity-seeking groups – and was seen as a priority for social justice? What understanding prevailed about the nature of social inequality and, hence, the nature of justice? In this chapter, I explore these questions through storytelling.

Michel Foucault's thoughts on dividing practices are useful for tracking what has become "gender equity" and "the other Others" in the academy.[10] His notion of governmentality is helpful for tracing the ways in which neoliberal orthodoxy and the corporatization of the academy have reinforced the divide, with gender equity increasingly pitted against "diversity."[11] Among academic feminists, this dividing practice is evident in the privileging of "gender diversity," meaning the recruitment, retention, and promotion of white women. At the same time, there is a thundering silence about the invisibility and inequitable experiences of the "other Others," including non-white and Indigenous women. I suggest that with this deepening divide, equity for the "other Others" is at risk of perpetual deferment – an empty theory of futurology that is always about *becoming* but never arriving; it is never something that is experienced in the here and now. Instead, the excuses persist: "we can't find any" or "we hire on merit," common justificatory gestures that conflate the academy's hegemonic whiteness with merit. Ironically, it also exposes the institutional failure: If, after several decades, the claim still remains that non-whites are "less" qualified or "lack" merit or have some other deficit which disqualifies their inclusion, then a prior failure must have occurred, such as during graduate training and mentoring, where the really difficult equity work occurs. Rather than deficit thinking, which assumes there is lack embodied in the "other Others," a critical gaze needs to be turned upon the academy and its culture, as well as the procedures and practices which vitiate change.

## A political theory of telling tales

The kinds of stories told about equity in the academy vary in how they account for the relationships and experiences between and among the four "designated" or "equity" groups identified by Justice Rosalie Abella in the final report of the Royal Commission on Equality in Employment.[12] The Abella Report uncovered systemic discrimination against women, non-whites (visible minorities), Aboriginal peoples, and persons with disabilities. It stated that "the obstacles in their [designated groups] way are so formidable and self-perpetuating that they cannot be overcome without intervention. It is both intolerable and insensitive if we simply wait and hope that the barriers will disappear over time. Equality in employment will not happen unless we make it happen."[13] The brute fact of systemic discrimination, Abella argued, justified the adoption of "employment equity," proactive policies and strategies to promote fair opportunities and outcomes for the designated groups. Abella argued further, "It is difficult to see how . . . an approach that does not include an effective enforcement component, will substantially improve employment opportunities." Moreover, she continued, "the seriousness and apparent intractability of employment discrimination, [makes] it . . . unrealistic and somewhat disingenuous to rely on there being sufficient public goodwill to fuel a voluntary program."[14]

Despite the broad vision of the Abella Report, over the past few decades equity discourses, policies, practices, and monitoring mechanisms have focused almost exclusively on "gender equity," that is, equity for women.[15] This focus has been supported by many academic feminists who advocate primarily, if not exclusively, on behalf of women's issues. Similarly, in many professional institutions, "women's issues" were separated from "equity issues." In fact, bodies like CAUT still have two committees, one for women's issues and the other for equity issues. (Note: CAUT is undertaking changes to this structure as this book goes to press. They will be implemented in April 2011.) Some success is notable as more women (primarily white women) have been hired in the academy, although arguably the glass ceiling continues to impede their advancement through the institutional ranks. At the same time, however, there has been little change and, in some cases, a decline in the hiring and advancement of the three "other equity groups" – non-whites, Aboriginal peoples, and persons with disabilities. How do we make sense of the differential fortunes of the equity-seeking groups?

Storytelling or "telling tales" on equity in the academy has multiple meanings.[16] In one sense it means "to tell *about*" or to describe the development of equity policies using narratives, historical and empirical data, and documentations of the when, what, how, and who of equity initiatives. In another sense, it means to "tell *on*" equity, the ways in which policies have unfolded, the disjuncture between equity-talk and practice, and how the latter may be obscured through stories that privilege hegemonic narratives and displace subaltern ones. And, in a third sense, it highlights stories that are "telling" or revealing, ones that expose the concealed operations of inequitable power relations and privilege and the ways in which these are maintained and reproduced, including among and between equity-seeking groups. With any storytelling, there is a need to differentiate between narratives that sustain the status quo and counternarratives that attempt to unsettle or transform it. Counternarratives interrogate stories in which the socially powerful construct "a form of shared reality in which its own superior position is seen as natural,"[17] and is reinforced in everyday institutional practices. How can these counternarratives inform a commitment to an embodied feminist ethics?

My own interest is in *what* stories are told about equity, the storyteller or *who* gets to tell them, *how* they are told and are received or taken up, and whether they function as hegemonic narratives or disruptive counternarratives. What are these stories – on university websites, in documents and reports, mission statements, and policies – designed to *do*? In stories about equity, what are the silences, gaps, and exclusions? How do they relate to particular bodies as well as bodies of knowledge in the academy? I suggest we think through competing narratives that purport to make sense of equity, that "talk about" as well as "talk back"[18] against such narratives. I am particularly interested in "disruptive storytelling,"[19] which narrates tales that trouble the prevailing common sense, underwriting structures, and relations of inequity. This Gramscian notion of common sense paradoxically points us to the area of the "un-thought" or the political unconscious in the academy, and it reminds us, as Himani Bannerji does, that even higher education institutions and the social practices within them are often rife with contradictions, myths, guesswork, and even rumours,[20] and thus always warrant a critical gaze.

Different stories, and differently told stories, construct various narratives of the academy as it relates to its raison d'être, its mandate, bodies who occupy it, as well as the bodies of knowledge it produces and privileges. In such a context, individual and institutional stories about equity can be told as quite "sincere fictions."[21] But sincere fictions can also be evidence of "motivated ignorance," a concept Cheshire Calhoun used to complicate feminist responses to troubling inequities which have become socially accepted practices that not only impede self-reflexivity but also whether and how people notice conditions of inequity.[22] Calhoun wanted to think through a feminist responsibility that may arise from knowledge of inequity at the level of social, and not just individual, practice. Such knowledge deepens what is at stake politically and ethically, as it suggests power and knowledge are inseparable from responsibility. Calhoun suggests there is motivation not to notice or acknowledge inequities, to deny or minimize them and, thereby, to distance oneself from any kind of political and ethical action.[23] Motivated ignorance is self-interested, and it allows ostensibly sincere persons to comfortably coexist with inequitable conditions. Power saturates social and institutional life, and although we may imagine ourselves in ways that conceal or obscure our own power, we are never above the fray. We are always implicated differently in the very same unequal relations of power which we defend, critique, resist, and seek to transform.

In the remainder of this chapter, I tell different stories about the dividing practices that have led to a "separate but equal" mentality and inequitable social trajectories between equity groups that have pitted gender equity against the "other Others." These stories unfold in four parts. First, I elaborate upon my critical storytelling methodology. Next, I explore the disappearance of equity as social justice-talk which emerged in the context of post-war social citizenship and is progressively being displaced by diversity-talk and the idea of market citizenship. I suggest these shifts have been shaped by particular governing philosophies and changing political rationalities. Then I offer an autobiographical story in the context of empirical data on equity as a way of thinking through the divide between gender equity and other equity groups. Related to this, I return to Ahmed's work on "this Other and other Others" in order to think through an embodied feminist ethics, one that may confront these dividing practices. Finally, I offer a few remarks about the possibilities and challenges for an embodied feminist ethics and politics in the context of a larger social justice project.

## Telling tales about equity in academia

As a feminist theorist of power and discourse located within the discipline of political science, my existence is often characterized by ambivalences, contradictions, and ironies. I have been *disciplined* to position myself as an expert who tells an authoritative story about my subject matter. Central to this recognition is that equity entails a struggle "over who has the authority to tell the stories that define us."[24] The process of *disciplining* – socializing one into a discipline – is also inextricably linked to internalizing how *not* to tell a story which may not be valued by the gatekeepers of received wisdom. Disciplinary legitimacy is, after all, a product of historical, intellectual, and social capital. Disciplining and institutional self-interest suggest it is "common sense" to work within the boundaries of dominant narratives or, at least, to stake a claim to its privileged margins, even if it reinforces the prevailing order of things.

Storytelling is a profoundly political act. Universities like "good news" stories, especially in an era of global ranking and branding. Institutional good is often conflated with stories that correspond to how universities want to imagine and position themselves. There is much at stake in how stories are told, by whom, and whether and how they historicize, contextualize, and explain equity and existing social relations. Hannah Arendt suggests storytelling should reveal meaning without committing the error of defining it.[25] Thinking through *what* stories are told, *how* they are told, and by *whom*, is important "for developing a more critical consciousness about social relations in our society,"[26] and for understanding that "[h]ow we portray the past, ourselves and our fellows can defend or contest social arrangements."[27] How the storyteller frames and tells the story of equity also has the power to shape how we see, or fail to notice, the social practices of equity and inequity. One way of delegitimizing stories about inequities is by characterizing them as "anecdotal" or as the result of personal experience, which is read as "biased." Of course, this critique exposes a certain methodological conceit; it assumes the role of a social science scholar is to advance a "scientific frame," one which offers an ostensibly objective account of social reality.[28] All scholars come to their research and writing with a perspective as well as with certain disciplinary currencies and methodological investments.

The critical tales which encourage a social majority to try and see the world from the perspective of a minority are not, however, merely anecdotal.[29] This recognition is vital for addressing those three notorious monkeys that enable the maintenance of hegemonic whiteness that does not see, hear, or speak about the stories of the disabled, non-whites, or Aboriginal peoples in the academy. Stories are a potential bridge between the anecdotal and individual, the social and collective, as they "communicate cultural assumptions and habits of thinking that transcend the individual and idiosyncratic."[30] While stories may be experienced as individual productions, they are also cultural and ideological, reflecting social relations of power and knowledge.[31] Consequently, stories told about equity in the academy inevitably "draw upon and reflect culturally and historically constructed themes that reverberate, often unconsciously, in individual accounts."[32] Stories are communicative forms that allow the organization and self-narration of minority experiences into "meaningful episodes,"[33] and that link together the historical and the contemporary with the prospects for an embodied future.

That notorious monkey that suggests we speak no evil must be confronted in order to disrupt both hegemonic whiteness and the deepening divide between women and the "other Others" that impede a broader commitment to social justice. Storytelling can be important to social change if we use it critically and in ways that do not suggest stories are simply suppressed knowledge or that language somehow represents reality rather than constituting it.[34] It reveals the excavated and submerged experiences, and engages subaltern voices without granting epistemic privilege to the oppressed or any pretension that those who are marginalized speak with one voice. The distinguishing elements of storytelling for social change, as reflected in the writings of Patricia J. Williams,[35] include the frequent deployment of autobiographies, parables, allegories, narratives, interdisciplinary studies, and an "unapologetic use of creativity" to disrupt the pretensions of scientific neutrality.[36] Williams invokes parables in order to tell critical tales about the subalterns and those who are traditionally left out, as well as to historicize the stories of those who have been erased, scorned, vilified, and perhaps even dehumanized in dominant narratives. My own critical race feminism builds on these perspectives in order to produce, portray, and perform social phenomena using words, writing, sounds, gestures, expressions, artwork, and images. Such an approach helps us to negotiate the paradoxes and ambiguities inevitable in the act of storytelling, the content of the stories, the context of telling and listening, and the unequally distributed risks, especially for those who are already vulnerable.

## Shifts in governing philosophies from equity to diversity

Understanding the fate of equity in our times requires an interrogation of the governing philosophies, the prevailing mentalities,[37] and the disciplinary conceits that generate blind spots or prevent us from grappling with the growing disjuncture between equity-talk and practice, and between an expressed commitment to inclusion and the fact of continuing social exclusion of non-white bodies from the academy. Since political theory is a form of storytelling, a different kind of tale about equity and power in the academy can be told by drawing on Foucault's notion of governmentality, a concept fundamentally concerned with the "conduct of conduct."[38] Governmentality concerns the "mentalities" or how we "think about" the governing of others and ourselves in a wide range of contexts.[39] Our conduct in the academy is governed not only by others but also by ourselves. Beyond this, it is useful to think through how new governmental rationalities[40] may be internalized and become common sense so that, over time, the governed will come to think of institutionally generated rationalities as *self*-regulation or *self*-governance. Because governmentality focuses on interpersonal conduct in a variety of institutional settings, it is also a productive way to assess the possibilities and the limits of academic freedom, the shifting rationalities guiding the governance of academic institutions, and our own conduct as academics. Specifically, governmentality draws our attention to how the very idea of the academic self is produced in the context of particular forms of governance, rationalities, and their related technologies or practices. Particular mentalities are not typically "examined by those who inhabit it,"[41] an observation that speaks to the possibilities as well as the limitations of self-reflexivity. This area of the un-thought has profound implications for how we think about equity and the position of equity groups in relation to the constitution of the academy and the academic self.

What I am suggesting, then, is that one way of thinking through the discourse and practices of equity within universities is in terms of shifts in governmental rationalities, or the mentalities that shape how the conduct of the ideal academic self is formed and performed over time and space. Governmentality offers a useful segue into the productive and disciplinary aspects of power, which is understood as not only – or even primarily – about creating docile bodies, as is the case when power is understood as hierarchical or top-down and aimed at conformity. Rather, the focus is on technologies of power, by which is meant "technologies imbued with aspirations for the shaping of conduct in the hope of producing certain desired effects and averting certain undesired ones."[42] A historicized and contextual focus on shifting governmental rationalities and productive power directs our attention to the production and reproduction of the ideal academic self and how that self's others and "other Others" are constituted within the academy.

Governmentality also broadens our understanding of governing beyond the institutions of the modern state, extending the purview to myriad "disciplinary institutions" which, for Foucault, included psychiatric institutions, prisons, schools, and universities. Discipline within universities takes on several meanings, such as the inculcation of a disciplinary subject matter, as well as the sculpting of conduct, as in discipline and punishment. While the tendency is to focus on the latter, the power of disciplinary institutions partly derives from their productive aspects, including the production of knowledge and discourses that shape conduct or the performance of the academic self. Academics not only can become experts in their respective disciplines but also may be valorized by their institutions and colleagues. In turn, they may valorize themselves to the extent they reflect a particular iteration of discipline in their behaviour. This is normally done by performing and producing output that enhances the "brand" of the academy, which I further explain below.

Equity-talk, policies, and practices emerged in the context of a specific governing philosophy and political rationality. These, in turn, were shaped by the social movements and struggles of particular historical moments. Two shifts in logic are notable in governing philosophies in the twentieth century, which produced, on the one hand, *equity as social justice* and, on the other hand, *diversity as management*. The first shift, marked by voluntary affirmative action and legislated equity programs, was lodged in the emerging social welfare state and shaped by civil rights and the women's movement during the 1950s and 1960s. This movement generated a host of human rights legislation, as well as equality and anti-discrimination institutions and mechanisms. These struggles were based on ameliorating conditions of social collectivities such as "women," "non-whites," or "people with disabilities." The particular governing philosophy and prevailing rationality and the social justice struggles and movements gave impetus to and enabled equity discourse and policies.

Since the late twentieth century, we have been witnessing a shift from broader notions of equity authorized by equality and human rights law to more sanitized notions of diversity[43] that are based on voluntarism and instrumental rationality, and are sanctioned by corporate logic and the new managerialism. This second shift in governing philosophy is lodged in the political rationalities of neo-liberal orthodoxy, which reverberates within the academy and broader civil society. The new governing philosophy rejects the very idea of social collectivities and, instead, promotes voluntarism and an individualized market-based logic. Neo-liberalism, like its classical iteration, only sees individuals as market actors that rationally exercise choice and individual preferences. What is particularly notable about the language of diversity, according to Ahmed, is that official university documents, policies, and statements often talk about it not as reflective of the broader academy as such, but rather as the difference that the "other Others" bring to the university. This additive sense of diversity allows the university to promote itself as a "welcoming" and an "inclusive" workplace.[44] What persists is the whiteness of the academy despite the diversity the "other Others" ostensibly "add" to it. This diversity is managed to ensure its conduct comports with the ideal academic self, thereby vitiating diversity's disruptive potential.

Unlike the welfare state, which recognized systemic discrimination as a barrier to citizenship equality, neo-liberalism promotes a form of market citizenship that is anathema to group claims and hence to equity as social justice.[45] When universities invoke diversity, they tend to do so strategically, as a response to what they call equity "fatigue" or "failure," where the argument is made that *equity* was insufficiently inclusive rather than that *institutions* failed to be inclusive. Neo-liberal rationalities may, at times, tolerate a particular iteration of diversity, but only to the extent that a business case can be made that such diversities can be managed, marketed in branding exercises celebrating the university, and made profitable particularly within niche markets, as can be seen in the uses of diversity in internationalization strategies. As such, diversity is a term that more readily lends itself to existing organizational ideals and, unlike equity, it is detached from the histories of civil rights and social justice struggles.

Neo-liberal governmentality also generates specific knowledge and discourses that enable the production and performance of the ideal academic self within the corporate academy. Academic life is regulated using various standardized indicators and performance measures that promote a self-interested individualism. It is not surprising, then, that the discourse of diversity *management* appears in the context of the corporate restructuring into an audit academy, one that defines value based on increasingly narrowly construed individualized and measurable performance indicators. In the audit academy, if it cannot be measured by some standard metric, it is not recognized or *e*-valuated. Individualism and an audit culture have also functioned as alibis for the re-emergence of notions of "merit," which historically has sheltered discrimination. Despite all the evidence to the contrary, neoliberalism tells the story of an autonomous, self-sufficient individual who can detach herself from historical, racial, and cultural markers in the pursuit of freedom and self-interest in the academy. Motivated by instrumental rationality, individuals collaborate and serve insofar as they comport within prevailing performance indicators and matrices.

This new shift informs an almost exclusive focus on a radical, self-interested individualism in the academy. It is accompanied by a narrowing of the number and type of indicators designed to produce the ideal-type academic, which prima facie are incongruent with diversity as praxis. Thus, despite the growing popularity of diversity-talk in the academy, governing practices and technologies function to contain the potentially unruly differences of the "other Others," those who come to the academy not only with different bodies and bodies of knowledge, but also with heterogeneous histories, experiences, and ways of knowing and being. The new governing mentality is such that these differences must be ironed out and "integrated." They must be sculpted, moulded, and measured to ensure uniformity by forms of governance and techniques of disciplinary power designed to produce a specific order of things. More concretely, there is incongruence between diversity-talk and standardized metrics of academic productivity. This process of disciplining under neo-liberalism is linked to discipline as punishment, generally in the form of denied opportunities, advancement, and remuneration. The techniques of power are not all top-down. Governmentality draws our attention to the ways in which an individual learns to modify her own conduct and to perform according to the new rationality not only because of the risk of institutional punishment, but also because she internalizes the new rationality and conduct as integral to the ideal-type academic self.

A dehistoricized analysis of equity and diversity discourses and practices within the academy can provide a new alibi for the persistence of inequities and their normalization as the prevailing common sense. Central to the shift in governing philosophy is the politics of renaming, and the legitimization of specific forms of truth-telling and truth-tellers. Under neo-liberal governmentality, initiatives to ensure equity in employment are being dismantled. Political rationalities tend to privilege specific vocabularies, such as equity under liberal conceptions of social citizenship and diversity under neo-liberal conceptions of market citizenship. With the "three notorious monkeys" as consorts, we see the shift in governing logic and a different narrative emerging, one that seeks to uproot and displace the embodied equity-talk authorized by social justice movements and policies with a hollowed-out diversity-talk authorized by market logic.

Governing philosophies and prevailing political rationalities produce their own procedures for seeing and representing the order of things. Neo-liberalism, as with its classical iteration, is sometimes able to recognize sexual difference narrowly construed as female and male, but is much more comfortable with the liberal myth of colour-blindness, despite the dominant tendency to hire primarily white scholars in the academy. As Williams puts it, although colour-blindness legitimately may be embraced as "hope for the future," there is a problematic tendency "to enshrine the notion with a kind of utopianism whose näiveté will ensure its elusiveness."[46] This naïve utopianism, combined with motivated ignorance, does nothing to disrupt hegemonic whiteness. What our ideals need, "from playground to politics," Williams suggests, is to be grounded, and to be treated with "a more thoughtful, albeit more complicated, guardianship. By this I mean something more than the 'I think therefore it is' school of idealism. 'I don't think about color, therefore your problems don't exist.' If only it were that easy."[47]

## Equity-talk as artful dodging

It is by no means an accident that I begin this part of my equity storytelling by invoking the artful dodger as a metaphor for the gap between equity-talk and equity practices in the academy. A critical gaze helps uncover the everyday relations of power and inequities that characterize academic life and work, in the institution generally and between women and the "other Others" specifically. Since Bannerji wrote what I believe is the single best essay on anti-racist feminism and class consciousness over two decades ago – "Introducing Racism: Notes Towards an Anti-Racist Feminism" – *plus ça change, plus c'est la même chose.* At that time, Bannerji explored the implications *within feminism* of what it means to be invisibilized, the silences and gaps of not only being "hidden in history" but also within herstories, and of "being organized *out* of social space or discourse, or *into apathy*."[48] Despite equity and diversity discourse, this phenomenon persists. It also continues despite the important scholarship of non-white feminists,[49] many of whom engage the academy as "guest" lecturers or "visiting" professors, or who, like Dionne Brand, M. Nourbese Philips, and Makeda Silvera,[50] work as writers, poets, and public intellectuals outside the academy. Or like Bannerji – whose work on feminism, Marxism, and India is globally recognized – persevered to have her position regularized. Not much has changed since Bannerji wrote that even within her own location of women's studies she rarely encountered white feminists who seemed to experience any discomfort, "any basic and fundamental sense of insufficiency with this feminism, which passes as *the* feminism."[51] After all of these years and despite equity-talk, most Canadian feminists work in spaces characterized by hegemonic whiteness, reinforcing the colour line in "who" is empowered to deploy the tools of knowledge production in the academy.[52]

Although a storytelling methodology facilitates the telling of equity tales that empirical data alone do not get at, such data are useful and can tell an important story about equity's fortunes within the academy. Among equity groups, I have suggested two shifts are evident: first, from equity broadly understood to its reduction to gender equity and, second, from the category "woman" to the privileging of white women. The shift is evident in an embodied sense to anyone who is *present* and wants to see. One cannot see and experience what is not there, the absences, the bodies and bodies of knowledge that speak to the "other Others" and our histories and experiences. In her research on women of colour in the academy, Audrey Kobayashi found that despite constituting nearly 20 per cent of doctoral degrees in Canada, women of colour represented a mere 10.3 per cent of continuing faculty positions.[53] Frances Henry and Carol Tator also found that women of colour continue to be under-represented in the academy.[54] Moreover, Bannerji suggests such exclusionary practices have become the common sense such "that they are not mostly (even for an anti-racist person) objects of investigation, for they are not even visible. They produce silences or absences, creating gaps and fissures through which non-white women, for example, disappear from any social surface."[55]

For feminists, the personal often is interwoven with the political, the cultural, and the institutional. At this moment I want to insert an autobiographical story as a way of further contextualizing the historical experiences that inform my thinking on the disjuncture between gender equity and the "other Others," and how this plays out in a predominantly white academic feminism. Mine might be called an ambivalent story, typical of the few non-white women who have gained entrance into the ivory tower. A formative academic experience was the noisily articulated opposition to employment equity in the academy, particularly aimed at non-whites and Aboriginal peoples; their joining the academic ranks was characterized as threatening to the meritocracy. Another important context relates to motivated ignorance about what Bannerji calls "people like us." The banality of racism is such that even someone who thinks of herself as, say, a feminist solidarity worker, or as sympathetic to the marginalized may comfortably coexist with hegemonic whiteness, "common sense racism," and a "passively racist aesthetic." Despite equity and even anti-racist talk, such a person can fail to register that she, for example, associates primarily or exclusively with white people like herself,[56] with few moments of meaningful and embodied encounters with the "other Others."

Yet where and when I enter this conversation is somewhat arbitrary. So, I want to return to the beginning of this chapter and the story that I began to tell about how equity became a dividing practice that, paradoxically, undermined a broader conception of social justice. Let me begin in the 1990s, when I was invited by the then Dean of Arts to serve on the faculty's Employment Equity Task Force, the first of its kind at the University of Alberta. I agreed and, in doing so, became one of two graduate students and the only non-white person on the task force. During that historical moment, I also was asked to serve – again, often as the only non-white person – on a host of other groundbreaking committees aimed at engendering greater equality in the academy, including employment equity, sexual harassment, and same-sex benefits. While one could argue that these invitations reflected my academic citizenship, my inclusion also testified to the small number of non-white faculty and graduate students in arts at that time.

A student of politics, there was never a moment when I was unaware of the power differentials on the committee, or of the many ways in which I was an outsider. At the time, I was temporarily in Canada – a visa student from the Bahamas completing doctoral studies – and at least two of the professors serving on the committee were in my home department. Most of the non-white continuing faculty within arts and the university were more like me, foreign-born. One of these faculty members, troubled by the committee's representation but afraid to make a wave, invited me to lunch off-campus and questioned why I, a graduate student, was the only non-white person on the committee. In this frank exchange, I was labelled the token representation. In hindsight, there was much I did not know about faculty governance: I did not know how the committee names had been generated, how my own name had come into play, or why certain people were selected. What I do know is this paradox: deliberative democracy can coexist with the everyday common sense that reproduces sexism, racism, and other exclusionary discourses. Ours was a highly consultative process involving a number of face-to-face encounters, which were saturated with power and expressions of entitlement among some, albeit not all, white male faculty. It often was destabilizing for me. As a committee, "we" entered spaces which were absented of "people like me" and were subjected to "words that wound" and the "assaultive speech,"[57] which constructed equity groups as unqualified and lacking in merit. The symbolic violence of this discourse was intended to belittle and devalue people like me and our contributions to the academy; it suggested whiteness and merit were inextricably linked.

These experiences were productive for helping me think through the possibilities and limits of salutary notions like "opening doors" or creating a "welcoming environment" in relation to the "chilly climate" in the academy. I also realized how unlikely it was that "people like us" would be hired by men "like them." Their hegemonic storytelling deployed common tropes in which equity was constituted as "reverse discrimination," efforts to create fair employment was constructed as hiring unqualified people and lowering standards, and hiring "people like us" would be "at the expense of" white men who would be denied jobs in the academy. Although the Equity Task Force focused primarily on institutional sexism, the consultations did expose the banality of racism in the academy generally and the blind spots of hegemonic whiteness.[58] The consultations revealed how power functions and circulates, and the disciplinary techniques by which a privileged "we" is constructed as separate from the under-represented, those who happened to be people like me. It seems "we," that is, we who were not white men, were the barbarians at the gates of civilization, and our entry into the academy would herald nothing less than its demise.

Shaped by the moment and the location, a strategic decision was made to prioritize gender equity and, as I have suggested, this de facto became privileging white women, a strategic move that reinforced hegemonic whiteness. While the report optimistically assumed a critical mass of women would lead to demands for greater inclusivity, this has not happened and instead, the divide between women and the "other Others" seems to be intensifying. As well, the current data suggest that rather than creating a broader sense of equity, the privileging of gender equity had the opposite effect; it led to the narrowing of the concept and the disappearance of the "other Others" from equity discourse and practices. Thus, when I requested and analyzed the employment equity data from the Office of Human Rights for the Faculty of Arts between 1993 and 2005, I found that there was a notable *decline* from the mid-1990s to 2005 in the representation of non-whites, Aboriginal peoples, and persons with disabilities. In fact, there were fewer persons from the other designated groups than when the policy was first implemented. The main group that benefited from equity policies and for which there was notable improvement was white women. The question of data is important for policy-makers, as its absence circumscribes what kind of story can be told about equity. This point was made in a recent CAUT equity report, which indicated it had data only for women. "While we know anecdotally that many equity-seeking groups remain seriously under-represented in Canadian colleges and universities, the lack of consistent and reliable data makes it very difficult to determine the full extent of this problem."[59]

The data and the everyday experiences over the past two decades do not suggest the academy has not been "walking the talk,"[60] at least not in relation to the "other Others." There is also a growing disjuncture between equity-talk and practices within academic feminism, where liberalism's focus on sexual difference is replicated as the fundamental difference that matters for academic transformation. This has a twofold implication for broader notions of equity: first, as noted, there is a reduction of equity to gender equity and, second, there is a discursive, embodied, and material reduction of the category "woman" to white women. Bannerji frames this in terms of the "emptying out" of the concept "woman," such that it is still possible to discuss the contemporary "woman question" without locating them or providing any historical and contextual background. To do so would undermine the "pseudo-universality which confers legitimacy and an interpretative and organizing status to this notion of 'woman.' "[61] The result is that equity-talk about women in the academy has come to mark non-white women, as Bannerji states, "by absence, subsumption and, if we are noticed at all, we are given an interpretative status by those who are in a position to control and generate forms of discourse."[62]

Within an increasingly white academic feminism, which performs *the* feminism, there are lacunae which need to be interrogated. The position of white academic feminism is saturated with an unacknowledged power, particularly in relation to non-white, Aboriginal, immigrant, and disabled women who are absent in discourse, written out of herstories, and organized out of social and institutional spaces. Problematically, when such women are engaged, even in women's studies, too often it is as if such women are temporary guest workers in the home of white academic feminists, a variant of what Nandita Sharma calls "homey racism."[63] This disembodied engagement reinforces a culture of whiteness in the academy.[64] The invisibilization of non-white women is normalized, even within academic feminist practice. It is a cautionary tale on how we all are, and can become, implicated in maintaining relations of inequity. It is thus important to remind ourselves of what Audre Lorde noted decades ago, "the master's tools will not dismantle the master's house," and when those same tools are deployed within feminism, they function as dividing practices that re/produce "sister outsiders."[65]

## Women, whiteness, and the other Others

In this part of my equity storytelling, I want to delve more deeply into the divide among equity groups, which plays out in the discursive constructions of women and the "other Others." In June 2008 I co-organized a series of anti-racism and equity panels at the Congress of the Social Sciences and Humanities, held at the University of British Columbia.[66] The invited speakers included, among other scholars, Janice Drakich, Enakshi Dua, Mahejabeen Ebrahim, Claudia Emes, Joyce Green, Yasmin Jiwani, Audrey Kobayashi, Joy Mighty, Roxana Ng, Carol Schick, Falguni Sheth, Sarita Srivastava, and Sunera Thobani. I name these scholars because the sessions became the subject of a question: Were these sessions about anti-racism *or* equity? Because of "who" spoke, they were deemed by some feminists to be about anti-racism. This artificial divide was captured in an encounter between two feminists, one white and the other non-white, which I re/produce in a fictionalized staging below. Although both characters are women, I have named them "White woman" and "Non-white" in order to emphasize how hegemonic feminism may become implicated in constructing "woman" as white and how the latter character masquerades as *the* feminism that demarcates who speaks authoritatively as a feminist.

*Dialogue: What – ain't I a (woman) feminist?*

*Non-white*: Are you coming to the anti-racism and equity panels?
*White Woman*: No, I don't think so. They seem to be more about anti-racism; I didn't see a lot on feminism and equity.
*Non-white*: What do you mean? The panels are primarily women, and all are feminists.
*White Woman*: Well, the panels seem to focus a lot on anti-racism.
*Non-white*: But didn't you notice? They also focus on intersectionality, gender, racism, disability, diversity, and decolonization.
*White Woman*: Oh, do they? Well, unfortunately, I have something else at the same time. Anyway, I must run. Good to see you, though.
*Non-white*: Yes, good to see you, too.

Despite all the talk about "sisterhood being global" and interlocking analyses, a Manichean thinking – either equity or anti-racism – persists and is emblematic of the dividing practice between white women and non-whites. The "Ain't I a woman (feminist)" dialogue self-consciously historicizes the dialogue between non-white and white feminist, which led to works such as Audre Lorde's *Sister Outsider* and bell hooks's *Ain't I A Woman.* By recalling such works, I want to suggest that this historical moment is witnessing older, less inclusive forms of feminist practice. In the dialogue, the encounter between "White woman" and "Non-white" also reveals how white feminists can become implicated in narrowly constructing feminism; theorizing that is not exclusively about gender equity is read as not being about equity or feminism. While some may read the dialogue as anecdotal, as I argued earlier, such stories are important communicative forms for organizing minority experiences into meaningful episodes, and individual stories reverberate in broader historical, social, and cultural experiences.

Ahmed's discussion of feminism and Otherness is also productive for thinking through the deepening divide between gender equity and the "other Others." For some feminists, there is a refusal "to locate otherness in the here and now,"[67] and Otherness tends to be associated with futurity. Privileging equity for women in the present, and subordinating or deferring equity for the "other Others" to the future is a difference that matters. It is a move that involves relations of power, epistemic subordination, and antagonism precisely at the moment when this ostensibly "innocent" gesture affirms women and the fact of gender inequity. The constitution of women as the privileged equity category is "a form of symbolic violence,"[68] as well as a source of material disadvantage. The discursive, political, and ethical effects of constructing such social categories are not neutral; the very assumption of innocence conceals the structures and relations of power that authorize and normalize such dividing practices.[69]

## Conclusion

As I conclude, it is useful to recall Arendt's view that storytelling should convey meaning without necessarily defining it. What is the meaning for a social justice project of an academic feminist praxis that privileges gender equity and remains silent on the "other Others"? A politics derived from encounters with "other Others" in the here and now is saturated with power and responsibility and "relationships of power mediate and frame the encounter itself."[70] Dividing practices that construct non-whites, Aboriginal peoples, and persons with disabilities as the "other Others" or that collapses them into the generic term of "diversity" are erasing practices and forms of symbolic violence, which fail to recognize particularities or, at best, gestures to a particularity that is deferred to the future. Of these "other Others" we can simultaneously profess to care and, at the same time, do nothing in this moment, because the hope for them is the future, not now. That future, however, is not yet here. Despite the desire, often an ethical one, to "celebrate otherness," a form of violence is enacted when that difference is encountered only as an appropriation or through efforts to contain it in the interest of establishing and asserting one's own identity; the "difference" is assimilated into "sameness."[71]

These discursive shifts present a fundamental challenge for a feminist ethics of alterity that pays attention to the particularity of Others: "how we can keep feminism open to other others in its very commitment to collective forms of struggle."[72] The ongoing need for collective activism, for embodied encounters that are face to face, requires a willingness to engage in serious work, a "painstaking labour," and a dialogue that requires working *with*, as well as speaking *to* and not simply speaking *about* the "other Others."[73] The collective ethical and political imperative of constructing a feminist "we" requires "a willingness to struggle with and for others who are faced in the present (a facing that is indebted to a past that cannot be left behind), and an openness to the future, as the promise and hope of what we might yet become."[74] For me, this suggests academic feminism must be at the forefront of rejecting a dividing practice that normalizes sexual difference as *the* difference that matters and that constitutes non-whites, Aboriginal peoples, and persons with disabilities as the "other Others" for whom justice can be deferred to an indeterminate future.

## Notes

1 Patricia J. Williams, "The Emperor's New Clothes," in *Seeing a Color-blind Future: The Paradox of Race* (New York: Farrar, Straus and Giroux, 1998), 5.

2 Patricia Ewick and Susan S. Silbey, "Subversive Stories and Hegemonic Tales: Toward a Sociology of Narrative," *Law and Society Review* 29 (1995), 197–226.

3 See Sara Ahmed, "This Other and Other Others," *Economy and Society* 31,4 (2002), 558–72.

4 See Sara Ahmed, "(Meta)fictions," in *Differences that Matter: Feminist Theory and Postmodernism* (Cambridge: Cambridge University Press, 1998), 142–65.

5 In this chapter I use non-white rather than "visible minorities," which the U.N. has called into question. The concept was invented and is used in the *Employment Equity Act* as a means of referring to those persons "who are non-Caucasian in race or non-white in colour." It is important to foreground the fact of white normativity. See Statistics Canada, Population Projections of Visible Minority Groups, Canada, Provinces and Regions, 2001 to 2017 (Ottawa: Ministry of Industry, 2005), ⟨http://www.statcan.gc.ca/pub/91-541-x/91-541-x2005001-eng.pdf⟩, accessed January 2, 2010.

6 Faculty of Arts, *Developing and Implementing Departmental Employment Equity Plans in the Faculty of Arts: Report and Recommendations of the Dean's Advisory*

*Task Force on Employment Equity* (Edmonton: University of Alberta, 1992), 2–3; emphasis added.

7 Ibid.

8 Ibid.

9 Canadian Association of University Teachers, "A Partial Picture: The Representation of Equity-Seeking Groups in Canadian Universities and Colleges," *CAUT Equity Review* 1 (November 2007), 1.

10 Michel Foucault, "The Subject and Power," in *Michel Foucault: Beyond Structuralism and Hermeneutics*, ed. Hubert Dreyfus and Paul Rabinow (Chicago: University of Chicago Press, 1983), 208–26.

11 Michel Foucault, "Governmentality," *Ideology and Consciousness* 6 (1986), 5–21.

12 Rosalie Silberman Abella, *Equality in Employment: The Report of the Royal Commission on Equality in Employment* (Ottawa: Supply and Services Canada, 1984).

13 Ibid., 254.

14 Ibid., 197.

15 Canadian Association of University Teachers, "A Partial Picture," 1–6.

16 Lee Anne Bell, "Telling Tales: What Stories Can Tell Us about Racism," *Race Ethnicity and Education* 6,1 (2003), 3–28.

17 Richardo Delgado, "Storytelling Oppositionists and Others: A Plea for Narrative," *Michigan Law Review* 87 (1989), 2412.

18 J.S. Simpson, "Easy Talk, White Talk, Back Talk: Some Reflections on the Meaning of Our Words," *Journal of Contemporary Ethnography* 25 (1996), 372–89.

19 Michelle Fine, *Disruptive Voices: The Possibilities of Feminist Research* (Ann Arbor: University of Michigan Press, 1992).

20 Himani Bannerji, "Introducing Racism: Notes Towards an Anti-Racist Feminism," *Resources for Feminist Research* 16,1 (1987), 12.

21 Lee Ann Bell, "Sincere Fictions: The Pedagogical Challenges of Preparing White Teachers for Multicultural Classrooms," *Equity and Excellence in Education* 35,3 (2003), 236–44; and Bell, "Telling Tales," 15.

22 Cheshire Calhoun, "Responsibility and Reproach," *Ethics* 99,2 (1989), 389.

23 Malinda S. Smith, "Racism and Motivated Ignorance," *The Ardent: Anti-Racism and Decolonization Review* 1,1 (2008), vi–vii.

24 Aurora Levins Morales, *Medicine Stories: History, Culture and the Politics of Integrity* (Cambridge, MA: South End Press, 1998), 5.

25 See Lisa Disch, "More Truth than Fact: Storytelling as Critical Understanding in the Writing of Hannah Arendt," *Political Theory* 21,4 (1993), 665–94; and Elizabeth Young-Bruehl, "Hannah Arendt's Storytelling," *Social Research* 44,1 (1977), 183–90.

26 Bell, "Telling Tales," 4.

27 Beth Ray, *Bitters in the Honey: Tales of Hope and Disappointment across Divides of Race and Time* (Fayetteville: University of Arkansas Press, 1999), 9.

28 Adalberto Aguirre, "Academic Storytelling: A Critical Race Theory Story of Affirmative Action," *Sociological Perspectives* 43,2 (2000), 323.

29 Ibid., 322.

30 Pierre Bordieu, "Language and Symbolic Power," in *The Discourse Reader*, ed. A. Jaworski and N. Coupland (London: Routledge, 1999), 502–13.

31 Bell, "Telling Tales," 4.

32 Ibid.

33 See Laurel Richardson, "Narrative and Sociology," *Journal of Contemporary Ethnography* 19 (1990), 118, and *Fields of Play: Constructing an Academic Life* (New Brunswick, NJ: Rutgers University Press, 1997).

34 Sherene H. Razack, "Storytelling for Social Change," in *Returning the Gaze: Essays on Racism, Feminism and Politics,* ed. Himani Bannerji (Toronto: Sister Vision Press, 1993), 83–100.

35 See especially, Patricia J. Williams, *The Alchemy of Race and Rights: Diary of a Law Professor* (Cambridge, MA: Harvard University Press, 1992), and *Open House: Of Family, Friends, Food, Piano Lessons, and the Search for a Room of My Own* (New York: Farrar, Straus and Giroux, 2004).

36 Derrick Bell, "Property Rights in Whiteness: Their Legal Legacy, Their Economic Costs," in *Critical Race Theory: The Cutting Edge*, ed. Richard Delgado (Philadelphia: Temple University Press, 1995), 71–79.

37 Mitchell Dean, *Governmentality: Power and Rule in Modern Society* (London: Sage, 1999), 16.

38 Michel Foucault, "Governmentality," in *The Foucault Effect: Studies in Governmentality*, ed. Graham Burchell, Colin Gordon, and Peter Miller, trans. Rosi Braidotti (Chicago: University of Chicago Press, 1991), 87–104.

39 Dean, *Governmentality*, 212.

40 D. Kerr, "Beheading the King and Enthroning the Market: A Critique of Foucauldian Governmentality," *Science & Society* 63,2 (1999), 174.

41 Ibid.

42 N. Rose, *Powers of Freedom: Reframing Political Thought* (Cambridge: Cambridge University Press, 1999), 52.

43 See Sara Ahmed, " 'You End Up Doing the Document Rather than Doing the Doing': Diversity, Race Equality and the Politics of Documentation," *Ethnic and Racial Studies* 30,4 (2007), 590–609.

44 Sara Ahmed, "The Language of Diversity," *Ethnic and Racial Studies* 30,2 (2007), 235–56.

45 See Janine Brodie, "Reforming Social Justice in Neoliberal Times," *Studies in Social Justice* 2,1 (2007), 93–107.

46 Williams, "The Emperor's New Clothes."

47 Ibid., 4.

48 Bannerji, "Notes Towards an Anti-Racist Feminism," 10.

49 See Sherene H. Razack, *Looking White People in the Eye: Gender, Race, and Culture in Courtrooms and Classrooms* (Toronto: University of Toronto Press, 1998); and Enakshi Dua and Angela Robertson, eds., *Scratching the Surface: Canadian Anti-Racist Feminist Thought* (Toronto: Women's Press, 1999).

50 See Dionne Brand and Krisantha Sri Bhaggiyadatta, *Rivers Have Sources, Trees Have Roots: Speaking Racism* (Toronto: Cross-Cultural Communications, 1986); M. Nourbese Philips, *Frontiers: Essays and Writings in Racism and Culture* (Stratford, ON: Mercury Press, 1993); and Makeda Silvera, ed., *The Other Woman: Women of Colour in Contemporary Canadian Literature* (Toronto: Sister Vision Press, 1995).

51 Bannerji, "Notes Towards an Anti-Racist Feminism," 10.

52 John Van Maanen, *Tales of the Field: On Writing Ethnography* (Chicago: University of Chicago Press, 1988), 128.

53 Audrey Kobayashi, "Now You See Them, How You See Them: Women of Colour in Canadian Academe," in *Feminist Issues: Selected Papers from the WIN Symposium in 2000–2001*, ed. S. Heald (Ottawa: Humanities and Social Science Federation of Canada, 2002), 44–54.

54 F. Henry, C. Tator, W. Mattis, and T. Rees, *The Colour of Democracy: Racism in Canadian Society*, 2nd ed. (Toronto: Harcourt Brace, 2000). See also F. Henry and C. Tator, "Racism and the University," *Canadian Ethnic Studies* 26 (1994), 74–90.

55 Bannerji, "Notes Towards an Anti-Racist Feminism," 11–12.

56 Ibid., 11.

57 Mari Matsuda, Charles R. Lawrence III, Richard Delgado, and Kimberlè Williams Crenshaw, *Words that Wound: Critical Race Theory, Assaultive Speech, and the First Amendment* (Boulder, CO: Westview Press, 1993), 89–110 and 111–32.

58 Bannerji, "Notes Towards an Anti-Racist Feminism," 11.

59 Canadian Association of University Teachers, "A Partial Picture," 1.

60 I borrow this phrase from Njoki Wane, Riyad Ahmed Shahjahan, and Anne Wagner, "Walking the Talk: Decolonizing the Politics of Equity of Knowledge and Charting the Course for an Inclusive Curriculum in Higher Education," *Canadian Journal of Development Studies* 25,3 (2004), 499–510.

61 Bannerji, "Notes Towards an Anti-Racist Feminism," 12.

62 Ibid.

63 Nandita Sharma, *Home Economics: Nationalism and the Making of "Migrant Workers" in Canada* (Toronto: University of Toronto Press, 2006).

64 Bannerji, "Notes Towards an Anti-Racist Feminism," 11.

65 Audre Lorde, *Sister Outsider: Essays and Speeches* (Trumansburg, NY: Crossing Press, 1984).

66 These panels for the 2008 Congress were co-organized with Donna Pennee, vice-president of the Canadian Federation of the Humanities and Social Sciences, and Maria Wallis, a sociologist and independent academic in Toronto.

67 Ahmed, "This Other and Other Others," 560; Zygmunt Bauman, *Postmodern Ethics* (Oxford: Blackwell, 1993).

68 Ahmed, *Differences that Matter*, 6 and 1–22.

69 Ibid., 12–13.

70 Ahmed, "This Other and Other Others," 570.

71 Ibid., 560; Drucilla Cornell, *Beyond Accommodation: Ethical Feminism, Deconstruction and the Law* (London: Routledge, 1991).

72 Ahmed, "This Other and Other Others," 569–70.

73 Ibid., 570.

74 Ibid., 558.

# 3 : Doubling discourses and the veiled Other: Mediations of race and gender in Canadian media

Yasmin Jiwani

> When social boundaries are imagined as matters of blood or
> stock, then women's bodies assume their age-old role as con-
> duits of male entitlement, power and identity. To attack and
> destroy an ethnic community, you attack and destroy their
> women in sexualized and dehumanizing ways – cut away this
> root of a people, and nothing else will grow, says the logic of
> ethnic cleansing.
> – G. Bhattacharyya, J. Gabriel, and S. Small, *Race and Power*[1]

THE EPIGRAPH QUOTED HERE underscores the centrality of women's bodies in the material and discursive realms. In this chapter, I focus on media representations of the female Muslim body, paying particular attention to the veiled discourses that construct her. The analysis focuses on Canadian mainstream media and its coverage of Muslim women within the domestic and international contexts. By centring the analysis on the strategic use of the hijab and the burqa as signifiers of the Muslim woman, my intent is to emphasize the relational dynamics that are at play in the contrasting opposi-tions and doubling discourses that frame representations of Muslim women "over here" and "over there."

I begin this chapter with a general overview of the mediated construc-tions of Muslim women in the West, focusing on the Orientalist gaze, under-scoring the doubling discourses that are inherent within them. I then proceed to examine contemporary representations of Muslim women in both "soft" media (entertainment) and "hard" media (news) within the con-text of their portrayals "over there," as in Afghanistan, and their representa-tions "over here" in the Canadian context. I conclude by linking these representations to an economy that prevails within the mainstream Western media, demonstrating how these representations serve to buttress strategies of exclusion, expulsion, containment, and commodification. But first, I provide a general backdrop to the main arguments of this essay – the terrain of mediated representations of race and gender signified through the bodies of women of colour within the theatre of the Western mass media, a context which is characterized by intense media concentration and conglomeration.

## Mediations of race and gender

In the dominant media, strategies of exnomination, naturalization, and universalization become the tools whereby dominance is affirmed as the normative frame of reference and whereby explanations that privilege race thinking are proffered as having the most explanatory value. The power of exnomination consists of the "power not to be named."[2] This is also the power of whiteness that forms the invisible backdrop against which stigmatized and valorized Others are profiled. As John Fiske eloquently argues, "The power to see while remaining unseen, the power to put others into discourse while remaining unspoken, is a particularly effective form of power."[3]

This power to define the situation and yet remain unnamed is materially grounded in the corporate concentration and convergence that characterizes the media landscape today,[4] most especially in Canada.[5] The Canadian context is marked by a handful of corporations that control most of the media outlets and publications across the country.[6] In such a situation, it is not unusual to find journalists and editors who are compelled, through threat of losing their jobs, to toe the corporate line and privilege the ideologies of those in power.[7] Indeed, commenting on his media empire and its explicit political position, CanWest founder "Izzy" Asper openly stated that an "anti-Israel bias is a cancer affecting Western media organizations,"[8] indicating that his papers (which at the time were the major dailies in most provinces and one national daily) would not take a pro-Palestinian position. Journalist Patricia Pearson commented, upon her resignation from the *National Post* (CanWest's national daily), that "when CanWest, controlled by the Asper family, acquired the paper from Conrad Black, I no longer dared to express sympathy for Palestinians."[9]

In light of the biases inherent in media monopolies and cartels, it is not surprising then that contemporary news portrayals of Arabs, Muslims, and Islam fare so negatively.[10] That aside, there is a long and entrenched history of negative representations that are circumscribed within a tradition of Orientalism, and thus, as Stuart Hall affirms, contemporary discourses bear these past traces.[11] However, just as Orientalist framings are pervasive in the media, so too are colonial tropes representing racialized groups in general. The economy of media representations works to privilege some groups over others, define particular groups in specific ways, and construct discrete groups as signifying distinct threats. Thus, Black males are often linked to crime in Canadian, British, and American newspapers,[12] and Muslim men are now associated with terrorism. Pnina Werbner argues that these representations signify different forms of racism, each drawing on specific historically inscribed stocks of knowledge.[13]

Stuart Hall's influential work on race and representations anchors this grid within a framework of colonial relations.[14] He argues that the binary relations of Manichean oppositions that constitute racist discourse are predicated on a base grammar of race. This grammar, he maintains, revolves around the following power co-ordinates manifest in colonial discourses about colonized Others: the naturalization of differences; the evacuation of history; and the fixed relations of power, wherein the dominance of one is secured by the inferiorization of the Other. Hall further argues that while this colonial form of "active" racism has now mutated into a more inferential form of racism, the premises on which it is based reflect continuity with previous discourses.[15] Contemporary representations of racialized groups thus bear the traces of previous histories, connoting relations of power, as well as naturalizing and dehistoricizing difference.

However, these representations are not "flat" and unidimensional. Rather, they are marked by an inherent ambiguity, a tension or a contradiction. Thus, Hall argues, within each representation, the ambivalence manifests itself in the tension between the "positive" and "negative" aspect of that representation.[16] The rebellious field slave forms one counterpart to the obedient and submissive house slave, yet both are contained within the representational construct of the slave as a subordinated object of possession. The figure of the "jezebel" is the inverse of the mammy, but both are circumscribed within relations of power. In his analysis of the representations of Indian women in Kipling's literary works, John McBratney also draws attention to this inherent tension conceptualizing it as a "doubling discourse."[17] In this context, the doubling occurs with the concurrent representations of Indian women as weak and helpless and in need of rescue, and at the same time, as evil temptresses that use white male colonizers for their own ends. Chandra Mohanty[18] and Ann McClintock[19] make similar arguments demonstrating the use of these representations in legitimizing conquest and colonization.

Abdul R. JanMohamed suggests that these internal tensions make it possible to experience both desire and repulsion, avowal and disavowal.[20] It is this doubling that enables the media to seize on particular representations at specific points in time, without contradicting the basic grammar of race. A representation of a racialized Other can be positively valorized as a state of exceptionalism at one point, but other representations of the same racialized group can be negatively constructed. In either case, the representations underpin and are contained within relations of power. However, the ideological purchase of these representations is contingent and relational: it is contingent on the ideologies framing the group at a specific historical juncture and it is relational insofar as it is reflective of the larger economy of representations prevailing within the mass media at a given time. This is why race is, as Hall remarks, a "floating signifier."[21]

It is these larger ideologies, grounded in a bedrock of historical knowledge and anchored in material realities, that we need to attend to in order to decipher contemporary representations. Here, I want to draw attention to a framework that Werbner proposes insofar as it allows us to tease apart the different threads and filaments that connect mediated representations to specific historical and material realities, while simultaneously enabling these representations to solidify around particular kinds of "folk devils."[22]

Drawing from Zygmunt Bauman and Michel Wieviorka, Werbner argues that racism is organized around three different logics. These logics are rooted in the Western historical exemplars of racism: American slavery, the Holocaust, and colonialism. She posits that these three logics can be articulated as follows: (a) self-purification that results in the elimination or physical expulsion of that which is considered a threat; (b) subordination that involves the physical exploitation of Others as cheap sources of labour; and (c) assimilation that entails the destruction of the Other's culture. She notes that each of these logics produces a particular variant of a folk devil. As she puts it, " . . . just as there are three logics of racism, so too there are three archetypal demonic figures which the racist imagination conjures up: the slave, the witch and the Grand Inquisitor." In following this logic, the slave represents the Black mugger on the street who is physically powerful and who "threatens the law and order of society." In contrast, the witch is the condensed sign signalling economic threat which in turn is signified by assimilated, successful minorities; the model minorities in the U.S. or the "middle man minorities."[23] Each of these groups is vulnerable to expulsion. Then there is the Grand Inquisitor. Here, Werbner draws on Frantz Fanon and others to explain, in psychoanalytic terms, the racist logic that underpins the figure of the Grand Inquisitor; a logic that she ascribes to the emergence of Islamophobia. Unlike the witch and slave, the Grand Inquisitor symbolizes resemblance with the Self, a resemblance which lends itself to producing a particular kind of intimacy and revulsion. As she explains it:

> The insurrectionist slave is a powerful iconic embodiment of the *id* – of sexuality unbound – but in the permissive society of today such an icon loses much of its terror. The nefarious Jewish or Hindu merchants, icons of sup-

pressed greed, seem less threatening in an age which celebrates consumption and individual self-gratification, thus necessarily less obsessed with the fear of hidden impulses of desire and greed. By contrast, the Muslim, the religious fanatic, the violent terrorist, negates all these impulses. He is, therefore, the folk devil *par excellence* of a post-modern age. The threat is not simply to the uneducated working class or petit bourgeoisie. Islam seems also to be a threat to the intellectuals and elites in Western society because it clashes with contemporary intellectual trends towards anti-essentialism and relativism.[24]

Werbner is, of course, talking about the threat represented by political Islam. As she is quick to point out, not all Muslims in the U.K. or elsewhere share the sentiments or the politics of this interpretation of Islam. Nevertheless, the Grand Inquisitor has been constructed as the contemporary folk devil responding to the specific kind of threat that Islam represents to the West. This threat, Werbner argues, can be located in Europe's history of "the long struggle to escape the Grand Inquisitor, the domination of the Church over the Soul, the stranglehold exerted over the bound body. In this respect, Islamophobia is like other phobias and racisms, an incapacity to cope not only with difference but with resemblance."[25]

This triadic framework offers a useful entry point into the Orientalist framing of Islam and its media representations. However, Werbner makes no room for women's representations in her analysis, nor does she differentiate between how slave women were portrayed as compared to slave men or look at the contemporary representations of Black women as "welfare queens"[26] as opposed to Black men as sex crime perpetrators. Likewise, she makes no mention of the Muslim or the Asian women who tend to be represented as quintessential victims of patriarchal ideologies associated specifically with their cultural and religious heritage.[27] Nevertheless, as iconic figures, the slave, the witch, and the Grand Inquisitor provide us with conceptual tools, albeit as condensed signs, to make sense of the varying and divergent representations that inhere within the mediated sign system of race. However, before turning to the issue of gendered representations of Muslim women, a brief detour is necessary in order to make more explicit the Orientalist roots that lend meaning to the figure of the Grand Inquisitor and to highlight the potential doubling discourses that are operative within it.

## Orientalist framings

In his now classic text, *Covering Islam*, Edward Said makes the argument that representations of Arabs, Islam, and Muslims have tended to be conflated.[28] Muslim communities and nations are constructed as static and homogenized entities. Drawing on his earlier work, Said points to the Orientalist frame as the organizing lens through which the West views the East, indicating that he has "not been able to discover any period in European or American history since the Middle Ages in which Islam was generally discussed or thought about outside a framework created by passion, prejudice, and political interest."[29] This situation has, one could argue, intensified with the events of September 11, which have come to represent a Rubicon, paving the way for the invasion of Afghanistan and subsequently Iraq.

Karim H. Karim's analysis of Orientalist representations of Islam and Muslims in the contemporary media coverage reiterates Said's central points, indicating that representations of Muslim men as "having fabulous but undeserved wealth (they have not *earned* it), being barbaric and regressive, indulging in sexual excess," and as "violent" are increasingly commonplace.[30] His findings are corroborated by Jack Shaheen's extensive analysis of Hollywood films, wherein figures of the veiled Muslim woman as the sexualized and evil Other are similarly pervasive.[31] Orientalism articulates with and encapsulates the grammar of race that Hall identified as underpinning colonial discourses of the Other. It is noteworthy that, as with colonial discourse, Orientalism posits Islam and Muslims as abstracted from history, their differences being naturalized and inferiorized in the process.

Feminist critiques of Said's work have noted the absence of women's subjectification, their role and complicity in shaping Orientalist discourse, and the muted emphasis placed on sexuality.[32] Said, for his part, did emphasize the feminization of the Orient, underscoring its designation as a zone of sexual conquest.[33] For the purposes of the present analysis, these critiques shed light on the importance of examining representations of women both as complicit facilitators of colonialist projects and imperial adventures, as well as subjected women whose material bodies and discursive representations are contested by patriarchal forces both within dominant and colonized groups. Here I draw on Claude Lévi-Strauss's argument,[34] which is also echoed by Floya Anthias and Nira Yuval-Davis,[35] concerning women's role as reproducers of the nation and therefore as critical sites on which the discourses of race and nation are inscribed.[36]

It is in this light that representations constitute the anticipatory ground fertilizing and nurturing subsequent actions that, through such processes, perpetrate a symbolic and discursive violence. This is not to suggest that representations are overdetermined and that audiences lack agency. Rather, in communicating preferred and dominant meanings that are privileged through the selection and combination of particular representations, the media legitimize certain actions and inactions, authorize particular ways of seeing the world, and lend credibility to specific interlocutors.

## Representations of Muslim women in Western media

Considerable literature has documented the stereotypical representations of Muslim women in the Western mainstream media. Here, what I wish to emphasize is the consistent media obsession with Muslim women's practices of veiling in contemporary settings. In previous eras, as for example during Hollywood's beginnings and later during its heyday, the veiled Muslim, Arab, Turkish, and Syrian woman – or whoever fit the notion of "Middle Eastern" woman at the time – was portrayed as a highly sexualized figure. Generally figured as the sensual belly dancer, or the princess (who often converts), or the quarrelsome queen, the Middle Eastern veiled woman represented the elusive, sexually tantalizing, and more often than not the wicked, duplicitous woman.[37] While this representation is still alive in some quarters, the tendency within the news media and current affairs programming has been to project representations of the veiled woman as essentially an abject and victimized Muslim figure.

In the sections below, I turn to the larger, current Western context within which the veil functions as a synecdoche for all manner of things associated with Islam and Muslims. By tracking the discourse surrounding the veil across international, national, and local contexts, we can understand its continuity as well as its symbolic values and the semiotic chains of signification that are amplified through the mass media. But for now I want to distinguish between representations of Muslim women and the hijab "over there" – as in Afghanistan, for example – and their representations "over here." I draw this distinction from Shahnaz Khan's work by the same title.[38] Khan makes the argument that the binaries between the oppressed Afghan women under Taliban rule and the liberated women in the West work to reinforce an ideological divide, elide the historical conditions and structures of power that connect them, while simultaneously suggesting that oppression only exists "over there." However, if this is a first order binary, the second level of the myth is the homogenization of all Muslim women – over here and over there.[39] As Khan puts it: "Such homogenized accounts often present the reader with a series of women who in a sense have been ripped out of their contexts, resulting in a re-plastering of their narratives onto Afghan women and other Muslim women in North America."[40] This "re-plastering" is the organization of Muslim women's representations within the same template of an oppressive, patriarchal Islam. However, I want to suggest another complicating layer – that of the mediating agent between "over here" and "over there." This is the native informant, and more often than not, the ex-pat or diasporic Afghan, a citizen of the West who is now relocated to the East. This assimilated figure, situated in the hyphen that bridges West and East, brings to the East the benefits of the West. Drawing from various examples, I will attempt to demonstrate the various layers of the myth of the veiled woman.

## Veiled intentions – Muslim women "over there"

As numerous scholars have documented, the veil in the West is weighted with semiotic significations that predate the War on Terror and that are installed within Orientalism.[41] To put it another way, the veil itself has become an iconic sign of difference, but one that is reified to the extent that its strategic use, within Western ways of seeing, veils the intentions or motivations of the definer. The veil thus comes to stand in for the mute, passive, and oppressed Muslim woman, a representation that discursively functions as a countersign to the liberated Western woman.[42] In speaking to the recent genre of documentaries that have been released about the veil and Muslim women, Sunera Thobani makes the argument that such representations can be described as "veilomentaries," in that "they are more about the constitution of the Western woman as an emancipated gendered subject, a constitution that relies on the Othering of Muslim women as gendered hypervictims."[43] And as Joan Scott has observed, the obsessive focus on the veil makes it seem "as if patriarchy were a uniquely Islamic phenomenon!"[44]

It is not surprising, then, that Western powers quickly harnessed the veil to legitimize their interventions into Afghanistan. As Eric Louw[45] has observed and Ann Russo[46] has corroborated, the Western feminist concern with the oppression of Afghan women emerged shortly after the Taliban came to power. Yet it was not until 2001 when the War on Terror was unleashed and the "coalition of the willing" exercised its intervention in Afghanistan that the veiled Afghan woman became a strategic pawn in the current geopolitical context. As I have detailed elsewhere, representations of Afghan women as helpless victims of the Taliban and as weak refugees fleeing war remain commonplace in the Canadian print media – so much so that the burqa (the full-body veil) has come to stand for all Afghan women – a metonym that is still in currency.[47] Sherene Razack argues that the imperilled Muslim woman, the barbaric Muslim man, and the white civilized European have become the stock-in-trade characters in the national and international imaginative landscape.[48]

Despite the "intervention" of the international coalition, the reluctance of Afghan's women to unveil – in spite of the forces of "liberation" freeing them from the tyranny of the Taliban – was not used to dismantle this stereotype of the veiled woman as a "gendered hypervictim" but rather to reinscribe it in the dominant discourse. Here, as Sedef Arat-Koç[49] points out, the culturalist argument was invoked to suggest that these women could not be liberated because they were so contained or imprisoned by their culture.

The veiled Afghan woman, as a symbol of oppression under Taliban Islam on the one hand and a victim of culture on the other, has become a floating signifier.[50] She remains mute in one instance and yet, in another, is the voice ventriloquizing a particular reality that fits Western preoccupations and assumptions. The real question, as Lila Abu-Lughod asks in her article on the subject, is: "Do Muslim women really need saving?"[51] But this raises the question as to how this floating signifier, in its gendered formation, is communicated discursively. In other words, what are the markers by which the victim status of Muslim women becomes apparent in ways that resonate with common-sense knowledge? In what contexts is the notion of victimhood made intelligible and how does the victimhood of Muslim women constitute them as "deserving" or "undeserving"/worthy or unworthy of Western benevolence and intervention?

Clearly, the answers to these questions depend on the context. As Jasmin Zine has argued, drawing from Mohja Kahf's historical analysis, Muslim women's representations were not always confined to a victim status.[52] Rather, these representations changed in conjunction with Europe's relationship with Islam, from the crusades to the contemporary stages of globalization. With colonization, the representations of Muslim women became increasingly condensed around this victim status such that it is now an entrenched signifier of difference replete with its associated identifier, the hijab. Miriam Cooke succinctly summarizes this link when she writes about the "four-stage gendered logic of empire."[53] This logic, she suggests,

> genders and separates subject peoples so that the men are the Other and the women are civilizable. To defend our universal civilization we must rescue the women. To rescue these women we must attack these men. These women will be rescued not because they are more "our" than "theirs" but rather because they will have become more "ours" through the rescue mission.... In the Islamic context, the negative stereotyping of the religion as inherently misogynist provides ammunition for the attack on the uncivilized brown men.[54]

Dana Cloud asserts that, "In times of war, images of enemy Others, represented as helpless and savage, are foils for the image of the national self."[55] One could argue that the "national self," in this regard, also changes in relation to the now-altered projection of the Other. If this is indeed the case, then as the War on Terror continues and as public support for it waxes and wanes, one can expect the discourse surrounding the representations of Afghan women to shift.

In examining stories circulating in *The Globe and Mail*, another of Canada's national dailies, it is apparent that the construct of victimhood is structured around an internal tension: there are good, worthy victims and unworthy, undeserving victims. This tension helps to define those victims that are worthy of saving as opposed to those that can be forgotten about.[56] As an ambiguity, it allows for a doubling discourse that lends itself to the kind of ideological harnessing required in recasting or telling a story within a hegemonic frame. Thus, in the case of Afghan women, while the representations in the initial coverage of the War on Terror emphasized the passive, oppressed, and subordinate status of these women, often speaking for them and highlighting their lack of agency, subsequent representations tended to follow an opposite trajectory. Early representations are marked by an obsessive focus on the veil, replete with images showing Afghan women sitting or standing in groups, their faces and bodies masked in anonymity by the burqa. In her analysis of AP wire photographs before and after the fall of the Taliban, Shahira Fahmy found that "women after the fall of the Taliban regime are portrayed as more involved, interactive, more socially intimate and symbolically equal to the viewer."[57] In a seven-year study of these representations that I conducted between 2000 and 2007, it was evident that Afghan women had become noticeably more "worthy," making the transition from victims to survivors.[58] In *The Globe and Mail* (Toronto), for example, the women were given more voice, their heroic efforts were underscored, and their emerging entrepreneurship was taken as a positive sign of "them" becoming more like "us."

It would seem that Western liberation through micro-business entrepreneurship, including that initiated by Beauticians Without Borders, served to make Afghan women worthy victims of rescue.[59] This brings to mind Slavoj Žižek's statement that our empathy "presupposes that in it, *we perceive ourselves in the form that we find likeable*: the victim is presented so that we like to see ourselves in the position from which we stare at her."[60] Consumer capitalism turns on the cultivation of potential Others as consumers, and Afghan women seem to fit the bill.

In September 2009, the floating signifier of the veiled Afghan women reappeared again, this time in *The Globe and Mail*'s week-long series entitled "Behind the Veil: Inside the Lives of Afghan Women." The series ran in both the online and print edition, and promised to unveil the lives of these women through online interviews, podcasts, and discussions.[61] The online version featured six stories about Afghan women. At the bottom of the website, one can scroll through various other links, which provide the reader with an introduction; a "behind the scenes" view (offering unedited footage); the foreign news editor's rationale for undertaking the series; the methodology and "creative journalism" used to get this information; a glossary of keywords; a discussion with Paula Lerner, the freelance photographer, and Jessica Leeder, *The Globe* reporter; an archive of previous stories about Afghanistan published by *The Globe*; a help link that offers a list of other charities and organizations "that can help you help Afghan women"; and a section called "The Observers," which covers the discussions between Sarah Hampson, a columnist, and Sally Armstrong, a well-known author who has written on Afghan women's issues before and who has also written opinion pieces for *The Globe and Mail*.[62] The list goes on with other hot links that invite audience participation: a "conduct your own online interview" with Rangina Hamidi, a human rights activist who is interviewed in the series; a timeline that delineates women's rights in Afghanistan; a reporter's notebook describing "what it's like to write and report from Afghanistan"; a photo gallery consisting of images from Kandahar; and, finally, a comment link that invites readers and viewers to comment on the series as well as on *The Globe*'s coverage of Afghanistan in general.

Website image from *The Globe and Mail*'s "Behind the Veil" series. Reprinted with permission.

Through this series, just as in crime drama serials, we as the audience are invited to be first-person voyeurs, watching the risks and dangers that Afghan women face from the safety of our chairs at home. In the introduction to the series, Jessica Leeder appears on screen and, through her voiceover, recounts to us what compelled her to engage in this venture of uncovering the lives of Afghan women. In her words:

My name is Jessica Leeder and I am a journalist for *The Globe and Mail*. In the past year, I have travelled twice to Afghanistan for the newspaper to work rotations in our Kandahar bureau. While female correspondents working in strict Islamic countries face many barriers that our male colleagues do not, we often gain a rare upper hand when it comes to accessing local women. In the conservative Afghan south, cultural and religious practices prevent females from talking to males who are not their relatives. That means the stories of what it is like to be a woman in this almost pre-historic slice of Afghan society have largely gone untold.

Last spring, I arrived in Kandahar to find security in a more precarious state than it was five months earlier at the end of my first trip. I wondered what this meant for the day-to-day lives of women in the city. While that question was still percolating, I found myself writing about the sad and gruesome public assassination of Sitara Achakzai, one of Kandahar's rare female politicians. I telephoned some of her colleagues that I had quoted before. But this time, they begged me through tears not to quote them, so terrified they had become for their lives. By now, I understood that Kandahar's women were even further from shedding their burqas than I had thought. Instead they were scrambling to put them back on. With the help of a local videographer and translator, *The Globe* set out to find out why.

Over the course of a month, we interviewed ten average women in the city who allowed us to film them, offering a rare window into both disturbing and mundane aspects of daily female life. For reasons of security and domestic obedience, some asked us to obscure their faces. But as our series unfolds this week, you'll meet all of them – widows, mothers, working women, and even a child bride. They'll tell you how improbable it seems that women will ever drive cars in Kandahar. You will hear what its like to be sold like livestock and you'll hear about hopes and far-off dreams.[63]

Throughout this introduction, Leeder's voice is accompanied by stills of Afghan women in various poses – cooking, walking, being interviewed, working, and so on. They are the visual objects creating a colourful backdrop to her narrative.

What is most interesting about Leeder's introduction is how she situates herself as a female reporter having more access to Afghan women than her male counterparts. Here, her discursive strategy of invoking a comparison with male reporters serves two functions. First, it legitimizes her as a credible authority (a working journalist returning to Kandahar) and her special status as a woman who can penetrate into the zones that men cannot, akin to the woman anthropologist who can enter a Zenana or harem, a space forbidden to men. Leeder thus has the kind of access that her male counterparts do not have, but this is also what highlights her special status: She is a woman like these Afghan women are and, hence, she can identify with them, bring out their stories in a way that resonates with the construction of a universal womanhood.[64] This stance is reminiscent of the imperial feminists who would publicize the oppression of their Third World sisters in a way that would also underscore their own superior status.[65] As Meyda Yeğenoğlu puts it,

> [T]he declaration of an emancipated status for the Western woman is contingent upon the representation of the Oriental woman as her devalued other and this enables Western woman to identify and preserve the boundaries of self for herself. . . . To be Western here implies feeling that one is entitled to universalize one's particular achievements and interests. The effacement/erasure of the particularity of Western women in the name of universality has the effect of legitimizing the colonial-feminist discourse as an act of generosity and as an act of conferring upon Middle East women the privilege of participating in Western women's universalism rather than a denial and negation of difference.[66]

Leeder's references to Kandahar as a "pre-historic slice of Afghan society," and a place where women beg through tears and are subordinated to "security and domestic obedience," invoke representations of Afghan society as ultrapatriarchal and Afghan women as fearful, submissive, and caught in the bind of tradition. These women are subject to "death by culture" as Uma Narayan describes it.[67] To recount Sitara Achakzai's assassination in April 2009 as "sad and gruesome" summons images of other Afghan women's murders under the Taliban, notably those that have circulated in popular culture.[68] Take, for example, *Beneath the Veil* (2001), an undercover documentary by British-Afghan filmmaker Saira Shah that focuses on women being executed by the Taliban, and *The Death of a Princess* (1980), a British docudrama that recounts the story of a love affair between a princess and her lover, an affair that resulted in their executions. These resonances raise the question as to whether *The Globe* was in fact mimicking Shah's documentary *Beneath the Veil* when it titled its series *Behind the Veil*.

Undoubtedly, the Taliban are patriarchal. My analysis above is not to suggest otherwise, but to underscore the perception that is being cultivated, a perception that effectively elides the patriarchal nature of Western societies and that of other non-Islamic societies. That Leeder can openly attest to the differential treatment of male and female reporters is a case in point, not only for women reporters in Afghanistan but also for women reporters in the newsrooms in Canada and across other Western nations.[69] The Western context of gender inequality remains concealed in her introduction.

Leeder's final and tantalizing promise to her viewers is that they will get to meet these women, all of whom are average, and even a "child bride." This effectively erases the sexualized violence that prevails against children in the West – children also who are not married but are nonetheless subjected to violence, sexual and otherwise. However, it is the tone of her voice when she says that we, as the audience, will actually meet one of these exotic creatures that introduces the element of sensationalism – the layers that invoke a certain structure of feeling, an emotional combination of anticipation and pity.[70] Interestingly, it is the picture of the child bride that viewers first got to see when they visited the website at the time when the series began.

Leeder's introduction paves the way to the individual interviews with each of the ten "average" women, who are interviewed with the aid of an interpreter. Most of them are wearing veils or burqas. We only see their faces when they are in an all-women's group doing work. Aside from the translator, the only other voice that is featured in some depth is that of Rangina Hamidi, a human rights activist working in Kandahar. Hamidi is described by Leeder as an "an Afghan-born woman who abandoned a comfortable ex-pat life in Virginia six years ago to pick up the fight for women's rights in Kandahar." Here again, the contrast between Afghan women who are born in Afghanistan and Afghan women who have come from elsewhere in the diaspora is accentuated. Unlike the other women who speak through the interpreter, Hamidi is well versed in English and able to recount the situation of women in Kandahar. She emphasizes the lack of security and the constant threat that women face on a daily basis. This strategic use of the diasporic voice to tell the stories and struggles of Afghan women raised and living in Afghanistan is similar to the manner in which *The Globe* has covered Afghan women's stories in the years preceding this series. As I have noted elsewhere, diasporic Afghan women are often used to portray the "civilizing" influence of the West as evident in their role of bringing Western notions of equality to their homeland.[71] They also become the native informants who model the "benefits" of the West and who provide insights into the world and lives of the colonized.[72]

In the midst of the individual interviews and Hamidi's account, printed words emerge in bold on the screen that highlight particular aspects of their travails. These words capture the points that the reporter/*The Globe* wishes the audience to retain in their minds. For instance, in the first article of the series entitled "Back behind the Veil," Hamidi relates her observations of the deteriorating situation in Kandahar. At specific points, her statements are bolded and centred on the screen with particular words capitalized: "I am questioning for the first time if it's worth my life. LIFE." Subsequently she says, "My right to live, my right to life, is not even in safety. SAFETY." The ten women who have been interviewed have their words transcribed at the bottom of the screen but not in this same fashion.

Overall, the series works to communicate the heightened fear and risk under which women in Kandahar live. In presenting them as worthy victims, the series deploys the following discursive devices: the women are portrayed individually; their narratives are told in a way that humanizes their concerns; and their struggles are depicted as being insurmountable, thereby offering us, as the audience, a way to support them. Ultimately, they are rendered as being just like "us," only a few decades behind it seems. Their agency is clearly underlined in the representations of their struggles against the oppressions they face. Hamidi's statement in one of these segments is to highlight the fact that women in the U.S. fought for "over thirty years" to get the vote; how then does one expect change to occur in Afghanistan overnight? Tribal and backward Muslim men are to be blamed for the situation, while historical and structural forces are eliminated from this story.

Overall, the message one gleans from these webcasts is that "we" (Canadians) need to remain in Kandahar to restore order, and that the order that exists is extremely fragile. Women are the ones suffering the most and, hence, it is "our" duty as concerned citizens (and as Canadians with an army stationed there) to remain in Kandahar. The worthiness of the Afghan women victims comes through and is facilitated by the website's link to charities and organizations to which "we" can donate in order to save our Afghan sisters. What is carefully elided in *The Globe*'s coverage is the continuing question of Canada's involvement in Afghanistan and the emerging reports of Canadian forces as being complicit in transferring Afghan prisoners to be tortured.[73] These questions are part of the larger context that is significantly muted by the media's obsessive focus on the veil.

I turn now to the representations of Muslim women in the veil "over here."

## Veiled intentions – Muslim women "over here"

By far, the most popular and well-known iconic representation of the veiled Muslim woman in contemporary Canadian popular media can be found in the figure of Rayyan (played by Sitara Hewitt, a non-Muslim), the second-generation, feminist Muslim physician featured in the popular and highly celebrated CBC comedy sitcom *Little Mosque on the Prairie*. However, Rayyan represents an exception to the normative treatment of veiled Muslim women in the Canadian press or in other television crime dramas.[74] More than that, she is the doubled Other – the inverse side of the oppressed veiled Muslim woman. Though wearing the hijab, she is sufficiently assimilated to be consumed as an exotic Other.[75] Through her representation, "we" as the audience, get to see past the stereotype, but at the same time, we also see that Rayyan is constrained by the patriarchal logic of the mosque (as evident in the episode concerning gender segregation within the mosque) and its male congregants.[76]

*Little Mosque on the Prairie* represents a form of "soft power"[77] – clothing its messages about the diversity of the Muslim *ummah* in a language that is at once appealing, comical, and humane.[78] The show stresses the universality of the everyday problems facing all groups, whether they are Muslims, Christians, or secularist zealots. In other words, through this universalizing discourse, the show enfolds and levels off the differences between these groups while, at the same time, underscoring and deconstructing the popular image of Muslims as threats, rendering their differences as peculiar. In the end, as Cañas emphasizes, "the form of the cultural text – a television comedy – can only use satire, parody, and mimicry in comedic ways that, while challenging orientalist discourse of the Muslim Other, produces its own silences."[79] These silences, as she points out, have to do with the deep cleavages within the *ummah*, the particularities and specificities of the different characters, and the notion of resolution as easily achieved through the forging of a harmonious multiculturalism. More to the point, these silences, I contend, have to do with the particular ways in which Muslim women are represented in a television show. The foil to Rayyan, the assimilated Muslim woman, is her mother, who is a Muslim convert, and not a "good Muslim" at that. Rayyan is the "hybrid" figure reflective of a mix between whiteness and Arabness (from her father's side). As a hybrid, she is "more like us" and, as I have pointed out in my analysis of Asian heroines, this strategy becomes one way in which to defuse or neutralize the threat of race.[80] She is then the figure "in-between" – mediating the links between the oppressed Muslim woman and her liberated white, Western, and secularized counterpart. As well, she mediates the contrasts between the "good" and "bad" Muslim woman (in the case of this sitcom, these figures are represented by Fatima, the African Muslim woman who tends to be more traditional, and Rayyan's mother, the "bad" Muslim convert).

While *Little Mosque on the Prairie* is emblematic of "soft power" in that the format is a situation comedy presented as a half-hour series and intended for familial consumption, news, as in television news programming, press reports, and current affairs magazines, which are laced with considerable credibility and legitimacy, can be construed as a form of hard power. This is not to suggest that all forms of "soft power" convey positive or benign representations of Muslim women.[81] Rather, "hard" news has an aura of authenticity that makes it more amenable to being incorporated within regimes of truth. Nonetheless, as I have shown in an analysis of the popular CBC crime drama *The Border*, Muslim women within this genre still occupy that zone of otherness – as the exotic, the erotic, and the dangerous.[82] Here, they are often portrayed as mute, passive, burqa-clad women or as white women who have "gone native" and therefore pose a substantial danger to domestic security. The only "in-between" figure is the hybrid Muslim woman – assimilated into Western ways but still retaining her Muslim religious allegiance and identity, and terribly conflicted by it all.[83]

Most representations of veiled Muslim women that are communicated through news and documentaries (those formats constitutive of "hard power") tend to cohere around the negative end of the binary, underscoring the entrenched media template of the oppressed Muslim woman living under ultrapatriarchal Islam. Since 9/11, there have been several events within Canada that have secured considerable press and television coverage concerning Muslim women; events that have centred on the veil, honour killings, and forced marriages. This has paralleled corresponding and heightened media coverage of terrorist attempts resulting in Muslim men held in confinement under suspicion. Razack has fittingly described the situation as one where Muslims are "cast out," bereft of any legal protection and held in a state of exception.[84] In a like manner, Shiraz Dossa has described the contemporary Canadian media representations of Muslim males as "Lethal" Others.[85] These representations are suggestive of Werbner's notion of the Grand Inquisitor – the Muslim folk devil – discussed earlier. Since gender is relational, the terrorist figure of the Muslim male stands in opposition to the hypergendered victim figure of the veiled Muslim female. While Muslim men are presented as proactive aggressors, Muslim women are portrayed as passive victims. Nevertheless, there are some doubling discourses at play even here, which I attempt to demonstrate in the discussion below, paying particular reference to Canadian examples of veiled women.

## Flashpoints

In a recent article, Jasmin Zine outlines the various flashpoints that have mobilized media attention on Muslim women and girls, raising questions about the viability of multiculturalism, national identity, and citizenship.[86] Briefly, these signal events occurred in 2007 and involved the Hérouxville Citizens' Code or "les normes de vie" that stipulated, among other things, that women are not allowed to be stoned, barred from public life, and veiled; the sharia law debate in Ontario that was sparked by a Muslim group wanting to mediate marital conflicts and divorces through the application of particular interpretations of Quranic law;[87] the expulsion of Asmahan Mansour, an eleven-year-old girl banned from playing an indoor soccer game in Laval, Quebec, because she was wearing a hijab; and the murder of Aqsa Parvez, a sixteen-year-old Pakistani teen who was killed by her father in Toronto. To these, I would add the alleged murder of Shemina Hirji by her husband in Vancouver that was alluded to in the media as an honour killing, and the Chief Electoral Officer's decree that women wearing the niqab would not be allowed to vote in the 2007 election in Quebec. It is noteworthy that all these incidents occurred within the period of one year. Coincidentally, by 2007, what had begun as a Canadian peacekeeping initiative in Afghanistan had grown into a fully operational militarized intervention.[88]

Zine identifies the explanatory frameworks offered by the media as cohering around three distinct tropes: (1) disciplining culture; (2) death by culture; and (3) death of culture. She categorizes the sharia law debate as a case of disciplining culture, whereby "the disciplinary technologies used to produce and reproduce the nation as a hegemonic cultural entity"[89] are invoked to contain and discipline the demands of unruly minorities. The murder of Aqsa Parvez by her father was framed by the media as a case of honour killing, fitting the paradigm outlined by Narayan as one of death by culture.[90] Within this framework, the culture of the Other is seen as being misogynist, and violence is seen as a part of the culture rather than as a universal attribute of patriarchy.[91] The Vancouver media also attempted to explain Shemina Hirji's death in the same manner, attributing her murder to the cultural values and norms of her murderer.[92] Zine attributes the actions leading up to and the coverage of Asmahan Mansour's ban from the soccer game to the "death of culture."[93] She notes that Mansour was banned from the field on the grounds that her hijab posed a threat to her safety. The argument used to legitimize the ban implied that it could strangle her, metaphorically suggesting her strangulation by her culture. Zine suggests that this fear is rooted in the perception of a "'civilisational danger' posed by a veiled Muslim woman."[94] Similarly, the Hérouxville Citizens' Code was "an attempt to preserve the 'homeliness' of the nation from the onslaught of estrangement and unfathomable cultural difference personified as the body of a veiled Muslim woman. Muslim women become 'imperiled Muslim women imperiling the nation.'"[95] Zine argues that through these tropes, Muslim women "unsettle the nation" by threatening the national imaginary of a tolerant, multicultural country. The strategies of containment, exclusion, and stigmatization (through the language of culture) keep threatening Muslim women at bay, which is evident in the language of the Hérouxville Citizens' Code.

While the Muslim woman as a threat to the nation is a significant theme in Zine's work, as it is in Joan Scott's analysis of the politics of the hijab in

France, there is another side to this representation that demands further interrogation.[96] I am referring here to the sexual discourses that are at work in not only presenting a concealed figure in the burqa-clad or veiled woman but also in the tyranny of the possession of the Muslim woman's body. An example of this can be found in the following exchange of an interview conducted by a Montreal radio talk show host with a Muslim female political candidate running for local office.

> The host, Benoît Dutrizac, invited [Samira Laouni] for a frank chat Wednesday. . . .
>
>     "It's very cute, your veil, the Islamic veil – it's very sexy," Dutrizac began.
>
>     "It's my headscarf," Laouni corrected him.
>
>     "No, but it's beginning to become sexy for us. Men in the West, miscreants like me, we're starting to find that sexy – be careful!"
>
>     . . .
>
>     After the break, Dutrizac went on the attack again. Can a "good Muslim woman" have sex with different men? Can she drink wine?
>
>     She's free to make her own choices, Laouni replied. "It's not up to me to judge anyone."
>
>     Did she know that under Muslim sharia law, "if I were to rape you here today, you'd need witnesses to testify that you weren't consenting?" Dutrizac asked.[97]

In this excerpt, the racist premises and propositions are abundantly clear. Yet it is the contextual framework that imbues these remarks with added significance. As Wendy Naava Smolash argues, "the meaning of any given raced identity, which justifies violence against those deemed 'Other,' is contingent on context."[98] Hence, this explicitly racist-sexist example is not, I would argue, a random occurrence. In this case, the Muslim affiliation of the wearer of the hijab is the constructed and construed source of stigmatization.

Laouni's insistence on wearing a hijab is construed by Dutrizac as an affront to the discourse of Quebec cultural sovereignty, an irritation that invokes anger and frustration but which, at the same time, is also seductive – seductive as in invoking the desire to possess the woman through the unveiling. This desire is signified through sexualized violence – the threat of rape. In her analysis of Orientalism from a feminist perspective, Meyda Yeğenoğlu observes, "this metaphysical speculation or mediation, this desire to reveal and unveil is at the same time *the scene of seduction*. The metaphysical will to know gains a sexual overtone."[99]

Hence, the simultaneity of the seductiveness combined with the perceived deception (marked by the concealment) makes it imperative for the veiled woman to be unveiled and, in the process, both subjugated through gender and possessed through sexual violence. It is not surprising, then, to see the threat of sexual violence being invoked in other such situations. For example, in 1994, when Émilie Ouimet, a twelve-year-old Québécoise student, wore a veil to school, she was expelled. The other students taunted her with threats of rape. The principal expressed concerns for her safety, indicating that it was her insistence on wearing the veil that made her vulnerable to such violence.[100]

There is yet another layer to the context that needs to be scrutinized in order to critically situate Dutrizac's interview with Laouni. The extract of this interview was published by *The Gazette* in Montreal, an English-language newspaper in a francophone milieu. In this context, the discursive construction of the veil and the Muslim woman is embedded in another discourse – that of the French–English conflict, itself a material testimony to the dual colonization of Quebec. Sharon Todd has aptly remarked that racial minorities are often used strategically by the two colonial powers in order to demonstrate each other's racism and lack of tolerance.[101] Hence, in the case of the media images of the veil, "veiling the other" unveils the dominant gaze.[102] As Sonya Fernandez observes, by "aligning the veil with hostility to democracy and the fear of fundamentalism, the language of violence weaves its way into the very fabric of the hijab."[103]

## Conclusion

The story of Afghanistan continues, as all war stories do. But this time, there is no clear victor; just a country of victims whose continual rescue has to be legitimized under different guises. Women, it seems, have become the quintessential victims in this geopolitical war, but their worthiness as victims can only be assured by their constant demonstration of struggle against the odds and their ability, through time, to become more like "us." In the meantime, the discourse has shifted to allow for the construction of "moderate" Talibans who can be trusted to look after their women. That this is so opportune at a time when Western military forces are seeking ways to leave Afghanistan is not surprising. The veiled Afghan woman remains the quintessential "floating signifier": ready to be called forth to legitimize another invasion or, more conveniently for the current situation, to legitimize the abandonment of a "failed state."

Representations of the veil in the Canadian domestic context point to the weight of the template of Islamic oppression which has so easily shifted terrains – from "over there" to "over here" – as evident in the furor generated over the sharia law debate and the quick and easy frame imposed on the murders of Aqsa Parvez and Shemina Hirji. Finally, the threat that the Muslim woman signifies in the case of the Hérouxville Citizens' Code, as in other European instances concerning the banning of the hijab, can be located in her role as reproducer of the culture. In this case, it is her role as reproducing Islam that invokes the paranoia of the cultural dilution on the part of the sovereign state (premised as it is on fictional blood lines and a presumed homogeneity). The threat of the veil is then the threat of an engulfing Islam, a threat that resonates with the historical archive of the crusades and that has to be contained somehow if not neutralized.

In terms of the economy of representations that prevail within the mainstream Canadian media, then, it can be surmised that the veiled Muslim woman remains the abject and passive Other in contrast to her purposive and aggressive male counterpart. Just as she is the gendered hypervictim, he is the ultrapatriarchal figure. However, each of these representations is organized around a doubling discourse. Whereas the traditional Muslim woman is constrained by her allegiance to Islam and imprisoned by her culture (as signified by her veil), the assimilated and Westernized Muslim woman is her doubled counterpart, reflecting the benefits of the West as they are embodied in liberated representations. She is "more like us." However, this liberated Other continues to play the role of a mediating agent, often as a native informant and, at other times, as the foil against which the traditionalism of the abject Muslim woman can be highlighted. The assimilated Other can be commodified and, through such commodification, consumed by popular media.

Whether as the gendered hypervictim in the East or the woman bound and killed by her culture in the West, the veiled Muslim woman has considerable currency in contemporary times. As a floating signifier, her representation can be corralled to fit particular hegemonic designs. And through her liberated, Westernized, and assimilated counterpart, the veiled Muslim woman "over here" or "over there" can be taught the benefits of the West, so that she, too, can become "more like us."[104]

## Notes

This research was supported by the Social Sciences and Humanities Research Council.

1 Gargi Bhattacharyya, John Gabriel, and Stephen Small, *Race and Power: Global Racism in the Twenty-First Century* (London: Routledge, 2002), 92.
2 John Gabriel, *Whitewash: Racialized Politics and the Media* (London: Routledge, 1998), 13.
3 John Fiske, *Media Matters: Race and Gender in U.S. Politics*, rev. ed. (Minneapolis: University of Minnesota Press, 1996), 217.

4 Edward S. Herman and Robert W. McChesney, *The Global Media: The New Missionaries of Corporate Capitalism* (Washington: Cassell, 1997).

5 Leslie R. Shade and Michael Lithgow, "The Cultures of Democracy: How Ownership and Public Participation Shape Canada's Media Systems," in *Mediascapes: New Patterns in Canadian Communication*, 3rd ed., ed. Leslie R. Shade (Toronto: Nelson Publishers, 2010), 200–20.

6 James Winter, *Democracy's Oxygen: How Corporations Control the News* (Montreal: Black Rose Books, 1997); James Winter, *Media Think* (Montreal: Black Rose Books, 2002).

7 Robert A. Hackett, Richard Gruneau, Donald Gutstein, Timothy A. Gibson, and NewsWatch Canada, *The Missing News: Filters and Blind Spots in Canada's Press* (Ottawa: Canadian Centre for Policy Alternatives and Toronto: Garamond Press, 2000).

8 Irwin Block, "CanWest Chief Attacks 'Cancer' in the Media: Anti-Israel Bias 'Destroying Credibility,' Fundamental Precepts of Honest Reporting Have Been Abandoned, Israel Asper Says," *The Gazette* (Montreal), October 31, 2002, A3.

9 Patricia Pearson, "See No Evil, No More," *The Globe and Mail* (Toronto), April 19, 2003, A19.

10 See Karim H. Karim, *Islamic Peril* (Montreal: Black Rose Books, 2000); Sina Ali Muscati, "Arab/Muslim 'Otherness': The Role of Racial Constructions in the Gulf War and the Continuing Crisis with Iraq," *Journal of Muslim Minority Affairs* 22,1 (2002), 131–48; Sherene H. Razack, *Casting Out: The Eviction of Muslims from Western Law and Politics* (Toronto: University of Toronto Press, 2008).

11 Stuart Hall, "The Whites of Their Eyes: Racist Ideologies and the Media," in *The Media Reader*, ed. Manuel Alvarado and John O. Thompson (London: British Film Institute, 1990), 9–23.

12 Travis L. Dixon and Daniel Linz, "Race and the Misrepresentation of Victimization on Local Television News," *Communication Quarterly* 27,5 (2000), 547–73; Travis L. Dixon and Daniel Linz, "Television News, Prejudicial Pretrial Publicity, and the Depiction of Race," *Journal of Broadcasting & Electronic Media* 46,1 (2002), 112–36; Travis L. Dixon, Cristina L. Azocar, and Michael Casas, "The Portrayal of Race and Crime on Television Network News," *Journal of Broadcasting & Electronic Media* 47,4 (2003), 498–523; Robert M. Entman, "Modern Racism and the Images of Blacks in Local Television News," *Critical Studies in Mass Communication* 7,4 (1990), 332–45; Fiske, *Media Matters*; Stuart Hall, Chas Critcher, Tony Jefferson, and Brian Roberts, *Policing the Crisis: Mugging, the State, Law and Order* (London: MacMillan Press, 1978); Mary Beth Oliver, "African American Men as 'Criminal and Dangerous': Implications of Media Portrayals of Crime on the 'Criminalization' of African American Men," *Journal of African American Studies* 7,2 (2003), 3–18.

13 Pnina Werbner, "Islamophobia: Incitement to Religious Hatred – Legislating a New Fear?" *Anthropology Today* 21,1 (2001), 5–9.

14 Hall, "The Whites of Their Eyes"; Stuart Hall, ed., *Representation: Cultural Representation and Signifying Practices* (London: Sage and The Open University, 1997).

15 See also Cornel West, "A Genealogy of Modern Racism," in *Race Critical Theories*,

ed. Philomena Essed and David T. Goldberg (Malden, MA: Blackwell Publishers, 2002), 90–111.

16 Hall, "The Whites of Their Eyes."

17 John McBratney, "Images of Indian Women in Rudyard Kipling: A Case of Doubling Discourse," *Inscriptions* 3,4 (1988), 47–57.

18 Chandra Talpade Mohanty, "Cartographies of Struggle: Third World Women and the Politics of Feminism," in *Third World Women and the Politics of Feminism*, ed. Chandra T. Mohanty, Ann Russo, and Lourdes Torres (Bloomington: Indiana University Press, 1991), 1–47.

19 Anne McClintock, *Imperial Leather: Race, Gender and Sexuality in the Colonial Context* (New York: Routledge, 1995).

20 Abdul R. JanMohamed, "The Economy of Manichean Allegory: The Function of Racial Difference in Colonial Literature," *Critical Inquiry* 12,1 (1985), 59–87.

21 Stuart Hall, "Race: The Floating Signifier (Transcript)," Media Education Foundation, 1997, ⟨http://www.mediaed.org/assets/products/407/transcript_407.pdf⟩, accessed October 7, 2009.

22 Werbner, "Islamophobia," 5.

23 A term coined by Edna Bonacich in reference to economically successful minority groups, as for example, the Asians in East Africa. Bonacich quoted in Werbner, "Islamophobia," 6.

24 Werbner, "Islamophobia," 8.

25 Ibid.

26 Wahneema Lubiano, "Black Ladies, Welfare Queens, and State Minstrels: Ideological War by Narrative Means," in *Race-ing Justice, En-gendering Power, Essays on Anita Hill, Clarence Thomas, and the Construction of Social Reality*, ed. Toni Morrison (New York: Pantheon Books, 1992), 323–61.

27 See Yasmin Jiwani, *Discourses of Denial: Mediations of Race, Gender and Violence* (Vancouver: UBC Press, 2006); Sherene H. Razack, *Looking White People in the Eye: Gender, Race, and Culture in Courtrooms and Classrooms* (Toronto: University of Toronto Press, 1998).

28 Edward Said, *Covering Islam: How the Media and Experts Determine How We See the Rest of the World* (New York: Pantheon Books, 1981).

29 Ibid., 23.

30 Karim, *Islamic Peril*, 62; emphasis in the original.

31 Jack G. Shaheen, *Reel Bad Arabs: How Hollywood Vilifies a People* (New York: Olive Branch Press, 2001).

32 Lisa Lowe, *Critical Terrains: French and British Orientalisms* (Ithaca, NY: Cornell University Press, 1994); Reina Lewis, *Gendering Orientalism: Race, Femininity and Representation* (New York: Routledge, 1996); Meyda Yeğenoğlu, *Colonial Fantasies: Towards a Feminist Reading of Orientalism* (Cambridge: Cambridge University Press, 1998).

33 For instance, Said argues that "the relation between the Middle East and the West is really defined as sexual: The association between the Orient and sex is remarkably persistent. The Middle East is resistant, as any virgin would be, but the male scholar wins the prize by bursting open, penetrating through the Gordian knot

despite 'the taxing task.'" Edward Said, *Orientalism* (New York: Random House, 1978), 309. See also, Sherene H. Razack, "Race, Space and Prostitution: The Making of the Bourgeois Subject," *Canadian Journal of Women and the Law* 10,2 (1998), 338–76.

34 Claude Lévi-Strauss, *Structural Anthropology*, trans. C. Jacobson and B.G. Schoepf (New York: Basic Books, 1963); Claude Lévi-Strauss, *The Savage Mind* (Chicago: University of Chicago Press, 1966).

35 Floya Anthias and Nira Yuval-Davis, *Racialized Boundaries: Race, Nation, Gender, Colour and Class and the Anti-Racist Struggle* (London: Routledge, 1992).

36 Such a depiction is, as Himani Bannerji notes, dehumanizing as it objectifies women as no more than "handmaidens of god, priest, and husband." Himani Bannerji, *The Dark Side of the Nation* (Toronto: Canadian Scholars' Press, 2000), 160.

37 See, for instance, the documentary *Hollywood Harems*, writ. and dir. Tania Kamal-Eldin, 25 min., Women Make Movies, New York, 1999, vhs/dvd; Shaheen, *Reel Bad Arabs*; Ella Shohat and Robert Stam, *Unthinking Eurocentrism, Multiculturalism and the Media* (London: Routledge, 1994).

38 Shahnaz Khan, "Between Here and There: Feminist Solidarity and Afghan Women," *Genders Online* 33 (2001), ⟨http://www.genders.org/g33/g33_kahn.html⟩, accessed June 15, 2003.

39 Here I draw on Roland Barthes discussion of the myth as an ideological sign constructed from the striations of different signifiers and signified. See Roland Barthes, *Mythologies,* trans. Annette Lavers (London: Paladin Press, 1973).

40 Khan, "Between Here and There," para 45.

41 Sedef Arat-Koç, "Hot Potato: Imperial Wars or Benevolent Interventions? Reflections on 'Global Feminism' Post-September 11th," *Atlantis: A Women's Studies Journal* 26,2 (2002), 433–44; Katherine H. Bullock and Gul Joya Jafri, "Media (Mis)Representations: Muslim Women in the Canadian Nation," *Canadian Woman Studies* 20,2 (2000), 35–40; Dana L. Cloud, " 'To Veil the Threat of Terror': Afghan Women and the 'Clash of Civilizations' in the Imagery of the U.S. War on Terror," *Quarterly Journal of Speech* 90,3 (2004), 285–306; Myra Macdonald, "Muslim Women and the Veil: Problems of Image and Voice in Media Representations," *Feminist Media Studies* 6,1 (2006), 7–23; Valentine Moghadam, "Afghan Women and Transnational Feminism," *Middle East Women's Studies Review*, 16,3/4 (2001), 1–12; Meghana Nayak, "Orientalism and 'Saving' U.S. State Identity after 9/11," *International Journal of Feminist Politics* 8,1 (2006), 42–61; Christine Noelle-Karimi, "History Lessons: In Afghanistan's Decades of Confrontations with Modernity, Women Have Always Been the Focus of Conflict," *The Women's Review of Books* 19,7 (2002), 1, 3–4; Carol A. Stabile and Deepa Kumar, "Unveiling Imperialism: Media, Gender and the War on Afghanistan," *Media, Culture & Society* 27,5 (2005), 765–82; Bradford Vivian, "The Veil and the Visible," *Western Journal of Communication* 63,2 (1999) 115–39; Yeğenoğlu, *Colonial Fantasies*; Jasmin Zine, "Muslim Women and the Politics of Representation," *American Journal of Islamic Social Sciences* 19,4 (2002), 1–23.

42 Mary Ann Franks, "Obscene Undersides: Women and Evil between the Taliban

and the United States," *Hypatia: A Journal of Feminist Philosophy* 18,1 (2003), 135–56.

43 Sunera Thobani, "Gender and Empire: Veilomentaries and the War on Terror," in *Global Communications: Toward a Transcultural Political Economy*, ed. Paula Chakravartty and Yuezhi Zhao (Lanham, MD: Rowman and Littlefield, 2008), 221.

44 Joan Wallach Scott, *The Politics of the Veil* (Princeton: Princeton University Press, 2007), 4.

45 Eric P. Louw, "The 'War against Terrorism': A Public Relations Challenge for the Pentagon," *Gazette: The International Journal for Communication Studies* 65,3 (2003), 211–30.

46 Ann Russo, "The Feminist Majority Foundation's Campaign to Stop Gender Apartheid," *International Feminist Journal of Politics* 8,4 (2006), 557–80.

47 Yasmin Jiwani, "War Talk – Engendering Terror: Race, Gender and Representations in Canadian Print Media," *International Journal of Media & Cultural Politics* 1,1 (2005), 15–21.

48 Sherene H. Razack, "Imperilled Muslim Women, Dangerous Muslim Men and Civilised Europeans: Legal and Social Responses to Forced Marriages," *Feminist Legal Studies* 12,2 (2004), 129–74.

49 Arat-Koç, "Hot Potato, Imperial Wars or Benevolent Interventions?"

50 Uma Narayan, *Dislocating Cultures: Identities, Traditions and Third World Feminism* (London: Routledge, 1997).

51 Lila Abu-Lughod, "Do Muslim Women Really Need Saving? Anthropological Reflections on Cultural Relativism and Its Others," *American Anthropologist* 104,3 (2002), 783–90.

52 Zine, "Muslim Women and the Politics of Representation."

53 Miriam Cooke, "Saving Brown Women," *Signs: A Journal of Women in Culture and Society* 28,1 (2002), 468–70.

54 Ibid.," 468.

55 Cloud, " 'To Veil the Threat of Terror,' " 290.

56 "Unworthy" victims, as I have outlined elsewhere, are often those who have no value to society, or whose values fall outside the normative boundaries of middle-class morality, as for example, sex trade workers and Aboriginal women. See Yasmin Jiwani and Mary Lynn Young, "Missing and Murdered Women: Reproducing Marginality in News Discourse," *Canadian Journal of Communication* 31,4 (2006), 895–917.

57 Shahira Fahmy, "Picturing Afghan Women: A Content Analysis of AP Wire Photographs During the Taliban Regime and After the Fall of the Taliban Regime," *Gazette: The International Journal for Communication Studies* 66,2 (2004), 106.

58 Yasmin Jiwani, "Helpless Maidens and Chivalrous Knights: Afghan Women in the Canadian Press," *University of Toronto Quarterly* 78,2 (2009), 728–44.

59 Beauticians Without Borders is a charitable organization funded by Clairol, Revlon, L'Oreal, and MAC, with many of these cosmetics companies supplying the products. The aim is to teach Afghan women how to be skilled beauticians. (See Hamida Ghafour, "Beauticians Without Borders Teach Basics to Afghan Women," *The Globe and Mail*, February 24, 2004, A1.) This presupposes that Afghan women

had no such skills before, as attested by the first-hand accounts of the Western beauticians who went over to train Afghan women. As Said has noted of Orientalism in general, the lens through which the Other is viewed bears no traces of history. Afghan women are suddenly discovered as needing beauty treatments and lacking beautifying skills. Said, *Covering Islam*.

60  Quoted in Franks, "Obscene Undersides," 146; emphasis added.

61  Online, the podcasts and interviews can be found at ⟨http://www.theglobeandmail .com/news/world/behind-the-veil/⟩. At the time when I began writing this paper, all the information on this website was freely accessible. However, since October 19, 2009, access to the different links has been suppressed and is only available to the GlobePlus members – those who have paid to subscribe to the online version of the paper.

62  Sally Armstrong, "Veiled Threat: Afghanistan's Women under Taliban Rule," *Homemaker's* (1997), 16–29; "Shrouded in Secrecy," *Chatelaine* (May 2001), 131; and *Veiled Threat, The Hidden Power of the Women of Afghanistan* (Toronto: Penguin Canada, 2003).

63  Jessica Leeder, "Behind the Veil" (September 2009), ⟨http://www.theglobeandmail.com/news/world/behind-the-veil/⟩, accessed September 20, 2009.

64  Chandra Talpade Mohanty, "Under Western Eyes: Feminist Scholarship and Colonial Discourses," in *Third World Women and the Politics of Feminism*, ed. Chandra T. Mohanty, Ann Russo, and Lourdes Torres (Bloomington: Indiana University Press, 1991); Russo, "The Feminist Majority."

65  Valerie Amos and Pratibha Parmar, "Challenging Imperial Feminism," *Feminist Review* 17 (1984), 3–19; Antoinette M. Burton, "The White Woman's Burden: British Feminists and the 'Indian Woman,' 1865–1915," in *Western Women and Imperialism: Complicity and Resistance*, ed. Nupur Chaudhuri and Margaret Strobel (Bloomington: Indiana University Press, 1992), 137–57; McClintock, *Imperial Leather*.

66  Yeğenoğlu, *Colonial Fantasies*, 102.

67  Narayan, *Dislocating Cultures*.

68  Achakzai was shot dead by four gunmen outside her home in Kandahar.

69  See Gertrude J. Robinson, *Gender, Journalism and Equity: Canadian, U.S., and European Perspectives* (Cresskill, NJ: Hampton Press, 2005); Karen Ross, "Selling Women (Down the River): Gendered Relations and the Political Economy of Broadcast News," in *Sex & Money: Feminism and Political Economy in the Media*, ed. Eileen Meehan and Ellen Riordan (Minneapolis: University of Minnesota Press, 2002), 112–29.

70  On the topic of sensationalism, see Joy Wiltenburg, "True Crime: The Origins of Modern Sensationalism," *American Historical Review* 109,5 (2004), 1377–404.

71  Yasmin Jiwani, "The Great White North Encounters September 11: Race, Gender, and Nation in Canada's National Daily, *The Globe and Mail*," *Social Justice* 32,4 (2005), 50–68.

72  Marnia Lazreg, "The Perils of Writing as a Woman on Women in Algeria," *Feminist Studies* 14,1 (1988), 81–107.

73 At present, there are 2,800 Canadian soldiers in Afghanistan, mostly concentrated in Kandahar. See the NATO International Security Assistance Force report at ⟨http://www.nato.int/isaf/docu/epub/pdf/isaf_placemat.pdf⟩.

74 See for instance, Yasmin Jiwani, "Soft Power – Policing the Border through Canadian TV Crime Drama," in *The Political Economy of Media and Power*, ed. Jeffery Klaehn (New York: Peter Lang, 2010), 275–93.

75 Suren Lalvani, "Consuming the Exotic Other," *Critical Studies in Mass Communication* 12,3 (1995), 263–86.

76 Jasmin Zine, Lisa K. Taylor, and Hilary E. Davis, "An Interview with Zarqa Nawaz," *Intercultural Education* 18,4 (2007), 379–82.

77 The distinction between "hard" and "soft" power is drawn from Nye and Owen's framework that focuses on the role of the media in promulgating hegemonic ideologies within international contexts. They argue that this is "soft" power in contrast to the "hard" military power of the state. See Joseph S. Nye, Jr. and William A. Owens, "America's Information Edge," *Foreign Affairs* 75,2 (1996), 20–36. However, my use of "hard" and "soft" also combines Bird and Dardenne's insight about the differences between "hard" news as factual reportage versus "soft" news, which includes columns and human interest stories. See Elizabeth S. Bird and Robert W. Dardenne, "Myth, Chronicle, and Story: Exploring the Narrative Qualities of News," in *Mass Communication as Culture*, ed. James Carey (Beverley Hills: Sage, 1988), 67–87.

78 *Ummah* or *uma* refers to the larger Muslim community.

79 Sandra Cãnas, "The Little Mosque on the Prairie: Examining (Multi) Cultural Spaces of Nation and Religion," *Cultural Dynamics* 20,3 (2008), 209.

80 Yasmin Jiwani, "The Eurasian Female Hero(ine): Sydney Fox as the Relic Hunter," *Journal of Popular Film & Television* 32,4 (2005), 182–91.

81 See, for instance, Catherine Burwell, "Reading Lolita in Times of War: Women's Book Clubs and the Politics of Reception," *Intercultural Education* 18,4 (2007), 281–96; Amira Jamarkani, "Narrating Baghdad: Representing the Truth of War in Popular Non-Fiction," *Critical Arts: A South-North Journal of Cultural and Media Studies* 2,1 (2007), 32–46; Cynthia Weber, "Not Without My Sister(s): Imagining a Moral American in Kandahar," *International Feminist Journal of Politics* 7,3 (2005), 358–76.

82 Jiwani, "Soft Power."

83 I am referring specifically to the first season of *The Border*. By the second season, this Muslim woman, played by Nazneen Contractor, has been killed and replaced by another, this time a woman of mixed racial heritage.

84 Razack, *Casting Out*.

85 Shiraz Dossa, "Lethal Muslims: White-Trashing Islam and the Arabs," *Journal of Muslim Minority Affairs* 28,2 (2008), 225–36.

86 Jasmin Zine, "Unsettling the Nation: Gender, Race and Muslim Cultural Politics in Canada," *Studies in Ethnicity and Nationalism* 9,1 (2009), 146–93.

87 Meena Sharify-Funk, "Representing Canadian Muslims: Media, Muslim Advocacy Organizations, and Gender in the Ontario Shari'ah Debate," *Global Media Journal, Canadian Edition* 2,2 (2009), 73–89.

88 According to Michael Byers, the escalation of troops signifying a full militarized intervention occurred in 2002 when Canadian troops participated in a full "combat mission under U.S. control in Afghanistan rather than participate in the British-led multinational force because [they] were 'tired' of acting as mere peacekeepers, according to a senior British defence official." See Michael Byers, "Afghanistan: The Wrong Mission for Canada," *The Tyee*, October 6, 2006, ⟨http://thetyee.ca/Views/2006/10/06/Afghanistan/⟩, accessed November 27, 2007.

89 Zine, "Unsettling the Nation," 152.

90 Narayan, *Dislocating Cultures*.

91 Razack, *Looking White People in the Eye*.

92 See Yasmin Jiwani, " 'Culture' Depends on Who's Defining It," *The Vancouver Sun*, August 8, 2007, Op-Ed Page.

93 Zine, "Unsettling the Nation," 152; emphasis in the original.

94 Ibid., 156.

95 Ibid., 158.

96 Scott, *The Politics of the Veil*.

97 Jeff Heinrich, "Politics 101: The Art of Staying Calm in the Event of Obnoxious Questioning," *The Gazette* (Montreal), September 13, 2008, A15.

98 Wendy Naava Smolash, "Mark of Cain(ada): Racialized Security Discourse in Canada's National Newspapers," *University of Toronto Quarterly* 78,2 (2009), 746.

99 Yeğenoğlu, *Colonial Fantasies*, 45–46; emphasis in the original.

100 Helle-Mai Lenk, "The Case of Émilie Ouimet: News Discourse on Hijab and the Construction of Québécois National Identity," in *Anti-Racist Feminism*, ed. Agnes Calliste and George Dei (Halifax: Fernwood, 2000), 73–88.

101 Sharon Todd, "Veiling the 'Other', Unveiling Our 'Selves': Reading Media Images of the Hijab Psychoanalytically to Move beyond Tolerance," *Canadian Journal of Education* 23,4 (1998), 438–51; also see Lenk, "The Case of Émilie Ouimet."

102 Meyda Yeğenoğlu further remarks, "The visible cultural effects one can induce by veiling or unveiling woman makes it a convenient signifier for the contending parties to fight out their differences through manipulating this highly charged symbol. The veil is thus transformed into a medium through which the male subjects of the nation can articulate their desires and fears, but, more importantly, can assert 'national' difference. However, the very construction of national difference is possible only through the mediation of woman, a mediation which nevertheless has to be repressed." *Colonial Fantasies*, 126.

103 Sonya Fernandez, "The Crusade over the Bodies of Women," *Patterns of Prejudice* 43,3/4 (2009), 284.

104 See Cooke, "Saving Brown Women," 468.

# 4 : Abandonment and the dance of race and bureaucracy in spaces of exception

Sherene H. Razack

> The state of exception is an anomic space in which what is at stake is a force of law without law (which therefore should be written: force of ~~law~~).
>
> – Giorgio Agamben, *State of Exception*[1]

ON MAY 21, 2009, SUAAD MOHAMUD,[2] a Canadian citizen of Somali origin, was prevented from returning to Canada from Kenya because a Kenyan airport official found that she did not look like her passport photo. For three months, Mohamud languished in Kenya while Canadian officials privately concluded that she was an imposter and publicly claimed that an inquiry into her case was ongoing.[3] Acquiescing several months later to Mohamud's demand for a DNA test, Ottawa finally relented when the test confirmed her identity and she was allowed to return home. When she sued the federal government in 2010, Mohamud became something of a cause célèbre, her experience leading many to wonder whether racialized Canadians enjoy the same rights as do other Canadian citizens.

Mohamud's predicament is a familiar one for people of colour who are nearly always assumed to be refugees or immigrants. Political discourses routinely feature the duplicitous refugee who lies about his or her identity to kind, unsuspecting Canadians (who are the embodiment of civility), forcing the latter to impose very strict rules about identity documents. Indeed, beginning with Bill C-86 to amend the *Immigration Act* in 1992, and followed by amendments in subsequent legislation creating an "Undocumented Convention Refugee in Canada Class," Canada joined other Western nations in ensuring that those who arrived without appropriate documents proving their identity would have fewer juridical and social rights. As I have written elsewhere, despite the fact that refugees routinely have trouble accessing travel documents (something that is acknowledged in UN Conventions), laws restricting the rights of those who do not have documents to prove their identity have been passed easily as politicians appealed to the idea that refugees (in this context principally from Somalia and Afghanistan but also the Middle East and Africa) were *inherently* duplicitous.[4] Suaad Mohamud's story was not therefore surprising to many, and its contradictions (demanding that she prove her identity but simultaneously making it difficult to do so) created a double bind that is all too familiar to refugees and immigrants.

What is worthy of close scrutiny in Mohamud's case is the role played by bureaucracy. When the affidavits of the federal government were made public, a picture emerged of the strange bureaucratic world Mohamud encountered. As the *Toronto Star* reported, "migrant integrity officer" Paul Jamieson maintained that there were four factors giving rise to his suspicion that Mohamud was not who she claimed to be: she bore only a resemblance to her photo; a younger sister Jihan was named on Mohamud's immigration application several years earlier and he suspected that the woman before him was Jihan and not Suaad; Mohamud knew her own biographical details (something imposters know); and imposters are usually related to rightful passport holders. Jamieson interviewed Mohamud three times in five days when she was first detained. For her part, Mohamud maintained that she had no sister in Kenya (and only half sisters elsewhere) and that someone else filled out her original immigration application. Jamieson's affidavit outlined that although he did not take notes, he remembered that Mohamud named Randy Jackson as a professor at Humber College but no such person could be found on the college's website. His suspicions were aroused because Randy Jackson is the name of a popular media figure from the show *American Idol*. Mohamud said that she attended Humber College but was thinking of attending Seneca College. Although she claimed to work for ATS, a courier company, she did not know what ATS stood for. She also could not name the Canadian prime minister, Toronto's mayor, or the teachers at her son's school, and she did not know that TTC stood for the Toronto Transit Commission. In a subsequent interview, Jamieson felt that her signature did not match the signature on her documents, and that her name was spelled several different ways. He found nothing but vagueness and evasion in Mohamud's responses to his questions; she would often cry and profess not to know why he kept calling her by the name Jihan. He was not impressed by the package of secondary documents she possessed and thought that she was "six or seven centimetres shorter" than what was described on her driver's license. At one time, Jamieson wondered if, from one day to the next, he was in fact speaking to the same person.

These details hint at an anxiety on Jamieson's part but one which the bureaucracy is unable or unwilling to resolve through the most obvious pragmatic means. Although Jamieson had serious doubts about Mohamud, no measures were taken (such as measuring her height or doing a DNA test) to establish the truth. Ottawa practised its own duplicity, evident in the email indicating that officials publicly said one thing and did another. In response to Mohamud's demand for a DNA test to prove her identity, officials privately opined that the $500 test was too costly and publicly announced that they had done all that was possible to establish identity. As an individual, Mohamud's fate was not Ottawa's concern and it did not trouble anyone in the consular office unduly. Consular officials did not act as her protector, making serious efforts to establish her citizenship, but rather as her prosecutor, anxious to secure Canadian borders against fraudulent claimants. More significant, however, than indifference and hostility is the bureaucratic impulse to ask for proof of identity and then refuse to make it possible for it to be given. In this respect, the Catch-22 in which Mohamud was caught up was not something we associate with liberal democratic nations such as Canada.

Suaad Mohamud's treatment by the state is perhaps one end of the continuum of abandonment. On the other, we might place Maher Arar and Omar Khadr, and other Canadians who were tortured with the complicity of the Canadian government. Arar was rendered to Syria where he was tortured, an act the United States undertook with the co-operation of the Canadian government. Omar Khadr is detained at Guantanamo, where he was brought as a fifteen year-old accused of participating in terrorist acts in Afghanistan. Canada has refused to request his extradition. Both men are Canadian citizens of Muslim origin. Canadians en masse still do not demand that Omar Khadr should be brought back to Canada to face our courts. The two ends of the continuum must be considered separately. Yet there is something to be gained in considering both ends of the continuum as one phenomenon of abandonment.

How might we understand this phenomenon of abandonment that ranges from rendition to torture to blocking the re-entry to Canada of racialized citizens? Are these simply moments of racial prejudice, as so many would have it, prejudice, nonetheless, that is officially sanctioned? Might they (only) reveal ignorance, incompetence, meanness, and arrogance? Or, are these glimpses into the racialized structure of citizenship in which people of colour, suspected of duplicity, must always be policed and kept at the margins of law and community? In this chapter, I reflect on these questions through an exploration of a group of individuals whose experience of abandonment predates 9/11. "Security delayed" individuals form a small group.[5] Although numbers are hard to establish, the term applies to refugees who have been granted asylum in Canada but whose full citizenship has been denied on the grounds that they pose a security risk. In exploring how individuals find themselves placed in this group and the effect this has on their lives, an effect best described as a social death, we are able to see the micropractices that create a class of individuals who are, as Zygmunt Bauman has notably described refugees, *in the national community but not of it.* When refugees are "suspended in a spatial void," as Bauman has suggested, they become extraterritorial.[6] While it is tempting to see abandonment as a feature of a post–9/11 world, the experience of security delayed individuals reminds us that states do in fact preserve spaces of abandonment – as Agamben has shown, a place where the lines of belonging to the national community are drawn.

I offer the argument that what happens to security delayed individuals as well as to individuals like Mohamud, Arar, and Khadr arises in the first instance because they are marked as a different order of humanity and are immediately ushered into a legal and bureaucratic zone where full legal rights do not apply. Race starts the process of eviction and is its main technological tool. Professional competence, context, and, paradoxically, rationality are all unnecessary in the zone of non-law. As Toni Morrison has noted, "contradiction, incoherence and emotional disorder 'fit' when the subject is black. . . . Difficult explanations are folded into the general miasma of black incoherence."[7] Race is not only necessary in order for abandonment to occur but also for the state of exception to function. We see its workings in bureaucracies such as the one Suaad Mohamud encountered, and in the ones which security delayed individuals confront, primarily in those Kafkaesque moments when nothing makes sense. The state of exception is a place where rationality and law are absent and where "black incoherence" fills in the gaps left by their authorized departure. In believing that zones of non-law invite and even mandate incoherence, I am speaking to those who have carefully charted the incompetence, the "stereotyping," and the "intellectual atrophy" so frequently in evidence in the security and immigration encounter.[8] I suggest that these aspects are intrinsic to spaces where law has authorized its own suspension. The law, Churchill famously saw, does not apply to barbarians. Competence, professional courtesy, and rationality, are not owed to barbarians. No sense makes sense, to restate Morrison's point colloquially, when the subject is one who has been evicted from political community and clearly confined to a lower order. No amount of training or cautionary notes about respecting the human rights of others will compensate for this foundational logic of the places where law has suspended itself. It will be the exceptional bureaucrat who withstands the temptation to do good, when evil is policy, Hannah Arendt reminded us.[9] In part one of what follows, I elaborate on the connections between abandonment, race, and the exception. In part two, I show how abandonment is practised in the case of the security delayed.

## Part One: Abandonment, race, and the exception

A space of exception, as Agamben has clarified, is a space in which the law has declared that it will not operate. Such spaces confirm the power of the sovereign to act outside his or her own law. I have argued elsewhere[10] that race is necessary to the operation of spaces of exception. That is to say, race thinking, a structure of thought that divides up the world between the deserving and the undeserving according to racial descent, accustoms us to the idea that the suspension of rights for those in spaces of exception is warranted in the interests of national security. Race thinking, captured in the phrase "they are not like us" and also necessarily in the idea that "they" must be killed so that "we" can live, becomes embedded in law and bureaucracy so that the suspension of rights appears not as violence but as the law itself. Violence against the racialized Other comes to be understood as necessary in order for civilization to flourish, something the state must do to preserve itself. It is the terrifying union of state machinery and race thinking, one that Irene Silverblatt refers to as "the dance of bureaucracy and race born in colonialism,"[11] that both gives birth to and sustains the space of exception. The state of exception is diffused through bureaucracy; like a virus spreading through the land, it attacks vulnerable populations, contaminating everyday bureaucratic practice.

If race has long been the hook that makes us accept places where there is the force of law without law, it is not surprising that when we examine state of exception mechanisms, we find them in emergency measures *and* in immigration law.[12] As legal scholars have noted, immigration law has remained largely outside of a human rights regime and, with rare exceptions, courts are generally willing to accept that non-citizens do not possess the same human rights as others.[13] As illustrated in the position taken by the Canadian Security Intelligence Service (CSIS) in a hearing defending its aggressive actions in the interrogation of a refugee for security reasons, bureaucrats and security professionals share the view that "courts have clearly stated that aliens have lesser rights than citizens."[14]

### The bureaucracy: Violence rendered civil[15]

In considering the situation of a Kurdish refugee who is internally displaced and who is the target of considerable state violence in Turkey, Anna Secor writes: "He is banished within the state. He is accused and always already guilty, subject to the mythical violence of the law over naked life. His only space is a space of invisibility."[16] Here Secor draws on Agamben's idea of the ban, noting that the subject who is banned exists in a threshold of indistinction, neither inside the law nor outside of it. For Agamben, as Secor writes, this zone of exception "permeates and overflows the spaces where the law operates in its various modes."[17] Here, Secor notes, is where we find "the everyday imbrications of violence and law." The police, she suggests, operate at this frontier of law, spreading zones of indistinction wherever they operate as law without law. When refugees encounter the police at the frontier, they are soiled. It is an "unholy space" where guilt and abjection reign. I propose below a similar reading of what happens in the spaces of bureaucracy to security delayed individuals. The bodies of those persons defined as sub-humanity become unholy spaces, spaces where there is no place for logic, competence, or understanding. Their bodies become spaces of exception, or concentration camps, where law has authorized that the full rule of law does not apply.

It is not surprising that those who implement state of exception measures – judges, lawyers, security professionals and bureaucrats, among others – do not experience themselves as engaging in violence or as denying fundamental rights to a group on the basis of race, but rather as fulfilling a duty. As David Goldberg suggests, echoing Hannah Arendt's analysis of imperialism, one feature of race in modernity is the fact that racist effects are routinized, entrenched in arrangements that "systematically close off institutional access on the part of individuals in virtue of group membership, and indeed that render hidden the very instrumentalities that reproduce that inaccessibility...."[18] The routines of bureaucracy mask the creation of the camp (the space of exception) and it is difficult to find individual wrongdoers in such a context. Violence is rendered civil through these arrangements. It is not the immigration or security officer whom we recognize as violent but rather the detainee whom the state official is required to keep in line. Hidden behind closed doors, "the conniving egoism and violence of men with a reputation for fine manners"[19] (a reputation acquired solely in the dominant group and not, in fact, among the subordinate themselves who know only too well their incivilities) clothes the state's violence in civility.

A very specific logic is in place in those routinized arrangements where access to full citizenship is closed off. Bauman describes its features:

> The "established," using their power to define the situation and impose the definition of all those involved, tend to enclose the newcomers in an iron cage of stereotype, "a highly simplified representation of social realities." Stereotyping creates "a black and white" design that leaves "no room for diversities." The outsiders are guilty until proven innocent, but since it is established who combine the roles of prosecutors, examining magistrates and judges and so simultaneously make the charges, pronounce on their truth and sit in judgement, the chances of acquittal are slim, if not nil.[20]

The refugee or concentration camp's inmates lose their right to due process in two ways: one person from one bureaucratic level is both judge and party to the case; and the camp is a place where there is only "a highly simplified representation of social realities." It is for these reasons that activists often describe the security hearing as Kafkaesque, a place where nothing can make sense because sense is so ruthlessly excluded from the start. The refugee must be made "unthinkable," Bauman reminds us. We refuse them the right to be imagined and, in so doing, we refuse them the right to be.[21]

## Part Two: Security delay as a camp

In June 1992, the Canadian government introduced Bill C-86, Amendments to the *Immigration and Refugee Protection Act,* which contained a new component for determining inadmissibility. Whereas in the past those who had committed violent acts were inadmissible, in C-86, refugees became inadmissible if there were reasonable grounds to believe that they *would engage* in terrorism. Further, persons could now be found inadmissible if they were members of an organization engaged in terrorism. The Bill offered no definition of terrorism or membership. It did provide, however, that those who met these criteria could nevertheless be admissible if they could satisfy the minister that their admission would not be detrimental to the national interest. Importantly, the amendments proposed that the Canadian Security Intelligence Service (csis or the Service) would identify possible terrorists while the Department of Immigration would retain the ultimate authority to decide who would be excluded. Asylum seekers would remain caught between these two agencies. As Sharryn Aiken has shown, when Bill C-86 became law in 1992, and terrorism became a new category of security inadmissibility overseen by the newly created Department of Public Security, a new era began, one in which security and immigration officials began to cross lines in refugee protection more vigorously than before.[22] Processes not only lacked rigour but refugees reported being threatened and asked to be informers in exchange for a positive report. Refugees appeared to be unfairly targeted, and those refugees involved in resistance movements back home, activities for which their own states had persecuted them, were considered by csis to be potential terrorists. The Canadian Council for Refugees documented nineteen cases in which it appeared that the majority of targeted refugees were not involved in direct terrorist action but instead were members of organizations in situations where membership was inescapable.[23] The discretion built into the revised *Immigration Act* itself, Aiken concluded, left "an unacceptably wide scope for xenophobic prejudices to inform administrative and judicial decision making. It also leaves certain groups susceptible to decision making based on popular and pervasive stereotypes."[24]

The amendments to the *Immigration and Refugee Protection Act* leave a great deal to an individual immigration officer's discretion, but it is not here that it first announces itself as a space of exception. That refugees who are granted asylum (and thus acknowledged as persecuted) now must undergo a second screening for their *potential* to commit violent acts shapes the security encounter as a place where proof of having committed violent acts is redundant. Law itself becomes redundant. There is no way to prove what a person will or will not do; screening invites, and even mandates, that security and immigration officials find recourse not in the laws of evidence but in assumptions about the nature of people and places, the very technology that is racism. The refugee, as Bauman powerfully suggests quoting Foucault, is locked in a drifting "place without a place, [a place] that exists by itself, that is closed in on itself and at the same time is given over to the infinity of the sea."[25] It is not surprising, then, that in this space of law without law, there is no need for logic, no need for context, no need for coherence. The coherence that exists is achieved at the outset: refugees are people to whom the normal rules do not apply. Tautologically, they must be screened for their abnormalities.

Aiken discusses the case of Suleyman Goven, a Kurdish refugee, illustrating, I believe, the three key features of the security delay experience: illogic, the absence of legal rules, and race. At the beginning of the 1990s, Mr. Goven fled Turkey in fear of persecution from the Turkish state. Accepted as a Convention refugee, he applied for permanent residence and received an "interview" with CSIS in the fall of 1994. In what he described as a day-long "interrogation" without food or water, where CSIS officers indulged in a good cop/bad cop routine, alternately threatening him that he would never receive his landing and assuring him that he did not have to be afraid, Mr. Goven was questioned about his support for a Kurdish group, the PKK, which was considered to be a terrorist organization. As a founder of a Kurdish community centre in Toronto, Mr. Goven was frequently involved in protests against the Turkish state. During the interview, he was shown pictures of members of the PKK who were dead and whose pictures were hanging on the walls of the community centre, and asked about the rank he held in the PKK. Denying that he was involved in the PKK, Mr. Goven nevertheless expressed admiration for them, although he condemned their recent acts of violence. Although he was not told directly that a member of his community had informed on him, he was told that his telephone calls had been monitored. Almost a year later, the Service informed Immigration of the results of the interview, the details and final decision of which were not revealed to

Mr. Goven. When he had not received an answer by 1997, Mr. Goven complained to the Security Intelligence Review Committee (SIRC) (an option that is now closed); his complaint was heard late in 1998 and then again early in 2000 in a hearing presided over by the Honourable Robert Rae.

The uniqueness of the legal terrain that is the state of exception is nowhere better demonstrated than when an attempt is made to treat the space of exception as though it were an ordinary legal space. The SIRC's report, written by Mr. Rae, concluded that CSIS had not demonstrated that Mr. Goven was a member of a terrorist group and recommended that he be processed for landing immediately.[26] Mr. Goven was then reinterviewed by immigration officials and an officer once again determined that there were reasonable grounds to believe that he was a member of a terrorist group. A judicial review of the officer's decision followed and here, too, it was determined that the officer had not properly considered the SIRC report in her finding. Although the court directed the case for reconsideration by another immigration officer, Mr. Goven remained in the labyrinthine world of security delay individuals for several years, pursuing information on his case, finding that his friends and acquaintances were still being questioned by CSIS, and pursuing a claim that his constitutional rights to security of the person and to equality had been infringed.[27] He was not cleared for landing until 2006.

If the lengthy processes and their circular nature (what is established in one place is swiftly discounted in another and no one agent can be held accountable for the outcome) do not already convey the nature of the bureaucracy through which Mr. Goven's eviction from the national community was accomplished, it is in the SIRC report written by Rae and in the Service's rebuttal to the report[28] that we can locate some of the practices of security professionals and the security paradigm that produces the "security delayed." In Mr. Goven's account, CSIS asked him to reveal information about other Kurds, something he refused to do. For its part, CSIS found him to be sympathetic to the PKK, something deduced from his own words (and, it appears, from an informant) and from his activities as a founder of a Kurdish community centre in Canada. CSIS considered Mr. Goven evasive and untruthful during the interview. One indicator of his untruthfulness concerned his declaration that he did not attend a protest in Montreal. CSIS noted that he had signed the form requesting authorization to attend the protest but at the SIRC hearing, when he finally had an opportunity to learn what some of the evidence was and had a chance to defend himself, Mr. Goven pointed out that he was in Toronto that day and did not attend the protest even though his name appears on the request for a permit.[29]

As Didier Bogo has written, security professionals operate from an ethos of secrecy and confidentiality made defensible by their claim that security concerns require a specialized knowledge and that the protection of national interests place security activities beyond the public's scrutiny. As a result, security professionals do not need to be precise, to fully prove their claims, or to operate within a structure of accountability.[30]

It is, however, security's role in the establishment of the state of exception (the eviction from the law of those who threaten our borders) that puts in place the absence of accountability. There is no one to call to account in a space of exception since there are no legal subjects. As Agamben reminds us, nothing committed against the inmates of the camp can be considered a crime.[31] In Mr. Goven's case, since he was not given the full information of what was being held against him, a number of misreadings and errors were made. More than this, however, a finding that Mr. Goven was possibly a member of the PKK, a terrorist organization, seemed to flow from the simplified approach taken towards proving membership. In his findings, Rae concluded that the Service utilized an understanding of membership in a terrorist group that lacked sophistication, and he recommended that "a more sophisticated analysis framework be developed for officials making assessments."[32] The Service had wrongly concluded that Mr. Goven was a member of a terrorist organization, indicting him for his sympathies and for his activities on behalf of his community. Principally, he noted that to make a determination that an individual was an active member of a terrorist group required context, an analysis that CSIS was not interested in doing. He pointed out that groups once considered terrorist organizations were no longer so (for example the ANC and the PLO). Further, many terrorist groups are complex and have branches that do not engage in terrorist activities. The Service had to make a greater effort to determine if support for an organization meant full participation in activities devoted to violence. Ironically, the Service itself, in its rebuttal to Mr. Rae's report, saw the pursuit of details and complexity as indulging in speculation. It wrote:

> The SIRC report's final conclusion, therefore, appears to result from a political assessment of a specific group as "freedom fighters," or "good terrorists," rather than terrorists. The danger of such an analysis is that the determination of who is or is not a terrorist becomes a purely speculative judgment depending on whether one sympathizes with the cause or not.[33]

If we abandon context simply because it may take us into political waters, our only other option remains judgement without analysis, a quick profiling against which individuals have little recourse. Pursuing context, however, and insisting on accountability, contradicts the very idea of the state of exception. Individuals without legal personality cannot be given a social existence where context matters; they have already been evicted from the social and the rational.

Membership in a terrorist group as well as the meaning of an individual's activities both in Canada and elsewhere are indeed difficult things to establish. As is clear from Mr. Goven's case, secret procedures where an individual is unable to defend himself, either because he has been intimidated or is not given an opportunity to rebut what is held against him, leaves the door open for abuses of due process and arguably limits the quality of information CSIS is able to gather. Mr. Goven relates that, during the interview, it quickly became evident that CSIS understood very little of the context in which the terrorist group in question operated. They did not appear to know, for example, that the PKK was primarily a military one – "like guerrillas fighting in the mountains" – a profile he did not fit.[34] His sense of being judged without recourse by individuals who did not know the context sufficiently is one shared by the security delayed individuals I interviewed, some of whom believe that the security "mindset" is not only unsophisticated and ill-informed but also sustained by racist assumptions.

The practices evident in Mr. Goven's case can be found in all of the nineteen cases examined by the Canadian Council for Refugees, and in the accounts of the seven security delayed individuals I interviewed.[35] They are also visible from the chart of thirty delayed individuals in one law firm's client list. Although there is an overlap between these data bases, the processes they reveal are typical of what Bogo has called "the securitization of migration."[36] Individuals have committed no specific acts that indicate that they are a security risk. Rather, they are considered to have a profile that suggests terrorism, an opinion rather than a fact, as CCR points out, and one in a context where terrorism remains undefined. Evidence consists of identifying markers and there is little or no investigation into the social and political contexts in which they originate.

In the view of the Canadian Council for Refugees, groups that have been the most likely to be among the security delayed include Iranians associated with the Mujahedin-E-Khalq (MEK) movement in Iran at the end of the 1970s and early 1980s, Kurds, Tamils, Sikhs, Algerians associated with Islamic groups, and Palestinians. The chart of cases in one law firm reveals that Ethiopians and Eritreans, those from other parts of the Muslim world, and a few Latin Americans can also find themselves marked as security risks. Security delayed individuals, therefore, are those with histories in conflict-ridden parts of the Third World; ironically, the very conflicts that have resulted in their seeking asylum, and in most cases being granted it, in the first place. Thus individuals who opposed the Shah and found themselves participating in, or simply caught up in his overthrow, through a formal, casual, or even tenuous association with the Mujahedin-E-Khalq, earn the marking of having associated with a group committed to violence, just as do those who associated with the Mujahedin fighting the Soviets in Afghanistan. Since it is the original branding that counts, the fact that individuals may have been marginally involved or fully involved in a legitimate struggle (which Canada might have even supported), or that they may have been fleeing persecution from these same groups, appears to have little influence on the outcome. Once a Mujahedin always a Mujahedin – country, context, or personal history notwithstanding. As the CCR concludes, individuals are condemned for their associations and not for specific acts for which they bear personal responsibility.[37] Aiken observes that the broad discretion built into the Act on the issue of guilt by association produces "a generalized bias in favour of designating the acts of non-state agents as terrorist, but not similar acts carried out by the state (particularly those which are strategic allies)."[38]

Error, misjudgement, and illogic mark the security encounter. N., a former journalist employed by a magazine owned by the PLO and controlled by its then leading faction, Fateh, found herself cast in security limbo in 1996 after being interviewed by CSIS without the benefit of a translator. Her interview with CSIS offered clues as to the source of her security problems. N. was asked if she was aware that the PLO was involved in hijackings and if she believed in violence. To the former, she replied no, since she interpreted the question to mean "do you have knowledge of hijackings?" Asked whether or not she attended the mosque, she at first replied no and then added that her son did because he was receiving Arabic lessons. N. was asked about her membership in an organization that did not exist, one that to her ears sounded Iranian rather than Palestinian. Once she was even asked about political events in 1962, a year in which she would have been seven years old. Twice interviewed by the same immigration officer whom she believed was politically biased against her, N. only learned the extent of her troubles when she received a letter in 2000 informing her that she was inadmissible due to her status as a former member of the PLO, and specifically of Yasser Arafat's Al-Fatah faction. In 2005, during a motion for discovery, her lawyer accidentally learned that the fact she had travelled five times with Yasser Arafat was being regarded as suspicious activity.[39]

F., also Palestinian, shared a similar experience, but one marked by an overt racism. Arriving in 1993 from Tunisia (after being forced to flee from Abu Dhabi), F. was interviewed in 1995 and asked (by a hostile interviewer of Coptic Egyptian background who appeared to have an open anti-Muslim bias), in reference to Arafat, if she knew "those terrorists." In a second CSIS interview, an interviewer asked her about suicide bombers after commenting to F. that she must be very happy to be in a society where she could wear what she wanted and where she could live on her own as a woman. Struck by the assumptions made by her interviewers about Muslim societies, F. was even more concerned that they did not seem to understand the material realities of the context from which she had just fled. For example, the Palestinian community in Tunisia at the time was a relatively small one where most Palestinians were employed by the PLO and where everyone knew everyone else. Asked about whom she knew and whom she worked for, F. could only indicate that she did in fact know PLO leaders. In her own account, F. recalled that she remained defiant during the interview, refusing to condemn the PLO.[40] Her defiance is one that the majority of those interviewed exhibited. Suleyman Goven, for example, refused to condemn the PKK outright. Others refused to condemn the Mujehedin or other liberation groups with which they were involved or familiar. Accidentally finding out that his claim was delayed because he was a leader in an Ethiopian resistance movement, Leenco Waqayyo remained proud of his involvement in armed struggle against the Mengistu regime in Ethiopia, believing that it was the only route to democracy. He continues to be an activist on behalf of his people and, ironically, is frequently consulted by the Canadian government among others as an expert on the region. Waqayyo was forced to accept the Norwegian government's offer of residence since he cannot easily continue his life in Canada under the conditions of security delay.[41] Chileans, condemned for their involvement in anti-Pinochet organizations in which there were both violent and non-violent factions, also do not concede that their activities were wrong. One can only speculate on the cost of this defiance.[42]

In a bureaucracy in which context matters very little and there is a legally sanctioned inattention to detail and due process, racism has free rein. Confronted with racism, the clear impression that the details of history and context do not matter, and perhaps more than anything the lack of direct information about what is held against them, many security delayed individuals conclude that their "crime" has been one of ideology. As N. succinctly put it, "Acts don't matter; it's thoughts and being Muslim."[43] Less certain of its systemic thrust, F. feels only that it was her bad luck to get a racist and ill-informed officer, but she, too, believes that her "crime" was the expression of "emotional support for the PLO."[44] A. feels that a "cold-war mentality" and incompetence of the officials with whom he dealt landed him in security limbo.[45] Other interviewees shook their heads in disbelief describing the instances in which security officials were simply "stupid," as S. repeated several times when I interviewed him.[46] These judgements of security and immigration officials, however, are deeply inflected with helplessness and frustration. In the end, N. reflected, "They can fabricate any story. They can accuse you, try you, convict you, all without letting you know what for."[47] As F. put it bluntly, "A certain person can define your fate, a person who knows nothing, and no one has the courage to say that's wrong."[48] You feel that there is nothing to defend yourself with, one individual summed up. It is this confinement to a space without law, one that ironically mirrors the stateless-ness of security delay individuals, that most marks and punishes and that provides such a hospitable environment for racism.

The contempt that many refugees feel from officials throughout the security process, one that several characterize as racist, is nowhere more evi-dent than in the difficulty they have in identifying and understanding how they have come to be labelled as security risks in the first place. Since the majority of security delayed cases are Convention refugees or protected per-sons, it is hard to understand why their stories entitled them to protection in one instance, often the refugee hearing, but not in another. The secrecy that surrounds the security process and the labyrinthine routes they must travel to get even the most basic information about their circumstances only com-pounds the fear and frustration. M.C. can only repeat with deep despair, "If I only knew what the trouble is. I don't know what the crime is that I have committed."[49] For him, Canada betrayed its own agreement. As an Iranian Kurd resettled to Canada by the United Nations High Commission for Refugees (UNHCR), M.C. believed Canadian officials when they granted him a ministerial permit in Turkey and when they assured him that permanent res-idency would be forthcoming. Unaware of the roadblocks ahead, M.C. only realized his precarious status when a friend pointed out the implications of a social insurance number that begins with 9, which marks an individual as someone without permanent residency status. Shortly after his arrival in 1993, at his CSIS interview, M.C. was told that he was cleared. In 1994, his name was published in an Iranian Canadian newspaper as someone the MEK was watching. Shortly after this event, CSIS came to his door but left appar-ently satisfied. More than twelve years later, M.C., his wife, and three chil-dren are still not landed. He was advised by Revenue Canada that he could not claim a child tax credit for his daughter who was born in Canada. Agi-tated by the retelling of his thirteen-year battle, M.C. wonders if all that is left to him is a hunger strike. As he comments angrily, "I don't need a letter [granting landing] when I am dead."[50]

## Blocking the exits

Bauman writes: "In refugee camps time is suspended; it is time but no his-tory."[51] The refugee can neither go back nor move forward; the exits are blocked. Security delayed individuals are mainly distinguished by a state of social death. Persons without permanent residence status in Canada, who are given the specially marked social insurance numbers beginning with the number 9, are quite literally marked. The number 9 immediately conveys their indeterminate status to employers, landlords, bank managers, and others. "Security delay" individuals apply yearly for a permit to work and for a health card; until recently, they were not entitled to apply for student assistance loans and were required to pay foreign rather than domestic fees if they attended university or college. They do not know what is being held against them, have no control over the bureaucratic processes to which they are subjected, and may wait years (often more than ten) before they are "cleared" for citizenship. It is now the minister of Public Safety and Emergency Preparedness who grants ministerial relief, a decision so enmeshed in post-9/11 security considerations that it is an option that appears to be rarely granted.[52]

M.C.'s wife found herself denied health care in 2003 when she became pregnant and was advised to "go to a church" when the time came to give birth. In a moment worthy of Orwell, she received a letter in December 2005, two years after her daughter was born, advising her that she had been entitled to continuous full health care coverage since 1993.[53] Leenco Waqayyo had his health card taken away by an official who decided that he ought never to have had it in the first place. The terror of getting sick drained the family. Denied the right to work, and, inexplicably, the right to be near children, Waqayyo found himself dependent on his wife who had acquired Canadian citizenship.[54] Since credit is also something denied to security delayed individuals, the prospect of starting a business is also slim.

It is perhaps the greatest irony that with so many roadblocks in their way and the delays produced by the various agencies themselves, security delayed individuals sometimes encounter officials who believe that their claims should be held up because they have not managed to be continuously self-supporting. Farkhondeh, for example, whose security issue is based on her association with the Mujahedin, an organization with whom her husband was very active and who was executed in Iran as a result, encountered an immigration officer who felt that she could not make a positive recommendation because she had not worked since she came to Canada.[55] The Omar family[56] travelled a particularly torturous bureaucratic path as outlined in the affidavit of Tareq Omar when he sought judicial review of the family's case. Between January of 1994 and 2001 when the father of the family died, the family was enmeshed in regulations requiring travel documents, security clearances, and medical certificates, each of which would each expire as the processes unfolded and as landing was refused on the grounds that they were all on welfare. Although some members received social assistance, it was hard to establish that this was not the case for all of them all the time. For example, on April 10, 1996, a memo entered into the family's file describes the family as "long-term welfare recipients" for whom "there are issues of poor documentation." The older children (Tareq and Meeza) were finally interviewed in September 1996, an interview to which they once again brought numerous documents attesting to their employment. An immigration officer prepared an updated report on March 19, 1998, which declared that the two young people were not collecting welfare benefits "at this time."

The dance of bureaucracy continued for the Omar family when they received a letter on January 18, 2000, which told them that they had to provide evidence that the family was self-supporting and that proper identity documents were still required. The letter confirmed that the family would be inadmissible since they were on welfare. In July 2001, the lawyer for Tareq and Meera informed CIC that their mother's social assistance benefits had been cancelled and that their father had died. He received no response and resent the letter in August and September 2001. On September 19, 2001, CIC undertook another welfare check. Satisfied on this score, the immigration officer, Ms. De Costa, nevertheless wrote to her supervisor (writing in capital letters) on October 16 that there was no proper ID and, that because of the events of September 11, she was "very very uncomfortable landing anyone without proper ID." The supervisor concurred and landing was refused. Soon thereafter, the family's security and travel documents expired once again. Tareq, Meera, and their mother were finally landed in 2005, fourteen years after arriving; an outcome we might speculate was due to the family's successful application to have their case considered in Federal Court.

The roadblocks to employment and social services are enormous, and the repercussions from these were evident in the health issues of all of those I interviewed. But those whose health suffered the most were the children. All of the children in the families I interviewed developed problems related to depression and illness. Parents were intensely concerned about how their children managed at school when the uncertainties and stresses of the home inspired rebellious behaviour. For those who were doing well in school and achieving high grades, the dreams of further education were stopped by the financial obstacles. The inability to fulfil this deep commitment to education is what was haunting most of those I interviewed. Not surprisingly, security delayed individuals reveal a deep despair. Y. wonders if "he came by mistake into this world."[57] F. declares bitterly that "everything I sacrificed for my kids was in vain." "I don't consider myself as living for the past fourteen years," she comments and wonders why, if she is such a threat, she is not simply deported.[58] M.C. rages that he would give anything to have a Canadian court tell him why he has been denied landing. "Khomeini may have shot me in the head," he says wryly, "but here it is like I am shot each day." His wife echoes his anguish, "My whole life is running away, running away," a flight that began more than sixteen years ago when her fourth child was only seven days old. Three of her children are now in their twenties and they believe that it is too late for them to get a post-secondary education.[59]

The isolation of security delayed individuals is intense; social death, we might speculate, may be contagious. Most cannot travel to see their families of origin. Others are so marked by their experience as security risks that they are reluctant to make links to their communities here. Suleyman Goven, for example, has ceased his activities with the Kurdish community centre, and M.C. fears the consequences of any association with Kurds in Canada. Yamani, targeted because of his involvement with the Popular Front for the Liberation of Palestine (PFLP) and once considered to be someone who "will engage in acts of subversion against democratic government, institutions or processes as they are understood in Canada,"[60] fears associating with any new immigrants in Canada. Bauman's words ring true for these individuals: "Having been abandoned or been forced out of their former milieu, refugees tend to be stripped of the identities that milieu defined, sustained and repro- duced. Socially, they are 'zombies': their old identities survive mostly as ghosts – haunting the nights all the more painfully for being all but invisible in the camp's daylight."[61] A camp exists whenever individuals find them- selves plunged into a space which law itself has created but where law does not operate. The camp, extended and diffused, is full of ghosts, the socially dead whose presence is never acknowledged.

## Conclusion

The legal and bureaucratic processes of states of exception clothe violence in rationality and render it legitimate. What is particularly insidious about the melding of race and bureaucracy is that the violence loses its blood red colour and shows itself only as a paradox: a commitment to legal rules that suspend the rule of law in the interest of national security. We imagine that people who are deported are simply "security risks" and not persons who "are disappeared." It all appears as the routines and practices of a civilized society. There are "truckloads of evidence," pages of legal decisions, long hours of cross-examinations, and appeals to precedents surrounding our actions. Law enforcement officers, legally authorized to focus on the profile of an "Islamic terrorist," ask what appear to be straightforward questions about how many times a day a suspect prays. In the end, we become con- vinced that the violence through which the nation is organized is not violence at all but the rituals of law and bureaucracy. It is this fiction that we must address.

When confronted with the oppressive practices of security and immigration officials, from the cases of Maher Arar and Omar Khadr to Suaad Mohamud, it is easy to find evidence of officials who have been incompetent. The immigration and security encounter is also one, to put it mildly, where two worlds collide and stereotyping operates. But these two explanations diminish the acts of callousness that ruin lives. The bureaucratic ethos that treats racialized peoples as extraterritorial, as neither inside the nation nor outside of it, is produced and sustained by the idea that there are spaces in law where law does not operate. If, as many scholars have noted, Canada is a liberal democracy in which Aboriginal peoples remain colonized, we can add to this that it is also a democracy in which spaces of non-law are preserved and in which increasing numbers of racialized peoples are finding themselves abandoned.

## Notes

I would like to thank all those who agreed to be interviewed, and Sharryn Aiken and Andrew Brouwer for sharing their files and thoughts about security delayed individuals.

1 Giorgio Agamben, *State of Exception*, trans. Kevin Attell (Chicago: University of Chicago Press, 2005), 39.

2 The details of Suaad Mohamud's case are taken from John Goddard, "Why Ottawa Saw an 'Imposter' in Mohamud Case," *Toronto Star*, September 30, 2009, A1, A19.

3 John Goddard, "Consular File Shows How Case Was Spun," *Toronto Star*, October 2, 2009, GT1, GT4.

4 Sherene H. Razack, "Simple Logic: The Identity Documents Rule and the Fantasy of a Nation Besieged and Betrayed," *Journal of Law and Social Policy* 15 (2000), 181–211.

5 The Canadian Council for Refugees estimates that there are approximately 100 security delayed individuals. Janet Dench, executive director, Canadian Council for Refugees, interview by author, Toronto, ON, December 20, 2005. One legal practitioner whose firm has a high case load of refugees considers this estimate too low and suggests that it is likely more than triple that number. Andrew Brouwer, interview by author, Toronto, ON, December 22, 2005.

6 Zygmunt Bauman, *Society under Siege* (Cambridge: Polity Press, 2002), 114.

7 Toni Morrison, "The Official Story: Dead Man Golfing," in *Birth of a Nation'hood: Gaze, Script, and Spectacle in the O.J. Simpson Case,* ed. Toni Morrison and Claudia Brodsky Lacour (New York: Pantheon Books, 1997), ix.

8 See, for example, Sharryn J. Aiken, "Of Gods and Monsters: National Security and Canadian Refugee Policy," *Revue québécoise de droit international*, 14,2 (2003), 1–51.

9 Hannah Arendt, *The Origins of Totalitarianism* (New York: Harcourt Brace Jovanovich, 1973), 199.

10 Sherene H. Razack, *Casting Out: The Eviction of Muslims from Western Law and Politics* (Toronto: University of Toronto Press, 2008).

11 Irene M. Silverblatt, *Modern Inquisitions: Peru and the Colonial Origins of the Civilized World* (Durham, NC: Duke University Press, 2005), 4.

12 Immigration acts have long contained provisions authorizing secret evidence for security cases; take the 1952 *Immigration Act* for example. The *Immigration Appeal Board Act of 1967* excluded "serious security cases" from appeal procedures. In 1967, MP David Lewis gave a revealing description to the House of Commons of the appeal process: "If security matters were involved . . . you could only guess that the refusal was for security reasons because you would not be given any reason at all. . . . When you inquired into the matter . . . you faced a blank wall. You had no information. You did not know what the source of evidence was . . . you argued as if you were punching a pillow. . . . I have had that kind of experience dozens of times." Quoted in Ninette Kelley and Michael Trebilcock, *The Making of the Mosaic: A History of Canadian Immigration Policy* (Toronto: University of Toronto Press, 2000), 344, and 344n208–209. See also *Regaldo-Brito v. Minister of Employment and Immigration* [1987] 1 F.C. 80 (C.A.) for the court's rejection of a challenge to security certificates. Security certificates have been integral to Canada's immigration legislation since 1978. See Canada Border Services Agency, "Fact Sheet: Security Certificates" (April 2005), ⟨http://www.cbsa-asfc.gc.ca/newsroom/factsheets/2005/certificate.html⟩, accessed March 18, 2006.

13 Sharryn J. Aiken, "From Slavery to Expulsion: Racism, Canadian Immigration Law and the Unfulfilled Promise of Modern Constitutionalism," in *Interrogating Race and Racism*, ed. Vijay Agnew (Toronto: University of Toronto Press, 2007), 55–111. For the American context, see Karen Engle, "Constructing Good Aliens and Good Citizens: Legitimizing the War on Terror(ism)," *University of Colorado Law Review* (2004), 64.

14 Canadian Security Intelligence Service, "General Comments on The Report's Findings"(henceforth csis, "General Comments"); and "Mr. Suleyman Goven and the Canadian Security Intelligence Service in the matter of the Complaints under the Canadian Security Intelligence Service Act by S.G. and S.D., sirc, 2000, expurgated Version" (henceforth sirc report).

15 David Theo Goldberg, *The Threat of Race: Reflections on Racial Neoliberalism* (Malden, MA: Wiley Blackwell, 2009), 45.

16 Anna J. Secor, " 'An Unrecognizable Condition Has Arrived': Law, Violence and the State of Exception in Turkey," in *Violent Geographies: Fear, Terror and Political Violence*, ed. Derek Gregory and Allan Pred (New York: Routledge, 2007), 39.

17 Ibid., 40.

18 David Theo Goldberg, *The Racial State* (Cambridge: Blackwell, 2002), 131.

19 Goldberg, *The Threat of Race*, 52.

20 Bauman, *Society under Siege*, 115.

21 Ibid., 113.

22 Aiken, "Of Gods and Monsters."

23 Canadian Council for Refugees, "Refugees and Security" (March 2001, updated February 2003), ⟨http://www.ccrweb.ca/security.PDF⟩, accessed March 18, 2006.

24 Aiken, "Of Gods and Monsters," 22.

25 Michel Foucault, "Of Other Spaces," *Diacritics* 16,1 (1986), 26, quoted in Bauman, *Society under Siege*, 112.

26 SIRC report.

27 Suleyman Goven, interview by author, Toronto, ON, December 22, 2005.

28 CSIS, "General Comments."

29 SIRC report, 12.

30 Didier Bogo, "Security and Immigration: Towards a Critique of the Governmentality of Unease," *Alternatives: Global, Local, Political* 27 (2002), 63–92.

31 Giorgio Agamben, *Homo Sacer: Sovereign Power and Bare Life*, trans. Daniel Heller-Roazen (Stanford, CA: Stanford University Press, 1998), 171.

32 SIRC report, 31.

33 CSIS, "General Comments," regarding Finding # 1, p. 20, 7.2.1, paragraphs 1, 2.

34 Goven, interview.

35 Canadian Council for Refugees, "Refugees and Security." To the extent that I can compare the profiles (the CCR report uses pseudonyms or initials for some of its cases and names for others), I interviewed four individuals of the nineteen cases discussed in this report and an additional three. Data of additional cases came from two key informant interviews and from the chart prepared by one law firm (in my possession). Unless names are already published, I have used pseudonyms for all security delayed individuals.

36 Bogo, "Security and Immigration," 65.

37 Canadian Council for Refugees, "Refugees and Security," 8, 9.

38 Aiken, "Of Gods and Monsters," 21.

39 Ibid., 16,17; N., interview by author, Toronto, ON, December 11, 2005.

40 F., interview by author, Toronto, ON, December 27, 2005.

41 M.K. on behalf of Waqayyo, interview by author, Toronto, ON, January 17, 2006.

42 Canada Council for Refugees, "Refugees and Security," 18, 19.

43 N., interview by author, Toronto, ON, December 11, 2005.

44 F., interview.

45 A., interview by author, Toronto, ON, January 13, 2006.

46 S., interview by author, Toronto, ON, December 22, 2005.

47 N., interview.

48 F., interview.

49 M.C. and his wife, interview by author, Toronto, ON, January 24, 2006.

50 Ibid.

51 Bauman, *Society under Seige*, 114.

52 Dench, interview.

53 M.C. and his wife, interview.

54 M.K. on behalf of Waqayyo, interview.

55 Canadian Council for Refugees, "Refugees and Security," 18.

56 In the case of Khadija Hassan, Mawaheb Osman Omar, Ezzedin Osman Omar, Mohammed Osman Omar, Meera Osman Omar, and Tareq Osman Omar (and the

Minister of Citizenship and Immigration and the Solicitor General of Canada) (court file IMM-230–05), an application for leave to commence an application for judicial review. This application was filed as a mandamus application, February 14, 2005, in the Federal Court of Appeal but the government dropped the case once the Federal Court granted leave. E-mail communication with Andrew Brouwer, the lawyer for the family, March 11, 2010.

57  Y., interview by author, Toronto, ON, December 11, 2005.
58  F., interview.
59  M.C. and his wife, interview.
60  A 1993 Security Intelligence Review Committee (SIRC) hearing report cited in Canadian Council for Refugees, "Refugees and Security," 23.
61  Bauman, *Society under Seige*, 116.

# Part Two

. . . . . . . . . . . . . . . . . . . . . . . .

# Race, gender, and class in Western power

# 5 : Indigenous women, nationalism, and feminism

Isabel Altamirano-Jiménez

DEVELOPMENTS IN FEMINIST THEORY AND PRACTICE since the late 1980s have enabled scholars to recognize how race, nationality, class, ethnicity, and sexuality inform axes of gender difference among women as a social group. Despite these contributions, Indigenous women and feminist issues remain underanalyzed. Although often assumed to fall within definitions of women of colour and post-colonial feminism, Indigenous feminism remains a site of racial, gender, and cultural identity struggle firmly connected to decolonization. The common assumption that Indigenous women should defend Indigenous nationalism, even if it is embedded in sexism, is extremely problematic and calls into question the relationship between Indigenous women, feminism, and nationalism.

The aim of this chapter is to examine this relationship by focusing on the political processes involved in constructing nationalism. I argue that race, gender, and nationalism are not hierarchical, but rather are relational categories of analysis in understanding the breadth of Indigenous women's oppression. Specifically, I contend that Indigenous feminism is in tension with Indigenous nationalist discourses and the construction of a political identity mimicking rigid definitions of Indigeneity, which constrain even while enabling Indigenous peoples. Nevertheless, Indigenous feminism can offer a more critical and liberating approach to decolonizing struggles.

I am aware of the diversity of Indigenous women's voices, of the existence of Indigenous feminist voices, and of women who deliberately ignore a gendered analysis. While all these perspectives are critically important, I consider a feminist analysis essential to connecting Indigenous political rhetoric about belonging with the lives of contemporary Indigenous women. My main context is my own Indigenous people along with the different places where I have developed my research on Indigenous women and nationalism, including Nunavut, Southern Mexico, and the Nass Valley, but I also draw examples from elsewhere. The discussion begins by investigating Indigeneity in relation to women and decolonizing struggles. Next, I explore feminism in relation to Indigenous women and the possibilities of using post-coloniality to frame an Indigenous feminism. Finally, I offer some concluding remarks.

## Indigeneity, gender, and nationalism

The transformation of a modern discourse of Indigeneity[1] into an internationally recognized legal and political identity[2] has been a strange process, which has had peculiar effects upon the communities that now find themselves cast as Indigenous.[3] Alcita Ramos has traced both the discursive frame and the *realpolitik* that has driven the development of this globally circulated politics, which she terms "Indigenism."[4] Ramos uses "Indigenism" in the context of Brazilian Indigenous politics to indicate new possibilities for the resolution of Indigenous peoples' political claims. These possibilities arise as a result of complex interactions between values, aspirations, and institutions that take place in the colonial setting. These include "regional prejudice, urban commiseration, state control, anthropological curiosity, religious commitment, sensationalism in the media, [and] Indigenous verbal, written, or gestural discourses."[5]

Although Ramos's definition of Indigenism includes the actions and influences of non-Indigenous peoples (even where these may be detrimental to Indigenous interests), her use of the term describes a range of institutions and practices that translate and, to some extent, distort the ongoing imperatives of the state, which paradoxically allows a resurgent sense of Indigenous autonomy while circumscribing it. Indigenism in this sense is not solely something "Indigenous," but is constructed in the context of highly complex and varied relationships between Indigenous peoples, the societies and the states in which they live, and various international organizations. The convergence spaces (to borrow Paul Routledge's term), in which these different actors' interactions occur are immersed in asymmetrical social and power relations.[6] Since places are important loci of collective memory and political identities, the capacity to mobilize those identities into configurations of solidarity depends upon the places in which these identities are constructed and maintained.[7]

As such, Indigenism is associated with a new process of relocalization, which expresses the dynamic relationship between the global and the local. As Turton observes, to make a claim to self-determination is to assert a global identity and occupy a position in the discourse of rights.[8] Nevertheless, what is problematic with this process is the tendency to reduce Indigeneity to an ethic and a logic of *preservation* that emphasizes commonalities and undermines Indigenous diasporic histories, roots, and different routes as sources of Indigenous experiences which are place-specific. Furthermore, as Eric Michaels points out, a prescribed version of Indigeneity ends up promoting centralization and homogenization, and ultimately demands compliance with "the State's objectives of ethnicization, standardization, even Aboriginalization, at the expense of local language, representation and autonomy."[9] In other words, it forces or induces Indigenous peoples to fit certain definitions of Indigeneity. The incorporation of this prescribed version of Indigeneity into the Indigenous political rhetoric reconstructs history as a meta-narrative of timeless cultural continuity that nonetheless clashes with dynamic social, political, and legal practices and gender relations. From this perspective, by being imbued with external political, hegemonic meaning, Indigeneity loses its very embeddedness in everyday life and is objectified as reflexively constructed and deployed.[10]

In this sense, the general, legal, and external definition of Indigenous identity becomes the condition of participation in the global dialogue. While such dialogue certainly facilitates Indigenous claims and the right to a political voice, this Indigenous political identity neither results from the prior existence of an ancient culture nor from the set of traditional practices that bound people together. Rather, this identity attains resonance to the extent that it is used by the state itself as a marker of inclusion and exclusion.[11] Consequently, there are many Indigenous peoples who identify themselves by their political-legal relationship with the state and other international legal instruments rather than by any cultural or social ties to their communities. Taiaiake Alfred and Jeff Corntassel have rightly argued that this is a continuing colonial process that pulls Indigenous peoples further and further away from their cultural practices and community aspects of "being Indigenous" and moves them towards an institutional politico-legal construction of Indigeneity.[12]

The power of defining extends beyond the national state. Indigenous identity is constructed at the global, local, and state level. The World Bank, the United Nations, the International Labour Organization, and other global actors contribute to the process of defining who are Indigenous and the meaning of being Indigenous. However, as Alfred has noted, demands for a precise, standard definition disregard the reality that group identity varies with time and place.[13]

In their efforts to turn their cultural difference into a political advantage, Indigenous peoples have integrated tradition into politics and transformed it into a significant symbolic capital with different functions and values according to different contexts. As Schochet has observed, the codification of tradition is among the more effective sources of social and political control and approval, as it is aimed at persuading the members of a community that their commonalities are more relevant than their differences. The codification and enforcement of tradition must be understood as attempts to institute unity to fit legal definitions of Indigeneity.[14] Difference is expressed in simple terms of white and black, and internal difference is rendered equally problematic. However, while these projects are imagined in affinity with local subjects, the logic upon which they are founded inhibits efforts to understand or empower those individuals who live "out of the way," as Anna Tsing puts it.[15] Furthermore, the integrating traditions are often those of, or at the service of, the dominant group, expressing economic and political control, as well as gender discrimination. Who gets to tell stories about Indigeneity, what stories are remembered, in what forums they are told, and for what purposes – all of these abilities are linked to memory and power. The fact that only certain Indigenous stories are emphasized has important implications for Indigenous women whose attachments to place, land, resources, and community have been mediated by gendered colonial legislations.

As such, these definitions of Indigenous political identity inform the construction of an "Indigenous way" that privileges hierarchical social organizations with all their class and gender inequalities, including inequalities in the access to culture.[16] Moreover, while this political identity serves an important purpose in the struggle to overcome past and present colonialism and to secure rights at the international level, it may also rule out distinctions between colonial oppressors and others escaping from colonial oppression, and justify oppressive practices of its own. From this perspective, while hegemonic definitions of Indigeneity both categorize and define, there is always resistance to these definitions because they are imbued with power and embedded in tensions between experience, language, and contradictions.[17] Indigeneity and identity politics have become divisive issues that have marginalized and disempowered some Indigenous women vis-à-vis other Indigenous women and in relation to the mainstream society. As Connor observes in the case of the Maori in New Zealand, identity politics creates artificial insider/outsider boundaries that separate those who know and those excluded from knowing.[18]

This identity politics extends to the issue of bringing together gender and nationalism as analytical categories, which have been seen either as divisive or as a threat to self-determination. Indigenous political rhetoric constructs women's rights and claims as "inauthentic," "untraditional," or threatening to the political and cultural liberation of Indigenous peoples. Often, gendered struggles against colonialism have been framed as "women's issues." Membership, poverty, property rights, colonization, or individual issues are then positioned as opposing the collective rights of the formal male leadership, and are presented as a wholesale threat to Indigenous sovereignty.[19] However, dismissing women's demands for inclusion and equality is ultimately a strategy that replicates colonial power relations. The use of tradition and culture to define who is "a real Indigenous woman," is not only reductionist but also undermines the potential site of political contestation. As Bird Rose argues, downplaying gendered experiences of colonization is about reproducing colonizing practices within decolonizing institutions and processes, and must not be understood simply as negligible side effects of essentially "benign endeavors."[20] This embeddedness conceals, naturalizes, or erases Indigenous women's voices and knowledge.

According to Linda Tuhiwai Smith, the "problems of 'voice' and 'visibility,' 'silence and invisibility' became particularly important to Indigenous women as they began to attend international conferences and attempted to influence international policies related to women's rights, population control, development and justice."[21] In the process of political recomposition, the roads newly opened by Indigenous women criticized a stagnant mythology that placed Indigenous women as a passive, subordinate group within their societies.

As James Scott argues, Indigenous women have kept "hidden transcripts" of resistance for a long time, and their relatively recent public militancy can be understood as a challenge to hegemonic forces. Hidden transcripts include gestures – discourses used by the marginalized to construct alternative possibilities.[22] Indigenous women's resistance challenges internal rhetorical images and dominant representations of Indigeneity. Indigenous women's critique and activism have focused on different paths and emphasized different experiences precisely because they are not a homogeneous social category. While feminists have stressed gender and identity as ways of contesting the state's national assimilative policies, legislations, and Indigenous politics that continue to ignore Indigenous women's demands,[23] others have accused feminists of being assimilated and against Indigenous self-determination, emphasizing a hierarchical relationship between nationhood and gender.[24]

Reyna Ramirez argues, however, that criticism of feminism among Indigenous scholars and leaders is, in fact, related to the prevalent sexism in Indigenous politics and the fear that feminism may engender conflict between women and men.[25] From this perspective, it is generally assumed that Indigenous women cannot be both Indigenous and feminist because the risk of mixing the two is seen ultimately as assimilation and the adoption of whiteness, which is understood as a regime of truth circumscribing the political possibilities of Indigenous peoples.[26]

This position is problematic because it downplays internal diversity among Indigenous women and reduces feminism to white, mainstream feminism, which no doubt benefits from white domination. However, the source of Indigenous women's oppression is not only racial but also is internally reproduced when an Indigenous woman has no choice but to adhere to what is defined as "authentic" or "traditional." As Lorraine F. Mayer states, the confrontation and recalling of traditions have influenced the misunderstanding between Indigenous women and Indigenous feminists.[27] Furthermore, as Julie Wuthnow notes, the issue of essentialized identities and authenticity raises a number of extremely political questions. Who defines what is authentic? What kind of violence needs to be done to difference in order to construct a stable identity for the authentic subject?[28] Thus, I believe the issue here is not about uncritically accepting dominant theories, nor is it about asserting that "traditions" are static or that identity is fixed. Rather, it is about adopting a reflexive criticism to understand both the potential and limits of Indigenous tradition and dominant theories.

The so-called women's issues need to be contextualized within a larger political frame, one that considers how dominant groups tend to control the rhetoric on tradition, identity, and culture in the process of constructing national identities. The contestable issue of gender usually remains submerged in political struggles emphasizing self-determination, cultural difference, and experiences of material and social inequalities. In this context, Indigenous women's voices remain "muted." Nevertheless, as Shirley Ardener has explained in her introduction to *Defining Females*, muted groups are not deficient in their capacity for language, nor are they necessarily quieter than the dominant group. Rather, the "mutedness" of one group may be regarded as the "deafness" of the dominant group.[29] Moreover, in every dimension of Indigenous life there is a variety of interpretations related to personal experiences and positions. These result from living in urban centres as opposed to communities, which affect how we see the world, organize our arguments, and engage with political activity.

## Towards an indigenous feminism

As a theory, Indigenous feminism is about engaging with the possibilities of decolonizing while not losing sight of the power relations that inform difference both internally and externally. Indigenous feminism is also about the ability to choose strategies and to construct relevant local meanings. From this point of view, it is about recovering rhetorical and political practices and centring our own experiences in order to reconceptualize the epistemological bases of our research to create an Indigenous feminist theory.[30] The questions include, How are we as Indigenous feminists claiming to be different from other feminists? How can both Indigenous feminists and Indigenous women "reinvent the enemy's language"?[31] How can Indigenous feminism empower women without losing touch with self-determination?

The first element involved in this "reinvention of language" is the fact that feminism is as external to Indigenous peoples as the concept of Indigenous peoples itself. While this concept has been adopted by Indigenous peoples and organizations for its political potential, feminism has been relegated as "foreign" to Indigenous communities. This situation undermines women. The link between nationhood and gender is fruitful not only to understand the many faces of gender oppression but also to construct a more expansive notion of nationhood, one that goes beyond preservation. While external definitions of Indigeneity open up political possibilities for Indigenous peoples, such definitions constrain and limit Indigenous peoples' liberation and self-determination precisely because they are aimed at preservation rather than at addressing the tension between equality and difference in the process of constructing identity. This tension is not merely an intellectual concern but a reality limiting Indigenous women's political involvement, as well as their access to culture and resources.

The need to secure the survival of the collective, while legitimate, has undermined the survival of the individual and has developed within a framework that is densely masculine. Indigenous feminism contests the powers behind this identity construction. Through selective memory and power, things are named, situations are defined, and decisions are made about who speaks on behalf of whom and who has the power to know. Indigenous feminism is concerned with these powers and asymmetrical relations, as well as with the social arrangements that allow and perpetuate such gender inequalities.

As mentioned earlier, in the same way that gender, nationalism, and race are relational, women's survival and Indigenous peoples' liberation are closely related. As Ramirez points out, peoples' survival is necessarily connected with the violence and sexism women confront in their everyday lives.[32] These are ultimately survival issues. Privileging nationalism and race over gender marginalizes women's survival and undermines their simultaneous oppression by race and gender. This hierarchical relation, as Bird Rose argues, reproduces colonial practices and appropriation in contexts and institutions meant to reverse colonization.[33]

Claiming "Indigenous feminism" can be the way to engage with what is knowledge, who can know, and what kind of powers are being exercised to justify Indigenous women's oppression. Being Indigenous and being feminist does not have to be an either/or identity. Both can be connected as a way of "talking back"[34] to the dominant society and mainstream feminism, and a way to enable Indigenous women as agents and knowers. Indigenous feminism is not about adopting feminism and whiteness altogether as practices that privilege and reproduce a white imperial subject. Rather, Indigenous feminism is about critically deciding which concepts better describe our experiences and struggles against sexism and gender discrimination.[35]

In this sense, post-colonial theory opens up new possibilities and dimensions for Indigenous scholarship focusing on feminism. Especially relevant is its critique of colonialism, its analysis of power relations in society, and its critical awareness of more subtle forms of colonization, which Spivak calls "epistemic violence," or the imposition and internalization of another worldview and set of values.[36] An obvious question is, to what extent is the label "post-colonial" useful when addressing current Indigenous peoples' experiences of colonization, particularly the experiences of Indigenous women?

Post-colonial feminists have contributed greatly to the discussion of the "double marginal" and have challenged other feminists to consider the intersections of gender with other axes of difference.[37] Chandra Mohanty's influential essay "Cartographies of Struggle," for example, redefines the Third World not within any geographical boundaries, but within particular socio-historical junctures.[38] Mohanty perceives important commonalities between Third World women and women of colour in the First World. As Mohanram argues, such redefinition is problematic because it reproduces a homogenous conception of the Third World, based on the global economy as an organizing principle.[39] At the same time, this redefinition underlines alliances that are relevant in multicultural contexts, while bypassing Indigenous rights and legal personality. Unlike other social groups, Indigenous peoples are attached to their homelands, which can be understood as meaningful habitats that have an emotional and material effect on people, their survival, and the practices that connect peoples with such places.

While the term post-colonial, which encompasses different national-racial formations has superseded the concept of Third World as a descriptor, it continues to neglect Indigenous colonization experiences. In this sense, the early iterations of post-colonial do not completely apply to Indigenous peoples. The question, however, is how can post-colonial discourses and feminism be defined differently in order to enhance rather than erase Indigenous ways of knowing and current concerns?[40] In other words, how can we reconfigure these models without reproducing marginalization and colonizing gestures that suggest colonialism is part of the past?

There are certainly some important differences between the issues that post-colonial feminists and Indigenous women raise in relation to nationalist projects. Critical differences between these perspectives result not only from their different racial and colonial experiences but also from their different locations and material circumstances. In other words, the material conditions of Indigenous women's oppression and their political interests are not only place- and history-specific but also are influenced by different legal divisions and circumstances. While some Indigenous women underline patriarchy as being a colonial imposition and draw instead on cultural constructions honouring and valuing womanhood and past women interventions within communities, families, and politics, others connect the social reproduction of their collective identities and communities to struggles for self-determination.[41]

Indigenous women's lives are diverse and defy easy generalization. Indigenous women within a community may experience a wide range of differences in their status, cultural settings, and voices, and individual women encounter considerable changes in their political position as a consequence of changing kinship status through marriage and motherhood.[42] These discrepancies between the actual functions Indigenous women perform and the gender roles imposed on them have created further paradoxes in the status of women relative to men. Quite often, Indigenous women experience inequality and unequal access to essential resources; however, some women use their domestic functions and status as a means to facilitate rather than hinder their opportunities for political participation. Others, in contrast, have adopted forms of political actions and discourses that emphasize gender equality as a crucial component to decolonization struggles.[43]

Along these lines, while there are Indigenous women who feel that separating women from the rest of their communities is foreign to their cultures, there are others who contest the images of "strong Indigenous matriarchs" often employed to brush aside Indigenous women's demands. While I do not intend to diminish the past political, social, and economic importance of Indigenous women, I wish to propose distinguishing between the desired ideal of Indigenous society and the contemporary, everyday reality of Indigenous women. As Kuokkanen observes in the Sami case,[44] and as I have experienced in the Zapotec case in Southern Mexico,[45] the image of the strong matriarch is often used against Indigenous women who advocate for "women's issues." This image is employed particularly by Indigenous men who have either internalized it or who simply benefit from the patriarchal system that has suppressed women.

Indigenous societies have been affected by different, interconnected colonial processes and social institutions. Thus, contemporary attitudes towards and perceptions of Indigenous women are the result of an entangled combination of situations, policies, conditions, time, and geography, hindering our ability to trace back traditional roles and the status of women, whatever the implication of "traditional" may be.[46] Moreover, Indigenous nationalist struggles may induce communities to honour a past and to conform to the image of a fixed culture and tradition that have, nonetheless, changed. In this context, the mobilization of an idealized image of the powerful woman entraps contemporary women in a situation where they may surrender to Indigenist aspirations of preservation and support the reproduction of discourses and practices that legitimize other forms of gender domination. Not only has the transformation of a modern discourse of Indigeneity affected the ways in which Indigenous peoples are forced to cast themselves but also it has justified the construction of a global geography in which contemporary Indigenous cultures stand for backward exclusions and the victimization of women.

In this global geography, culture and gender are blamed for everyday poverty, marginalization, and discrimination.[47] From this perspective, it would seem that Indigenous cultures and essentialism motivate or naturalize certain gender discriminatory practices. However, as recent feminist geography research has shown, this cultural global geography is embedded in neo-colonial power relations, political and economic structures of domination, and cultural subordination, all of which obscure structural violence and Indigenous women's agency. These combined elements shape gendered politics of inequalities, difference, and resistance in specific communities.[48]

Indigenous women are neither subject to unified racial and gendered identities nor victim subjects, as the familiar colonialist imagery would suggest.[49] Rather, Indigenous women are agents constructing reflexive discourses and practices aimed at challenging male-only Indigenous leaderships, gender discrimination, and state intervention that reinforce women's exclusion. Indigenous women are also defending territorial sovereignty, autonomy, human rights, control over natural resources, health and body, and traditionalism. This diversity of Indigenous women's voices may be understood as immersed in complex power relations, racial, political, and economic structures of domination, and cultural subordination that shape their gender experience vis-à-vis their own people and vis-à-vis mainstream society.

As agents claiming to construct and mediate meaningful complex subjectivities, Indigenous feminists aim at transforming the interface between the discourses of place, culture, tradition, and politics in Indigenous decolonizing struggles. In this sense, Indigenous feminism is not only about contesting the everyday practices that discriminate against women but also the knowledge that informs those conventions. It is precisely this transformation that challenges dominant discourses of tradition and dominant external representations of Indigeneity.

Connecting nationalism, gender, and race means bringing women's concerns and aspirations to the forefront. Indigenous women's demand for attention to their contemporary political or socio-economic marginalization and the different forms of violence they experience in their own communities are not women's issues that threaten to sabotage the decolonization struggle. They are part of contemporary reality. Labelling this reality as "women's issues" is a patriarchal tactic that results in women losing political opportunities. Acknowledging that sexism and patriarchal relations of power exist in most Indigenous societies today is necessary to integrate Indigenous women's claims and aspirations into the centre of the survival project. Considering models and visions of nationhood and self-determination that stem from understandings informed by contemporary Indigenous women and men and not from external notions of Indigeneity, which may promote homogenization and compliance with the state, ultimately requires distinguishing between idealized pasts and contemporary presents. This consideration also requires the deconstruction of patriarchal hegemony and colonizing discourses, power relations, and practices that are embedded in the decolonization struggle.

As Indigenous peoples, we can organize and disentangle the circumstances and processes determining legal and political identities, gender relations, and racial and economic hierarchies that have come to coexist within the decolonization process. In this process, Indigenous epistemologies can be extremely useful in constructing and validating knowledge in changing cultural contexts. They embody change and conflict, and provide the background for an Indigenous critical praxis in which people reflect on their culture, history, politics, economies, and the socio-political context in which they live. This critical praxis is about how people see themselves and how they are recognized by others. This process goes beyond pitting Indigenous women against Indigenous feminism or preserving collective rights against individual rights.

## Indigenous feminism: Sketching theoretical and practical strategies

It is important to develop a conceptualization of the Indigenous subject that includes notions of embodiment, history, and place but avoids essentialism, in order to legitimize situated experience and history.

Indigenous women's lives and experiences must be analyzed as a process mediated through the simultaneous operation of gendered and racialized hierarchies, spaces, and places. Gender is not the only difference that matters in Indigenous women's lives. Location also matters. By emphasizing these dimensions, we focus on a material, multi-layer view of the power relations and practices affecting women, their relation to national states, and other groups of women.

The material conditions of Indigenous women and their varied political interests are historically place-specific and are reflections of the asymmetry that exists between Western and non-Western understandings of women's agency and oppression. A flexible conception of the "local" as a spatial and temporal concept provides the mechanisms for grounding political legitimacy and resistance.

The creation and ownership of Indigenous knowledge is embedded in power relations; thus, knowledge is not neutral and is immersed in competing interests. Claims to authenticity undermine social-changing dynamics within Indigenous communities and deepen women's oppression.

There is strategic potential in constructing knowledge that places Indigenous women at the centre.

It is not very productive to distinguish between gender relations produced in pre-colonized and colonized societies: in both cases, gender practices and roles are defined in relation to both men and women. While in some past societies Indigenous women had a rich political life, this is not a monolithic image, and may in fact have a negative impact on contemporary women's agency.

The intersection of multiple geographical scales allows us to understand the ways in which neo-colonial relations of power and political economic structures of domination and subordination combine to shape place, identity, gendered politics of inequalities, and resistance in specific communities.

Multi-scale research, for example, shows how global discourses affect the ways in which Indigenous peoples see themselves. It also shows the specific forms in which women and men are drawn into arrangements shaped by communal discourses of honour, respectability, tradition, and social institutions, and by how the national state and legal structures reinforce the public/private dichotomy.

Without seeing them as timeless, fixed, or hermetic, we can bring forward notions of history, knowledge, the local, the colonized, and the Indigenous woman to construct an Indigenous feminism that is expansive, liberating, and committed to decolonization.

## Notes

1 Elazar Barkan and Ronald Bush, "Introduction," in *Prehistories of the Future: The Primitivist Project and the Culture of Modernism*, ed. Elazar Barkan and Ronald Bush (Palo Alto, CA: Stanford University Press, 1995), 1–22.
2 Benedict Kingsbury, " 'Indigenous Peoples' as an International Legal Concept," in *Indigenous Peoples of Asia*, ed. R.H. Barnes et al. (Ann Arbor, MI: University of Michigan Association for Asian Studies, 1995), 13–34.
3 Brigham Golden, "The Lessons of 'Indigenous' Women for Theory and Activism in Feminist Anthropology," *Voices: A Publication of the Association for Feminist Anthropology* 5 (2001), 1–8.
4 Alcita Ramos, *Indigenism* (Madison: University of Wisconsin Press, 1998).
5 Ibid.,7.

6  Paul Routledge, "Critical Geopolitics and Terrains of Resistance," *Political Geography* 15,6/7 (1996), 509–31.

7  Paul Routledge, "Convergence Spaces: Process Geographies of Grassroot Globalization Networks," *Transactions of the Institute of British Geographers* 28,3 (2003), 333–49.

8  David Turton, "Introduction," in *War and Ethnicity: Global Connections and Local Violence*, ed. David Turton (Rochester, NY: University of Rochester Press, 1997), 1–15.

9  Eric Michaels, "For a Cultural Future: Frances Jupurrurla Makes TV at Yuendumu," *Art and Criticism Monograph Series* 3 (1987), 1–80.

10  Ingo W. Schröder, "The Political Economy of Tribalism in North America: Neo-Tribal Capitalism?" *Anthropological Theory* 3,4 (2003), 335–56.

11  Courtney Jung, "The Politics of Indigenous Identity: Neo-Liberalism, Cultural Rights and the Mexican Zapatists," *Social Research* 7,2 (2003), 433–62.

12  Taiaiake Alfred and Jeff Corntassel, "Being Indigenous: Resurgences against Contemporary Colonialism," *Politics of Identity IX* (Oxford: Government and Opposition Ltd., 2005), 599.

13  Taiaiake Alfred, *Peace, Power, Righteousness: An Indigenous Manifesto* (Oxford: Oxford University Press, 1999), 85.

14  Gordon Schochet, "Tradition as Politics and the Politics of Tradition," in *Question of Tradition*, ed. Mark Salber Phillips and Gordon Schochet (Toronto: University of Toronto Press, 2004), 309.

15  Anna Tsing, *The Realm of the Diamond Queen* (Princeton, NJ: Princeton University Press, 1993).

16  Arif Dirlik, "Place-Based Imagination: Globalism and the Politics of Place," in *Places and Politics in the Age of Globalization*, ed. R. Prazniak and A. Dirlik (Lanham, MD: Rowman and Littlefield, 2001), 16.

17  Shari Stone-Mediatore, "Chandra Mohanty and the Revaluing of 'Experience,'" in *Decentering the Center: Philosophy for a Multicultural, Postcolonial and Feminist World*, ed. Uma Narayan and Sandra Harding (Bloomington: Indiana University Press, 2000), 122.

18  Helen Connor, "Reclamation of Cultural Identity for Maori Women: A Response to 'Prisonisation,'" in *Bitter Sweet: Indigenous Women in the Pacific*, ed. Alyson Jones, Phyllis Herda, and Tamasailu M. Suaali (Otago, NZ: University of Otago Press, 2000), 130.

19  Bonita Lawrence and Kim Anderson, "Introduction to 'Indigenous Women': The State of Our Nations," *Atlantis: A Women's Studies Journal* 29 (2005), 1–6.

20  Deborah Bird Rose, "Land Rights and Deep Colonising: The Erasure of Women," *Aboriginal Law Bulletin* 3,85 (1996), 6–14.

21  Linda Tuhiwai Smith, *Decolonizing Methodologies: Research and Indigenous Peoples* (London: Zed Books, 1999).

22  James C. Scott, *Domination and the Arts of Resistance: Hidden Transcripts* (New Haven: Yale University Press, 1990), 11–52.

23  See Joyce Green, ed., *Making Space for Indigenous Feminism* (Halifax: Fernwood, 2007).

24 See M.A. Jaimes-Guerrero, "Patriarchal Colonialism and Indigenism: Implications for Native Feminist Spirituality and Native Womanism," *Hypatia* 18,2 (2003), 58–69; Patricia Monture-Angus, *Thunder in My Soul: A Mohawk Woman Speaks* (Halifax: Fernwood, 1995).

25 Reyna Ramirez, "Race, Tribal Nation, and Gender: A Native Feminist Approach to Belonging," *Meridians: Feminism, Race, Transnationalism* 7,2 (2007), 22–40.

26 Aileen Moreton-Robinson, "Troubling Business: Difference and Whiteness within Feminism," *Australian Feminist Studies* 15,33 (2000), 348.

27 Lorraine F. Mayer, "A Return to Reciprocity," *Hypatia* 22,3 (2007), 35.

28 Julie Wuthnow, "Deleuze in the Postcolonial: On Nomads and Indigenous Politics," *Feminist Theory* 3,2 (2002), 198.

29 Shirley Ardener, "Introduction," *Defining Females*, ed. Shirley Ardener (New York: Wiley, 1978).

30 Elizabeth Archuleta, " 'I Give You Back': Indigenous Women Writing to Survive," *Studies in American Indian Literatures* 18,4 (2006), 88–114.

31 Joy Harjo and Gloria Bird, *Reinventing the Enemy's Language: Contemporary Native Women's Writing of North America* (New York: W.W. Norton, 1997).

32 Ramirez, "Race, Tribal Nation, and Gender," 23.

33 Bird Rose, "Land Rights and Deep Colonising," 10.

34 bell hooks, *Talking Back: Thinking Feminist, Thinking Black* (Boston: South End Press, 1989).

35 Ramirez, "Race, Tribal Nation, and Gender," 31.

36 Gayatri Chakravorty Spivak, "Response to 'The Difference Within: Feminism and Critical Theory,' " in *The Difference Within: Feminism and Critical Theory*, ed. Elizabeth Meese and Alice Parker (Philadelphia: John Benjamins, 1989), 208–20.

37 See Spivak, "Response to 'The Difference Within' "; Chandra T. Mohanty, "Under Western Eyes: Feminist Scholarship and Colonial Discourses," *Feminist Review* 30 (1988), 61–88; Daiva Stasiulus, "Relational Positionalities of Nationalisms, Racisms and Feminisms," in *Between Woman and Nation*, ed. Caren Kaplan, Norma Alarcón, and Minoo Moallen (Durham, NC: Duke University Press, 1999), 182–218.

38 Mohanty, "Under Western Eyes."

39 Rhadika Mohanram, "The Construction of Place: Maori Feminism and Nationalism in Aotearoa/New Zealand," *NWSA Journal* 8,1 (1996), 51.

40 Wuthnow, "Deleuze in the Postcolonial," 193.

41 See Jaimes-Guerrero, "Patriarchal Colonialism and Indigenism"; Lisa Udel, "Revision and Resistance," *Frontier: A Journal of Women Studies* 22,2 (2001), 43–62; and Lawrence and Anderson, "Introduction to 'Indigenous Women.' "

42 Christine Conte, "Ladies, Livestock, Land and Lucre: Women's Networks and Social Status on the Western Navajo Reservation," *American Indian Quarterly* 6 (1982), 105–24.

43 See Anne Teresa Nahanee, "Indian Women, Sex Equality, and the Charter," in *Women and the Canadian State*, ed. Caroline Andrew (Montreal: McGill-Queen's University Press, 1997), 89–103; Green, ed., *Making Space for Indigenous Feminism*; Rauna Kuokkanen, "Sámi Women, Autonomy, and Decolonization in the Age of Globalization," *Act 4: Finnish Sapmi* (2006), 1–37.

44 Kuokkanen, "Sámi Women, Autonomy, and Decolonization in the Age of Globalization."

45 Isabel Altamirano-Jiménez, "The Politics of Tradition: Aboriginal Nationalism and Women. Mexico and Canada in a Comparative Perspective" (PhD diss., University of Alberta, 2006).

46 Kuokkanen, "Sámi Women, Autonomy, and Decolonization in the Age of Globalization," 4.

47 Vivian Newdick, "The Indigenous Woman as Victim of Her Own Culture in Neo-Liberal Mexico," *Cultural Dynamics* 17,1 (2005), 73–92.

48 R. Nagar and V. Lawson, "Locating Globalization: Feminist (Re)readings of the Subjects and Spaces of Globalization," *Economic Geography* 78 (2002), 257–84.

49 Lata Mani, *Contentious Traditions: The Debate on Sati in India* (Berkeley: University of California Press, 1998).

# 6 White innocence, Western supremacy: The role of Western feminism in the "War on Terror"

Sunera Thobani

TOWARDS THE END OF THE TWENTIETH CENTURY, white feminists in North America – activists and academics alike – were publicly deliberating whether feminism's transformational potential had been exhausted. Movement politics were floundering in the face of the twin assaults of neo-liberal restructuring and the angry white male backlash that accompanied it.[1] While the former was eroding the socio-economic gains women had made since the 1960s by decimating social programs and fundamentally reshaping the workforce, the latter, articulated in the politics of the newly emergent and highly vocal men's rights movement, set its target on women's access to abortion and child custody rights, as well as on the anti-violence movement.[2] A number of prominent women, including some who had previously identified as feminists, often fed – if not outright led – the anti-feminist politics of the period.[3] Many of these women claimed that feminism had turned women into nothing but perpetual victims, denying them any recognizable form of agency. They also accused "feminazis" of imposing a stifling political correctness on public discourse that they considered inimical to women's interests.

Disagreements – even struggles – among the different politico-theoretical traditions internal to feminism were also taking their toll. Some feminists pronounced the death of feminist politics in the face of the multi-faceted challenges posed by Indigenous women, women of colour, women with disabilities, and queer women to the white middle-class heterosexual woman who had long reigned as the "real" subject of feminism. Others worried that feminism's radical potential had been diluted through its institutionalization and professionalization within the academy (as women's studies became increasingly disengaged from movement politics) and its bureaucratization in the state (as feminism became incorporated into the machinery of women's ministries, secretariats, and gender mainstreaming policies).[4] Yet others fretted that perhaps feminists had become too comfortable with the

*see J. Brodie*

127

status quo and, having lost touch with disenfranchised women, were increasingly becoming theory-obsessed, elitist, or simply politically disillusioned.[5]

Then came the attacks of 9/11 and the War on Terror. Suddenly, presidents and prime ministers declared themselves willing to go to war to fight terrorism and secure women's rights. Feminism became all the rage as the status of women in the Muslim world became a key concern of international politics. As the invasions of Afghanistan and Iraq unfolded, women were suddenly visible in highly prestigious positions at the White House, in Congress, at the State Department, in the Pentagon, and in Parliaments around the Western world. Women's rights activists appeared on prime time news and talk shows on radio and television. They were featured prominently in films and documentaries, at festivals and international human rights gatherings. Almost overnight, feminism acquired a new lease on life, as enthusiastic women – and men – clamoured to discuss the abject status of the oppressed Muslim woman, whether in Afghanistan, Iraq, or in their nearest immigrant ghetto. Well, a particular kind of feminism became exercised with this burning desire.[6]

The War on Terror has been waged with a historically unprecedented level of participation by women on its various front lines: Western women have made great inroads in journalism, politics, the military, international development, publishing, filmmaking, the beauty industry, and in practically every other field of industry and opportunity touched by the war. This chapter thus examines white/Western feminist responses to the post–9/11 state of affairs. How have Western feminists theorized the War on Terror and, most importantly, its relation to gender? Given the centrality of the idea of the "clash of civilizations" in the discursive framing of the war, how have these feminists articulated their own relation to the dominant construct of the "West" and its Islamic Other?

Western feminists and white women's organizations have, of course, been divided in their responses to the war. While some supported all aspects of the War on Terror, others opposed it. Some were ambivalent about the Afghan war, but nevertheless came to support it as necessary. Many opposed the Iraq war, defining it as unnecessary and a war of choice. Given these divided political responses to the war, were Western feminists likewise divided in their theoretical assumptions and political analysis of the war and its causes?

The responses of a number of prominent, North American–based white feminists across a broad range of theoretical traditions, from liberal to socialist and post-structural/postmodern feminism, are examined. In the following sections, I argue that although these feminists have been divided in their political responses to the War on Terror, there are a number of surprising similarities in the foundational assumptions informing their analysis. More disturbing, using their analytic perspectives, they have buttressed hegemonic constructs of the "West" and its Islamic "Other." Thus, these feminists have constituted their subject positions as endangered by Islamic terror, violence, and misogyny. In the process, they have helped revitalize "Western" feminism through a focus on the global that constitutes the West's gendered subject as the mark of the "universal," and the world of the Muslim gendered subject as that of death, violence, and misogyny. Since the responses of these feminists map out the parameters for the (im)possibilities of anti-racist and anti-imperialist solidarity among women in their differing locations, my interest lies primarily in identifying the discursive practices and political strategies that sustain the power of the West and whiteness in the War on Terror, albeit in its "feminist" forms.[7]

## White feminism's war on Muslims

With the launch of the War on Terror, many white feminists publicly supported the invasion of Afghanistan, drawing heightened attention to what they defined as the essential trait of the Taliban, an adherence to Islam and a misogynist hatred of women.[8] Speaking on behalf of "more than 220 leading human rights and women's organizations in the U.S. and around the world," the Washington-based Feminist Majority Foundation not only backed the war on Afghanistan but also called on the Bush Administration to increase the level of American troops in Kabul and extend their presence into the rest of the country.[9] Canadian feminist Sally Armstrong called for a similar expansion of the reach of American, Canadian, and other North Atlantic Treaty Organization (NATO) forces in her documentary *Daughters of Afghanistan*. This feminist politics with its global reach was not unconnected to the domestic activism of these feminists. The National Organization of Women, for one example, was reported to have "use[d] the terrorist attacks to flak its own domestic agenda," declaring that "in this time of national and global turmoil, the reasons we celebrate 'Coming Out Day' are more visible and important than ever and proceeded to call for a permanent lifting of the ban on gays in the military."[10]

As these feminists and their organizations urged an extension of the Afghan war, some feminists went further and called for an expansion of the War on Terror from Afghanistan into the entire Middle East. This position was articulated most strongly by Phyllis Chesler, one of the founding figures of second wave feminism. Her book *The New Anti-Semitism: The Current Crisis and What We Must Do About It* was a fairly uncomplicated tract arguing that the U.S. and Israel were targets of a common deadly enemy, Muslims, and the "terrorist" politics they espouse. She concluded that the two countries needed to band together to defeat this threat to their respective populations.

In this view, the 9/11 attacks were essentially an attack on Israel and Jewish people everywhere. Claiming "[t]his fight against the Jews is as old as the Jews," Chesler identified a "new" anti-Semitism which she named as the cause of the 9/11 attacks and the subsequent global crisis.[11] Linking Islamists to Nazis, and using the parlance of the neo-conservatives, she argued the U.S. had become a target of "Islamofascists"[12] only because of its support for Israel. Defining as "old" the anti-Semitism based on biological notions of racial inferiority, Chesler identified its "new" form as being distinct in that "acts of violence against Jews and anti-Semitic words and deeds are being uttered and performed by politically correct people in the name of anticolonialism, anti-imperialism, antiracism and pacifism."[13] Pointing to the support of intellectuals – including Jewish intellectuals – for the Palestinians, and for the anti-globalization, anti-colonial, and anti-racist movements, she charged them with a "betrayal of the Jews."[14] Chesler drew on the apocalyptic view of the "clash of civilizations" earlier promoted by Samuel Huntington and Bernard Lewis, which had become central to the neo-conservative foreign policy of the George W. Bush Administration. Chesler's contribution was to give this neo-conservativism, which had earlier been defined by most feminists as anti-women, a feminist veneer by highlighting a gender dimension of this "clash."[15] Her framing of the war as a battle between the "West" and Islam, it should be noted, was shared by some Muslim feminists in the West.[16]

If the dangers were clear to feminists who shared Chesler's perspective, so too was the remedy. Among other strategies, Chesler urged her readers to "[f]orm Jewish-Christian Alliances."[17] Her identification of any criticism of Israel as a "new" form of anti-Semitism contributed to a climate that has strengthened the hand of neo-conservative governments outside the U.S., including the Harper government in Canada. In 2009, a parliamentary committee was set up to combat "new" anti-Semitism on the basis of "new fears" that were said to threaten Jews and other supporters of Israel in Canada. What the committee defined as "new" about this anti-Semitism were "accusations of blood libel . . . being directed against the State of Israel, such that anti-Zionism is being used as a cover for anti-Semitism."[18] That Chesler's brand of feminism sits very comfortably with such neo-conservative rebrandings of anti-Semitism and Zionism points to the imperialist politics shared by both.

Keeping the focus on a partial view of the oppression of Muslim women

and normalizing Zionism as a core aspiration of the West, Chesler dehistoricized and decontextualized the conflict between the U.S. and its opponents
in the Middle East and Central Asia from contemporary geopolitics. Situating
it instead in an eternal primitivism of Islam characterized by its ostensible
hatred of Jewish peoples and by Muslim men's hatred of women, she presented this primitivism as having marked human history for centuries. This
framing did not allow for attention to be drawn to the asymmetrical power
relations between the West and the Muslim world, between the state of
Israel and occupied Palestine, or between the United States and the Islamist
movements that oppose U.S. imperialism. Politically, she engaged in a fear-
mongering bordering on the paranoid in her representations of Muslim
men.[19] Chesler's was thus a familiar colonial narrative that lent feminist cre-
dence to the racialized fantasy of an eternal war of the "civilized" West –
defined as the Judeo-Christian world – against the forces of Islamic bar-
barism. Although Christians had participated in the pogroms against Jewish
populations in Europe, which culminated in the horrors of the Holocaust,
Chesler effectively exonerated them by arguing that the Church had
"evolved" and had "begun to rethink and regret some of its earlier positions."[20] Claiming that "[u]nlike the Jews in France or in Argentina, America
has, so far, been good to the Jews," she presented Muslims as the world's
leading anti-Semites and unmitigated enemies of both Christians and Jews,
while defining Judeo-Christianity as allied against Islam.[21]

Chesler's definition of a "new" anti-Semitism, which she argued is based
in, and of the same quality as, the historical persecution of the Jews that culminated in the Holocaust, was a move that has been identified as deeply
problematic by critical race scholars. David Goldberg has argued that the
Holocaust has been turned into the "the mark par excellence of race and
racially inscribed histories" in Europe. This singular focus on the Holocaust
makes "Europe's colonial history and legacy dissipate if not disappear," he
cautioned.[22] Goldberg's critique of the obscuring of Europe's colonial legacy
and the present removal of "race" from scrutiny through such a focus on the
Holocaust is relevant to Chesler's work, for she reproduced these problematic approaches in her eagerness to present Jews as the "eternal" – and only –
victims of racial hatred. There is little to be found in this perspective that is
different from the Bush Administration's division of the world between "us"
and "them," between "good" and "evil."

Chesler's purchase of the fantasy of the West, which presents it to itself as
endangered but nonetheless enlightened benefactor of the Other, is total: "As
a feminist, I have long dreamed of rescuing women who are trapped in
domestic and sexual slavery against their will with no chance of escape." In
keeping with this imperial feminist fantasy, Chesler revealed how her own

feminism was spurred by her recognition of the primitivism and misogyny of the Muslim world:

> My so-called Western feminism was certainly forged in that beautiful and treacherous country [Afghanistan], where I observed and experienced the abysmal oppression of women, children and servants. Forever after I was able to see gender apartheid anywhere, even in America. Although I appreciated my relative freedom as an American woman back on American soil, I no longer believed that American women were free – only privileged.[23]

The conditions which grant this "privilege" to American women, and men, namely, colonialism, imperialism, and globalization, were not taken up for discussion. Nor was the recognition that defending this "privilege" is precisely the imperative driving the War on Terror.

## Imperial precariousness

In contrast to the white feminists urging for an expansion of the War on Terror, others strongly opposed it.[24] Most prominent among them was Judith Butler, who argued in *Precarious Life: The Powers of Mourning and Violence* that the distinction between anti-Semitism and anti-Zionism is vital to recognize. Unequivocal in her condemnation of anti-Semitism and violence, she noted that the charge of anti-Semitism was increasingly being used post–9/11 to silence both dissent in the U.S. and critiques of Israeli state violence.[25] Arguing for the need to address the "root causes" of 9/11, Butler's book undertook an examination of the basis for "community" in the face of violence and mourning. She also addressed the suspension of the law in the name of national security and ethical and moral responses to the demand from the Other. Butler's main concern was with "the conditions of heightened vulnerability and aggression"[26] left in the wake of 9/11, and she criticized the Bush Administration's decision to respond with violence abroad and the erosion of civil rights in the U.S. She was also extremely critical of the media's dehumanization of the Other, arguing that in not reporting on the violence done to them, the media made their lives "unknowable" and their deaths "ungrievable." Butler's intervention was very significant politically, given her standing as a prominent feminist intellectual and a founding figure of post-structural/postmodern feminism.

Butler's analytic frame was centred on the injury done to the U.S. in the 9/11 attacks: "That US boundaries were breached, that an unbearable vulnerability was exposed, that a terrible toll on human life was taken, were, and are, cause for fear and mourning; they are also instigations for patient political reflection."[27] Nevertheless, the numerous breaches of the boundaries of other countries by the U.S. in the decades preceding 9/11, although mentioned in passing, were not allowed to shape the analytic frame. Although she acknowledged that "others have suffered arbitrary violence at the hands of the US,"[28] this suffering, concretized most relevantly in Afghanistan and Iraq *prior to the 9/11 attacks*, among the many other well-known victims of U.S. aggression, was made irrelevant in her analysis. Instead, she situated the injury to the U.S. at the heart of her construct of the generalized suffering of a generic humanity, and for her philosophical and political deliberations on violence, grief, and mourning.

This framing foregrounded – perhaps unintentionally – the imperial subject, who had suddenly and graphically discovered its own vulnerability, and thus implicitly reproduced the Bush Administration's claims of American innocence. That this subject was disturbed by the war, that it did not glorify in, nor deny, the obvious violence being done to the Other, made it no less imperial. This subject was primarily disturbed by the war because of the violent *response* it was likely to generate in the future, and not because of this subject's unconditional opposition to the violence done to its Other.

Searching for an understanding of the injury done to the self, as well as to the Other, Butler posited a vulnerability to violence that she defined as central to the human experience: "To be injured means that one has the chance to reflect upon injury, to find out the mechanisms of its distribution, to find out who else suffers from permeable borders, unexpected violence, dispossession, and fear, and in what ways."[29] Although she acknowledged such vulnerability was not equally distributed, her analysis nevertheless proceeded on the assumption that it was, as she reflected on the possibility of political community based on this shared (American) experience of loss, mourning, and vulnerability. This community became the "we" of her text: "Despite our differences in location and history," she argued, "my guess is that it is possible to appeal to a 'we,' for all of us have some notion of what it is to have lost somebody. Loss has made a tenuous 'we' of us all. And if we have lost, then it follows that we have had, that we have desired and loved, that we have struggled to find the conditions for our desire."[30]

In spite of having cautioned against the assumption of a universally shared human condition by saying, "I do not even mean to presume upon a common notion of the human, although to speak in its 'name' is already (and perhaps only) to fathom its possibility,"[31] her analysis was grounded in just such a notion of a universal (degendered, deracialized) human subject:

I am referring to violence, vulnerability, and mourning, but there is a more general conception of the human with which I am trying to work here, one in which we are, from the start, even prior to individuation itself, and by virtue of bodily requirements, given over to some set of primary others: this conception means that we are vulnerable to those we are too young to know and to judge, and hence, vulnerable to violence; but also vulnerable to another range of touch, a range that includes the eradication of our being at the one end, and the physical support for our lives at the other.[32]

Butler thus grounded her narcissistic analysis of an imperialist war, its breaching of the national boundaries and destruction of national sovereignties in Afghanistan and Iraq, of invasions and occupations, in a shared, primal, pre-individuated psychological construct of human vulnerability. This theoretical move suppressed the alterity that was historically constituted between those doing the occupying and invading and those being invaded and occupied.

The commonality of the human experience posited by Butler served to make the Other the same as the Self, erasing the experience of the Other as the Self moved back into a position of centrality, into the epistemically violent position of determining what constitutes *the* human experience. Her use of the Self's experience of a "primal vulnerability" to analyze the war ejected the analysis of power relations in the geopolitical order put on the global agenda by the 9/11 attacks, and situated it instead in an abstract, liberal, individualist frame. With this move, the specific forms of vulnerability and violence that sustain imperialist relations became invisible, as the vulnerability of the condition of human infancy was defined as primary and thus dominated the discursive frame. Consequently, Butler's imposition of the collective "we" in prioritizing this infant condition, for both the Western Self and its occupied Other (if they were to be included in her conception of the human), denied recognition to the specific forms of vulnerabilities, injuries, and losses experienced by the invaded and occupied Other, which are significantly different from those experienced by imperial subjects. In assuming the primacy of the infant condition in which she anchored her theorization of the "vulnerability" experienced by the U.S. as the point of departure for the Other's ontological fashioning, and therefore its experience of vulnerability, the Other's experience of loss and injury was equated with, and subsumed within, that of the imperial subject. In this manner, Butler could approach the invaded and occupied object as being essentially the same as the imperial, white self. Such a commonality of experience is, of course, practicably impossible in the absence of the transformation of the conditions of U.S. imperialism.

My concern with Butler's approach is not so much that the psychoanalytic and philosophical approaches she used cannot be useful in shedding light on the war. After all, many critical race theorists, from Frantz Fanon onwards, have drawn on both very fruitfully for their theorization of violence, suffering, and pain.[33] What is problematic about Butler's use of these is her reproduction of the universalist pretentions of Western philosophical and pyschoanalytic traditions, and implicitly, of the Western Self as the only truly human subject. Commenting on Freud's insistence that the "individual factor" demanded attention, Fanon had cautioned that "the Black man's alienation is not an individual question. . . . Beside phylogeny and ontogeny stand sociogeny."[34] Butler, like other white feminists, avoided engagement with the many theorizations of "sociogeny" developed by critical race scholars.

Butler's analysis thus reinforced the denial of the historical scale and magnitude of the violence done to the Other by the Western Self, even as it furthered the discourse of a wounded and injured, but essentially innocent Western subject. It led to a failure to name the U.S. as an imperialist power, and to overlook the facticity of its foundations in the genocidal violence of the European conquest of the Americas. Placing the 9/11 injury to the U.S. at the centre of the analysis enabled her to make the surprising move of representing the world's only – and militarily unmatched – superpower as equally vulnerable to violence as the impoverished societies that have been the victims of its colonial and imperial aggression.

Butler thus repeated the very practices she criticized by recentring and thus restabilizing the West and the white subject. A frame that might have taken as its starting point the injury done to the Other by the Western Self would have not only been more accurate historically, but also might have revealed that the violence committed by the Other was not the original violence. Unfortunately, Butler's vague, ahistorical, and decontextualized references to "state terror" were no substitute for such a discussion. Her problematic framing led to a strange conclusion, where the violence of the U.S. came to be understood as essentially a "tragic" and defensive violence:

Tragically, it seems that the US seeks to preempt violence by waging violence first, but the violence it fears is the violence it engenders. I do not mean to suggest by this that the US is responsible in some causal way for the attacks on its citizens. And I do not exonerate Palestinian suicide bombers, regardless of the terrible conditions that animate their murderous activities. There is, however, some distance to be traveled between living in terrible conditions and suffering serious, even unbearable injuries, and resolving on murderous acts. President Bush traveled that distance quickly, calling for "an end to grief" after a mere ten days of flamboyant mourning. Suffering can yield an experience of humility, of vulnerability, of impressionability and dependence, and these can become resources, if we do not "resolve" them too quickly;

they can move us beyond and against the vocation of the paranoid victim who regenerates infinitely the justifications for war. It is as much a matter of wrestling ethically with one's own murderous impulses, impulses that seek to quell an overwhelming fear, as it is a matter of apprehending the suffering of others and taking stock of the suffering one has inflicted.[35]

It was a curious logic indeed that made an equation between the "murderous acts" of Palestinian suicide bombers and those of an American president, who had the power to mobilize the biggest military machine amassed in human history to carry out his "impulses." Did Butler really mean to suggest such a moral equivalence? This logic got even more curious when it was suggested that a similar experience of "suffering" gave rise to the "murderous impulses" of Palestinian suicide bombers and the president of the United States! Moreover, her demand that Palestinians renounce violence even when living with "unbearable injuries" in order to become "ethical" subjects so completely subjugated the Other's epistemic and ontological experience and priorities that it rendered impossible almost any consideration that the Other's actions might also be construed as having foundations within a different system of moral and ethical values.

Perhaps Butler's criticism of the media for not covering the deaths resulting from the war was the most revealing of her ethical preoccupations. Arguing that the media should give visibility to the war dead and hence make their deaths "grievable,"[36] she explained that the mourning such witnessing would provoke would allow the war dead to be recognized as having been worthy of life. In other words, viewing the dead would allow her community of the "we" to not only "see" their annihilated Others, but through their (dead) visibility, the community witnessing the deaths would *make* these lost lives "grievable" and hence grant them some value. This call to make visible the war dead is very interesting, because the act of "seeing" is presented as the key to a radical humanizing of the Western Self, in that the "seeing" would enable the self to feel grief, and through the subsequent mourning, feel a common bond with the humanity of its Other. What might the Other have to say about this act of being "seen" in the moment of its annihilation, about a grief and mourning that is initiated in the observer only in the moment of observing the Other's death?

Palestine reveals an insight into this politics of deadly/deathly grief and mourning, for if there are a people whose lives have been rendered utterly "ungrievable" by the Western media, it is that of the Palestinians. But if the Western media has accomplished the dehumanization of Palestinians in the popular Western imaginary, Palestinian cinema has been a major site of confronting and reversing such dehumanization. Consider what Hamid Dabashi has to say about the politics of visibility by way of his discussion of the accomplishments of Palestinian cinema, which he describes as being driven by "the mutation of [that] repressed anger into an aestheticized violence – the aesthetic presence of a political absence."[37] The documentaries made by Palestinians, he argues, are a form of visual " 'J'accuse' – animated by a tireless frenzy to create an alternative record of a silenced crime, to be lodged in a place that escapes the reach of the colonizer as occupier."[38] This cinema, standing as the testament of the quintessential Other to the West, is unconcerned with Israelis and other Westerners mourning the loss of Palestinian lives. Instead, its main function is defined as an accusation of those who have committed crimes against its people, who have dispossessed them, and seem to be bent on their utter destruction. What on earth would Butler have to say about such a media, and its accusation of the imperial subjects who Butler would "mourn" over the sight of the Others' dead bodies? Did Butler believe that Iraqis and Afghans were not aware of the deaths of their loved ones, and that they did not grieve over these lost lives and broken bodies whether the Western media covers their deaths or not? Did she really think they did not value the lives of their loved ones, or did not believe their own lives had value? So utterly centred and dominant is the white subject in Butler's frame that such questions do not even give her pause for concern. _Her U.S. citizen imagining is merely that of the white person.

## Sexual terrorism and gender apartheid

If Butler claimed a shared experience of vulnerability to displace the specific claims of the Other by recentring the imperial subject-as-victim, the notion of "gender apartheid" in the Muslim world became popular among other white feminists in a similar fashion to construct themselves as endangered subjects akin to the Muslim women whom they tied to themselves by the bonds of sisterhood. Such a feminist alliance was used to erase the privileged location of white women as imperial subjects, albeit gendered ones, in relation to Muslim women *and men*. An interesting example of this sort of response can be found in Zillah Eisenstein's book *Against Empire*. Setting out "to uncover the relations and histories of power more fully ... to move towards a more inclusive viewing of humanity by looking for absences, listening for silences, and imagining beyond my own limits," Eisenstein stated her opposition to the U.S. Empire, which she noted had a long history of violence and exploitation, from the conquest of Native peoples to the slave trade, and into the present.[39]

Drawing on a socialist-feminist framework, Eisenstein's analysis began with the argument that a "class war is being waged in the US while all eyes look abroad."[40] She pointed out that the U.S. government was engaged in a neo-liberal and neo-conservative assault on the gains of the civil rights and women's movements, cutting taxes for the rich, supporting corporate corruption, and undertaking a dangerous remilitarization.[41] Tracing the War on Terror to the policies of previous administrations, Eisenstein rejected the East/West binary, noting that flows have always existed between them.[42] Linking current U.S. imperialism to the history of the colonization of the Americas and slavery, Eisenstein's frame of analysis promised a more fruitful approach. Her elaboration on the violence of colonization and slavery, and her linking of this violence to the historical development of capitalism, patriarchy, and racism is certainly not commonly found in the writings of white feminists. However, after outlining this history, Eisenstein's theoretical lens became fixed on gender, stunting her analysis of race and processes of racialization.

Eisenstein challenged the dominant framing of the war as an intervention to "save" Afghan women, but she did so only to restate the argument popular among white feminists who opposed the war, that the Bush Administration had "hijacked" feminism.[43] Drawing attention to male domination and violence against women in the U.S., she analyzed the causes of the war as follows:

> A masculinist-military mentality dominates on both sides of the ill-named East/West divide. The opposition implied by this divide is not simple or complete. . . . Flows between these locations have always existed, and they occur today more than ever. Furthermore, the two sides of the divide share foundational relations, even if differently expressed, especially in terms of male privilege. Neither side embraces women's full economic and political equality or sexual freedom. In this sense fluidity has always existed between the two in the arena of women's rights and obligations. The Taliban's insistence on the burqa and the US military's deployment of women fighter pilots are used to overdraw and misrepresent the oppositional stance.[44]

In this formulation, "gender apartheid" in Afghanistan and "sexual terrorism" in the U.S. became conflated, and the status and power of American men was equated with that of Afghan men, the "patriarchy" of both being treated as essentially of the same order, with the same consequences. Eisenstein then presented the control of women's sexuality as a major motivation of al Qaeda in the 9/11 attacks:

> I do not agree with columnists who attributed September 11 solely to the anger of bin Laden and his followers toward the excessive greed and irresponsibility of global capitalism and its white supremacist ways. Nor did Septem-

ber 11 happen simply because the global economy is displacing men from their earlier livelihoods. These explanations are valid, but September 11 must also be viewed in relation to the way that male patriarchal privilege orchestrates its hierarchical system of domination. The age-old fear and hatred of women's sexuality and their forced domestication into womanly and wifely roles informs all economies. Global capitalism unsettles the pre-existing sexual hierarchical order and tries to mold women's lives to its newest needs across the East/West divide.[45]

By attributing a sexual motive to the 9/11 attacks, and by relegating race and racism mainly to the past, Eisenstein's argument furthered the view that Islamists are motivated by a "hatred of women's sexuality" with little attempt to actually examine al Qaeda's political demands, or with the West's racialization of Muslim men as misogynists.

Eisenstein's insistence that the male domination and sexual violence pervasive in the U.S. remains visible was certainly a welcome departure, particularly in a political moment where the demonization of Islam and Islamists relied on rendering invisible Western secular forms of patriarchal practices. Unfortunately, this insistence was not enough to undermine the dominant racialized and gendered construct of Third World men, including Muslim men, as hypermisogynist.[46] The cultural construct of Third World "machismo" has been pervasive in the West for centuries, and surprisingly, Eisenstein ignored this established historical tradition.

Moreover, in presenting a "global misogyny"[47] as the cause of the current conflict, Eisenstein posited an experience of gender oppression that was shared by Western and Muslim women, that is, that the "patriarchy" that both were subjected to was defined as being basically the same. Her rejection of the East/West binary was thus replaced with a gender binary; the East /West divide was disavowed while the woman/man binary was reinforced, as she elevated gender to primacy in her analysis of the global order. Yet, despite her attempt to reject the East/West divide, Eisenstein ultimately remained unable to displace this from her own analysis, as reflected in her discussion of feminism. Contesting the idea that feminism was solely a Western phenomenon, she went to great lengths to draw attention to "alternate feminisms" from "elsewhere."[48] In naming these (non-Western) forms of feminism as "alternate" and being from "elsewhere," she centred white, Western forms as normative.

Certainly, one cannot argue with Eisenstein's contention that sexual economics underpin the global economy, nor can one deny the realities of the violence against women that exists in both the "East" and the "West." However, in the absence of an equally rigorous emphasis on the social relations of race, as well as a substantive critique of white supremacy, Eisenstein's analysis often dovetailed with the very imperial feminism that she attempted to reject. In claiming a shared experience of gender oppression with Muslim women without examining the racialized experiences of Muslim women (and men), Eisenstein treated white women's oppression as essentially the same as that of Muslim women, with the result that her analysis concealed the unequal power relations between white women and Muslim women.

While Eisenstein drew some attention to race and racism, she either relegated both to the past, or attributed them solely to "capitalist" and "imperialist" structures, and to white male elites. In this way she rendered invisible the very tangible benefits that accrue to Western women through their access to the privileges of whiteness. "Western" women have made their arguments for a "global sisterhood" on this very basis, securing their own privileged location at the forefront of this sisterhood by often leaving this privilege unnamed and unexamined.[49]

Eisenstein acknowledged the need to examine whiteness in her text, yet in the end, remained unable to actually integrate such an imperative into her own analysis. By emphasizing the violence that is done to Afghan women by Afghan men, she implicitly downplayed the violence done to these women by the men *and women* of the Western imperialist nations that invaded and occupied that country. It was thus less than convincing for her to argue that it was the Bush Administration's hijacking of "the language of women's rights" that was the main issue, or that the few women she identified in the Bush Administration as being "showcase[d] masquerad[ing] as a masculinity in drag"[50] were the only women to benefit from U.S. imperialism.

In the absence of a rigorous critique of the racially exclusionary forms of feminism that abound in the U.S., Eisenstein was back on the familiar, colonial terrain of white women claiming their own experience as gender victims to present themselves as the "natural" gender allies of women in the Third World, and thereby evading substantive interrogations of their own power and privileges. Presenting the benefits of imperialism as accruing only to the elite and corporations, she argued it was the few women who "shore up white patriarchy for global capital by making it look gender – and race – neutral" that benefited from the war.[51] This perspective allowed the imperial (feminized) subject to claim proximity to the position of the Third World Muslim woman and from this vantage point, contribute to the demonization of Muslim men.

Predictably, Eisenstein criticized Black and Third World anti-racist and anti-colonial male leaders for sexism, but little criticism was to be found of white women's reproduction of racial supremacy, or of Western feminists and their exclusionary feminisms.[52] Unfortunately, Eisenstein's analysis demonstrated that the rejection of the East/West binary can sit quite comfortably with a re-inscription of the white gendered subject as innocent of, and far removed from, the reproduction of imperialist relations.

## Conclusion

At the end of the Cold War, the United States emerged as the world's only superpower, confident in its hegemony and concerned only with the form of leadership it should demonstrate, not with the fact of the leadership itself. But this confidence was short-lived. The 9/11 attacks destroyed it by demonstrating to the world that the U.S. was not invincible. The U.S. and its allies launched the War on Terror to reassert their dominance of the Middle East and central Asia. In this chapter, I have argued that white feminists have helped to restabilize the idea of Western innocence and its superiority, even if this innocence is presented as gendered.

Western feminism has emerged from different theoretical traditions throughout its history. Yet despite the varied sets of concerns and perspectives of the feminists discussed above, their foundational assumptions converge in a number of interesting ways. Drawing attention to these similarities I have sought to identify the discursive strategies that reproduce white innocence and Western supremacy in feminist tracts. These revolve around the universalizing of the white imperial perspective and its representation of imperial subjects as vulnerable, victimized, and threatened by the Muslim Other. Key among the strategies these feminists share with the neo-conservative architects of the war is their refusal to engage with the actual socio-economic critiques or political demands of the Islamist movements that challenge U.S. hegemony. Yet another strategy is their equation of the reach and power of the U.S. (with its immense military might) with that of al Qaeda, the Taliban, and Saddam Hussein. Rather than an accurate (or even rational) reflection of reality, this equation, more than anything else, reveals the paranoid fantasies of the white women who have historically imaged themselves to be imperilled by those who are actually dominated and exploited by the West.

White feminists who supported the war, including Chesler, revelled in demonizing the Islamic "enemy" and were clear about their political vision: eliminate them. Although white feminists, including Butler and Eisenstein, were opposed to the war, they refused to engage with an analysis of the racialized inequalities within the global economy, or with Islamists in their *political* specificity. Their analysis strengthened the dominant discourse that the motives and demands of Muslims-as-terrorists are unspeakable and unknowable. Refusing to acknowledge this Other as a *political* opponent makes it easier for him or her to be presented as the *existential* enemy of the

West. The Other remains a mythic, abstract figure, the looming face of death and destruction.

The feminist perspectives examined in this chapter cannot be read outside the context of the political deployment of a discourse on terror in which the "terrorist threat" is said to be of global proportions, bent on destroying the security of Western nations and their subjects. Western feminist perspectives have embraced their own location in the category of the "West" as its most innocent, endangered, and exalted subjects, although each has done so in a different manner and to a varying extent.

Whether feminists analyze the war from a materialist perspective or from philosophical and psychoanalytic perspectives is moot. The global order needs to be analyzed from all these theoretical traditions and perspectives, as well as a good many more. What is indispensable, however, is the disruption of the practices that reproduce Western supremacy and white racial power, even in their feminist incarnations.

## Notes

This chapter is based on a paper first published in *Feminist Theory*, "White Wars: Western Feminisms and the War on Terror," 8 (2007), 169–85.

1 For analysis of the backlash and emergence of the men's rights movement, see S. Faludi, *Backlash: The Undeclared War Against American Women* (New York: Crown Publishers, 1991); D.E. Chunn, S.B. Boyd, and H. Lessard, eds., *Reaction and Resistance: Feminism, Law and Social Change* (Vancouver: UBC Press, 2007).

2 See Janine Brodie and Isabella Bakker, *Where Are the Women? Gender Equity, Budgets and Canadian Public Policy* (Ottawa: Canadian Centre for Policy Alternatives, 2008).

3 Prominent among these were scholars, journalists, and public commentators, including Camille Paglia, Daphne Patai, Phyllis Chesler, Barbara Amiel, Anne Coulter, and Donna La Framboise.

4 See J. Brodie, "Canada's 3-D's: The Rise and Decline of the Gender-Based Policy Capacity," in *Remapping Gender in the New Global Order*, ed. M. Cohen and J. Brodie (London: Routledge, 2007), 166–84.

5 See J.W. Scott, ed., *Women's Studies on the Edge* (Durham, NC: Duke University Press, 2008); B. Epstein, "What Happened to the Women's Movement?" *Monthly Review* 53,1 (2001), 1–13; L.P. Rankin and J. Vickers, "Women's Movements and State Feminism: Integrating Diversity into Public Policy," in *Feminisms and Womanisms: A Women's Studies Reader*, ed. A. Prince and S. Silva-Wayne (Toronto: Women's Press, 2004), 43–51; E. Messor-Davidow, *Disciplining Feminism: From Social Activism to Academic Discourse* (Durham, NC: Duke University Press, 2002); and D. Patai and N. Koertege, *Professing Feminism: Cautionary Tales from the Strange World of Women's Studies* (New York: Basic Books, 1994).

6  Anti-colonial and anti-racist feminists who spoke out against the invasions and occupations of Afghanistan and Iraq were publicly attacked and reviled as ungrateful
   upstarts and apologists for terrorists. See Sunera Thobani, "War Frenzy," *Atlantis: A
   Women's Studies Journal* 27,1 (2002), 5–11.

7  I have discussed my own position on the War on Terror, as well as my experiences
   in opposing this war, elsewhere. See Thobani, "War Frenzy."

8  See S. Arat-Koç, "Hot Potato: Imperial Wars or Benevolent Interventions? Reflections on 'Global Feminism' Post-September 11," *Atlantis: A Women's Studies Journal* 26,2 (2002), 433–44; C. Hirschkind and S. Mahmood, "Feminism, the Taliban
   and the Politics of Counterinsurgency," *Anthropological Quarterly* 75,2 (2008),
   339–54.

9  "Eleanor Smeal Urges President to Fulfill Promise to Afghan Women," *Feminist
   Daily News* (Washington) May 22, 2002, ⟨http://feminist.org/news/newsbyte/
   uswirestory.asp?id=6544⟩, accessed June 6, 2002.

10 C. Stolba, "Feminists Go To War. The Women's Quarterly, Independent Women's
   Forum" (2002), ⟨http://www.iwf.org/pubs/twq/Winter2002i.shtml⟩, accessed June
   16, 2002.

11 P. Chesler, *The New Anti-Semitism: The Current Crisis and What We Must Do About
   It* (San Francisco: Jossey-Bass, 2003), 41.

12 For a critique of this caricatured use of words during wartime, see Niall Ferguson,
   Interview by Lawrence A. Tish, "The War of the World: Conversation with Niall
   Ferguson," Institute for International Studies, University of California-Berkeley,
   2006, ⟨http://globetrotter.berkeley.edu/people6/Ferguson/ferguson06-con5.html⟩,
   accessed March 10, 2010.

13 Chesler, *The New Anti-Semitism*, 88.

14 Ibid., 12.

15 Chesler describes the impact of her visit to Afghanistan as a young woman as important in shaping her subsequent feminist politics. Ibid., 16.

16 Irshad Manji's deeply emotive attack on Islam and Muslims and its exaltation of
   the "West" is a fine example of the attempts of some Muslim feminists to give cre-
   dence to the "clash of civilizations" narrative. The conditions of her book's reception in Canada, the United States, and Europe speak to the important role of Mus-
   lim feminists in legitimizing the ideological aspects of the War on Terror. See I.
   Manji, *The Trouble with Islam: A Wake-Up Call for Honesty and Change* (Toronto:
   Random House, 2003). For an excellent analysis of the writings of Irshad Manji,
   Phyllis Chesler, and Orianna Fallaci on the War on Terror, see Sherene H. Razack,
   "Unassimilable Muslims and Civilized White People: The Race/Culture Divide in
   Law" (paper presented at the annual meeting of the Law and Society Association,
   Chicago, IL, May 27, 2004). Also see Sherene H. Razack, *Casting Out: The Eviction of
   Muslims from Western Law and Politics* (Toronto: University of Toronto Press,
   2008).

17 Chesler, *The New Anti-Semitism*, 213.

18 Faculty for Palestine, "Submission to the Canadian Parliamentary Coalition to
   Combat Anti-Semitism" (August 31, 2009), email to author, read on January 15,
   2010.

19 Here is Chesler's view on the threat presented by Islam and Muslims:

> It begins with the Jews, but if we do not stop them it will, soon enough – it already has – spread to Christians, Hindus and Buddhists, and to all Americans of all religions and races. Appeasement is no longer an option. If we do not stop them, Islamic jihadists will surely remove the precious jewels from our houses of worship and our museums, melt down the gold and the silver, and blow up our most beautiful churches and synagogues, or they will build mosques right over them. Muslims have been doing exactly this in the Islamic world for more than a thousand years, and they continue to do so today. The moderates among them have not stopped them. Jihadists will destroy our most beautiful paintings and sculptures, especially those of non-Islamic religious figures and those of naked women – just as they blew up the beautiful Buddha of Bamiyan in Afghanistan. (*The New Anti-Semitism*, 21)

20 This is how Chesler analyzes the relations between Jews and Christians, and the possibilities for their "alliance": "I do not wish to alarm you but I am fairly and accurately describing how most Islamic extremists have treated 'the infidel' for centuries (even when life was still soft and easy). Unlike the Catholic Church, which has evolved and begun to rethink and regret some of its earlier positions, fundamentalist Islam has not yet evolved. With some exceptions, it is exactly the same today as it was when Muhammad was alive. Sameness is what is valued; difference is feared and hated" (ibid., 21). She further discusses the relationship between these two groups:

> Please understand: I am not quarreling with the rights of Catholics or Christians to worship Christ as the Messiah in any way they so choose. I am horrified, saddened, outraged – a mite prickly – about the Church's centuries-long mistreatment of Jews, its acts of both omission and commission. I am not saying that because the Church persecuted Jews – or did too little to rescue Jews endangered by the princes of the Church – that all Christians are therefore evil (I do agree, however, with Harvard political scientist Daniel Jonah Goldhagen that it is time for the living Catholic Church to acknowledge its role in the persecution of the Jews that culminated in the Holocaust and to make serious retribution). I am not saying that each and every Christian persecuted Jews as God-killers. Many did, some did not; some saved Jews, but most chose not to endanger themselves to prevent pogroms or Jewish extermination. (ibid., 29)

In another section, after criticizing Catholicism for "frightening" and "enraging" her, she extols on its virtues, especially for women: "Thus, I do not mean to sound overly harsh about Catholicism. Forgive me if I do. In many ways it is a good religion for women." Here, she points to Mary as a positive "female role model and deity"; to convents for "guarantee[ing] poor girls and women literacy, a roof over their heads, and a God-centered communal life; and to the concept of redemption" (ibid., 30).

21 Ibid., 209.

22 D.T. Goldberg, "Racial Europeanization," *Ethnic and Racial Studies* 29,2 (2006), 336.

23  Chesler, *The New Anti-Semitism*, 16.

24  See Betsy Reed, ed., *Nothing Sacred: Women Respond to Religious Fundamentalism and Terror* (New York: National Books, 2002).

25  The essay in which Butler argues for the need to confront anti-Semitism and also oppose Israeli state violence without always equating the two is part of a debate she had with Lawrence Summers, president of Harvard University, who argued that actions such as boycotts of Israel are "anti-Semitic in their effect if not their intent."

26  Judith Butler, *Precarious Life: The Powers of Mourning and Violence* (London: Verso Books, 2004), xi.

27  Ibid.

28  Ibid., xiv.

29  Ibid., xii.

30  Ibid., 20.

31  Ibid., 31.

32  Ibid.

33  F. Fanon, *Black Skin, White Masks* (London: Pluto Press, 1986).

34  Ibid., 13.

35  Butler, *Precarious Life*, 149–50.

36  Butler argues that certain deaths are publicly mourned and acknowledged as losses within the U.S., while other deaths are not given any consideration. The former are grieved, while the lack of recognition afforded to the latter makes their deaths, and lives, "unthinkable and ungrievable" (ibid., xiv).

37  H. Dabashi, ed., *Dreams of a Nation* (London: Verso Books, 2006), 11.

38  Ibid.

39  Z. Eisenstein, *Against Empire: Feminisms, Racism and the West* (London: Zed Books, 2004), xv.

40  Ibid., xix.

41  Eisenstein argues that "the downsizing and corporate restructuring of the US economy through the 1980s and 1990s has now been accompanied by a restructuring of the CIA, FBI, and Pentagon. . . . This new security-state monitors and conducts surveillance in the name of democracy" (ibid., xix).

42  This is how Eisenstein traces the beginnings of the Iraq war:

> The US war against Iraq preceded the post-September 11 "war on terrorism." It has been a more-than-decade-long war with three noted episodes: Desert Storm, in 1991, orchestrated by Bush Sr.; the renewed bombing of 1998 designed by Bill Clinton and Madeleine Albright; and the "war on terrorism"/Operation Iraqi Freedom of 2003 led by Bush Jr. and Donald Rumsfeld. Economic sanctions were in place this entire time, devastating the country as a whole, while Saddam amassed incredible wealth for himself. Through the sanctions, the US blocked shipments of milk, yogurt, printing equipment for schools, dialysis and dental supplies, chlorine for purifying water, and textbooks for medical schools. Children suffered the most: hundreds of thousands died of malnutrition and radiation poisoning. (ibid., 12)

43 Eisenstein takes the Bush Administration and its "women helpmates" to task for taking " . . . the post–September 11 moment and appropriat[ing] the language of women's rights for a right-wing and neoliberal imperial agenda" (ibid., 148).

44 Ibid.,151.

45 Ibid.,152.

46 See also Mishra Smeeta, " 'Saving' Muslim Women and Fighting Muslim Men: Analysis of representations in *The New York Times*," *Global Media Journal* 6,11(2007), ⟨http://lass.calumet.purdue.edu/cca/gmj/fa07/gmj-fa07-mishra.htm⟩; Lila Abu-Lughod, "Do Muslim Women Really Need Saving? Anthropological Reflections on Cultural Relativism and Its Others," *American Anthropologists* 104,3 (2002), 783–90; and Sherene H. Razack, "Imperilled Muslim Women, Dangerous Muslim Men and Civilised Europeans: Legal and Social Responses to Forced Marriages," *Feminist Legal Studies* 12,2 (2004), 129–74.

47 Eisenstein, *Against Empire*, 150.

48 Ibid., xv.

49 There are, of course, some exceptions to this general tendency. See, for example, Ruth Frankenberg, *White Women, Race Matters: The Social Construction of Whiteness* (Minneapolis: University of Minnesota Press, 1993).

50 Eisenstein, *Against Empire*, 156.

51 Ibid., 157.

52 See A.K. Wing, ed., *Global Critical Race Feminism* (New York: New York University Press, 2000); and Chandra Talpade Mohanty, *Feminism without Borders: Decolonizing Theory, Practicing Solidarity* (Durham, NC: Duke University Press, 2003).

# 7 : New whiteness(es), beyond the colour line? Assessing the contradictions and complexities of "whiteness" in the (geo)political economy of capitalist globalism

Sedef Arat-Koç

WE ARE LIVING IN A WORLD that has been radically made over in the last two to three decades. The period since the late 1970s has marked the collapse of the Second and Third Worlds, and every country on the planet has been significantly restructured by neo-liberal capitalist globalization. The remaking of the world requires an assessment of what race and racism mean today. Nevertheless, such an assessment may be a rather confusing process. There are not only ongoing experiences of inequality, exclusion, injustice, and stigmatization in the economic, social, cultural and political realms but also heightened experiences of racism in new forms. At the same time, it appears as if racism has lost legitimacy as a state or societal discourse, as mainstream discussions and practices of race become increasingly sophisticated in the Western world, taking the forms of the self-proclaimed "non-racism" of liberal "colour-blindness" and, more recently, neo-liberal multiculturalism portraying a post-racist world of freedom and opportunity.

What complicates and confuses the picture at present are the huge contradictions that have emerged as a result of the limited entry of individuals from racialized backgrounds into the middle class or into positions of decision-making power, even as racial inequality and injustices continue full steam ahead. In South Africa, Black poverty has not only continued but, according to some reports, has gotten worse more than a decade after the end of apartheid, despite the fact that a Black middle class has emerged in the same period. In the United States, what has been called the "prison-industrial complex" continues to stand as a central institution of society. The complex houses more than two million people, the majority of whom are racialized, while an African American president resides in the White House. During Hurricane Katrina, at the same time as New Orleans had a Black mayor, poor Black people in the city received threats rather than the support they needed from the National Guard, whose mission was apparently more about protecting property than about providing rescue and aid. In the aftermath of the hurricane, even as public debates continued on the significance of race and class in experiences of a so-called natural disaster, some of the same people who experienced the worst forms of deprivation during the hurricane found themselves ethnically cleansed from the city. Canada's Governor General, a woman of colour originally from Haiti, paid a "working visit" to Haiti in 2009. Before, during, or after the visit, neither she nor the media asked any critical questions about the nature of Canada's role in the kidnapping and overthrow of Haiti's democratically elected president, Jean-Bertrand Aristide, in 2004, or the nature of Canada's presence in the country since the 2004 intervention. What has been significant as much as the stark reality of these contradictions themselves has been how they are popularly interpreted and presented. Rather than being problematized in popular opinion, these contradictions are either celebrated as a reality slowly changing in a positive direction towards a raceless state, or are taken as signs of individual differences between "good" and "bad" racialized people.

With a specific focus on whiteness, this chapter[1] argues for the need to historicize and contextualize the complexities and contradictions of "race" in the post–Cold War era of neo-liberal globalism and an age of new imperialism. Such a project requires an approach to critical race theory that takes political economy and geopolitics seriously. As a result of neo-liberal economic globalization, class inequalities are increasing at national and global levels and large numbers of white people in white-dominated societies are becoming socio-economically marginalized, whereas a very small minority of non-European people are being welcomed into a transnational bourgeoisie. This involves not just a relative "browning" of the transnational bourgeoisie, but also a "whitening" of the (former) Third World elite in relation to the people of their countries. In this environment, there is an increased urgency related to identifying and clarifying what "race" means in relation to class. The task is to recognize race as a technology of power that goes beyond skin colour to identify some of the ways race involves "historic repertoires and cultural, spatial, and signifying systems that stigmatize and depreciate one form of humanity for the purposes of another's health, development, safety, profit and pleasure."[2] When we approach race in this way, it seems that a race logic and a race-like language can be used in the exclusion, stigmatization, and subordination of people *beyond*, as much as *along*, the colour line.

Exploring the complexities and contradictions of whiteness in the current period, the first section of this chapter demonstrates how racial logics don't just apply along the colour line alone. This section focuses on "cracks" along the colour line in three different contexts, reflecting some of the developments in the former three worlds in recent decades. It underlines, however, that even when whiteness operates with "cracks" along the colour line, becoming more conditional on class, it is still based on a race logic and ideals of white supremacy that are the foundations of West European middle-class norms and standards of capitalist modernity. The second section of the chapter qualifies some of the arguments in the first section. While neo-liberal globalization and some of the geopolitical processes of the post–Cold War era have complicated and destabilized "whiteness" in some respects, I argue that they have not marked the end of a race as ideology or materiality. On the contrary, several important developments in the last few decades have represented a return to racism and white supremacy with a vengeance. In addition to the "War on Terror" that redefines geopolitics along so-called civilizational lines, the explosion of anti-immigrant and anti-refugee discourses and policies in the global North mark the continuing centrality of race to the current structuring of societies and the world. They also redefine the current context as one in which the "wages of whiteness" and empowerment offered through civilizational and new nationalist discourses in Western countries may prove irresistible to whites otherwise facing socioeconomic threats to their white privilege.

## Cracks on the colour line? Destabilizing whiteness: Developments in the post–Cold War era

*The decline of the welfare state, reconfiguration of class relations, and decline of universal whiteness for "whites"*

The dismantling of the welfare state that has accompanied neo-liberal globalization in countries in the North has meant that cracks have appeared in some of the privileges associated with the rights of citizenship that the white working class has come to take for granted for almost a century. As the whiteness of the working class in some Western countries has been historically contingent on the development of the welfare state, it is not clear what form the whiteness of the "white" working class will survive in the weakening of the welfare state, or whether it will survive at all.[3] On the one hand, there are indicators suggesting that the impact of dismantling the welfare state, like its historical formation, is taking racially differentiated forms. On the other hand, it is possible to argue that the changes taking place through neo-liberalism – economic, as well as political and ideological – are also affecting the white working class.

There are now numerous studies that show significant percentages of the population being treated as "surplus" or "waste" in the global North, as well as in the global South.[4] A significant proportion of those marginalized in the North are racialized sections of the working class. As Manning Marable argues, there is a "new racial domain" in the United States based on "mass unemployment, mass incarceration, and mass disfranchisement."[5] Loic Wacquant identifies the prison as the main racial institution in the United States at present, following the previous institutions of slavery, Jim Crow segregation, and the ghetto. According to Wacquant, the prison system serves as a highly racialized and "race-making" institution not only during the period of incarceration but also in the way it leads to exclusions from social welfare, denial of cultural capital, and political disenfranchisement long after the actual incarceration is over.[6] So central is the "prison-industrial complex" to the contemporary structures of capitalism that some academic analysts and activists have made prison abolition central to their anti-racist, anti-capitalist, and anti-imperialist struggle.[7]

As I will demonstrate throughout the chapter, neo-liberalism has significantly transformed perceptions and representations of class in different parts of the world. Recent studies on the depictions of the working class in the United States and Britain suggest that sections of this group are seen not simply as economically marginalized but rather are conceptualized as a form of humanity culturally apart. The overwhelming popularity of the term "underclass"[8] in media and public discourses in the U.S. and Britain over the last few decades is significant in fostering this perception. It may indicate a simultaneous meaning of racial difference and potential cracks in whiteness. Even though the term is clearly heavily racialized, I would argue that it also cultural*izes* and racial*izes* poverty, potentially implicating poor whites. The term is reminiscent of Victorian references to the poor as "dangerous classes" and "paupers," references that represented a language of class and race fixated on the body and the culture of the poor.

Since the 1980s, the term "underclass" has become increasingly popular in the U.S. Introducing the term to a broad audience, a 1977 *Time* magazine cover story stated, "Behind [the ghetto's] crumbling walls lives a large group of people who are more intractable, more socially alien and more hostile than almost anyone had imagined. They are the unreachables: the American underclass."[9] Summarizing some of the critiques of the category of underclass, Charles Mills argues that it is "inherently biased, racially coded and methodologically vacuous."[10] Despite its enormous problems and limitations as an analytical category,[11] "underclass" has grown in its ideological appeal. In the post–civil rights era, when overt racism may not have the social legitimacy it once enjoyed, it has provided a language for Othering the poor that goes beyond describing economic deprivation. The naming that the term and discourse of "underclass" engages in is heavily loaded with presuppositions and normative judgements. In his critique of William J. Wilson's use of the term, Goldberg argues that "(n)aming the underclass *makes* the underclass, *nominates* it into existence, and *constitutes* its members at once as Other."[12]

"Underclass" emphasizes social and cultural differences that are assumed to go far beyond what class inequalities would produce, a form of marginality, a pathological form of existence outside what are thought to be the "normal" structures of society and economy. "The underclass is treated as somehow different from the rest of society and indeed as standing outside of society. . . . The underclass is seen as composed of aliens and outcasts: 'A Nation Apart' as one US newspaper described it."[13] The term "underclass" is used to describe not so much the poor, but rather those who are seen to be "morally degenerate, a class of people which *by its nature* is dissolute, debauched, depraved and sinful."[14] According to these representations, poverty is portrayed as a moral issue, not a social one. *& the legitimacy to cut social services & support structures*

Even though the discussion about the "underclass" is used predominantly for racialized groups, the political and ideological climate of neo-liberalism has a tendency to individualize and pathologize poverty and to blame it on the poor themselves. Thus, it has implications for all poor people, including poor whites. One could also argue that what is said about the "underclass" has significant implications for the working class "proper," including the white working class. In her work on Britain, Beverley Skeggs argues that significant shifts have taken place in recent years on the position of the working class in British society. According to Skeggs,[15] Britain has moved from historical attempts to incorporate the working class into the nation to delineating them as a hazard to modernity:

> The class struggle is being waged on a daily basis through culture as a form of symbolic violence, through relationships of entitlement that are legitimized and institutionalized, and it is these processes that set limits on who can and cannot belong, be, and have worth on a national and global stage.[16]

Skeggs mentions that there is an "understated ubiquity of class" in Britain, that class is "continually referenced even when not directly spoken."[17] She argues, however, that there is a shift in the meaning of class from an economic category to one popularly conceived as being based in cultural characteristics and practices. Closer to the nineteenth century rather than twentieth century in how it is characterized, the working class in Britain is once again being identified with excess, waste, entertainment, lacking in taste, unmodern, backward, escapist, dangerous, unruly, and immoral.[18]

Skeggs refers to processes in which economic deprivation is understood increasingly through moral deprivation, whereby "class is being increasingly defined as a moral-cultural property of the person, related to their attitudes and practices (not named and known directly as class)."[19]

In her study on welfare reform and discourses of social inclusion in Britain, Chris Haylett looks into how these discourses have focused not on the economic predicament of the poor but on their "culture" or "cultural impoverishment, a poverty of identity based on outdated ways of thinking and being."[20] Haylett argues that in the "modern multicultural" Britain, "there is no legitimate space for class-based discourses" but that the "impulse is for class to be remade as an ethno-difference."[21] In the hegemonic discourses of multiculturalism, the white working class comes to represent "the unmodern," with a generalized "backwardness," "a culturally shameful and burdenous whiteness," whereas "a representative of the middle class is positioned at the vanguard of 'the modern' which becomes a moral category referring to liberal, cosmopolitan, work and consumption based lifestyles and values."[22]

Significant in these analyses are the ways in which the "white" working class might be losing its unconditional membership in modernity. In addition to the mockery of the lifestyles of the working class, the poor, and the marginalized as tasteless, crude, and unsophisticated, there is often a tendency to blame them for what is now presented as unacceptable in bourgeois culture. Certain forms of overt racism, sexism, and homophobia are no longer associated with middle-class values, but are rather considered the attributes of racialized groups or the white working class.

## Post-socialist Eastern Europe: European identity and its pitfalls

The end of the Cold War has led to an ambiguous status for East Europeans in "post-socialist" countries. On the one hand, there have been hopes for belonging to a united Europe and, for some, formal realities of accession to the European Union. On the other, the hopes, aspirations, and possibilities for European belonging have not automatically translated into unqualified European status. Contradictorily, the eastern expansion of Europe has been accompanied by new discourses of Europeanness, constructing Europe in an East/West binary – different from the Cold War one – distinguishing between Europe "proper" versus an Eastern Europe reinscribed as its Other.[23] What has developed since the end of the Cold War has been "a multitier patchwork of Europe with varying degrees of Europeanness and Eastness."[24] Rather than transforming into "the imagined community of a united Europe," expansion of Western Europe to the East has created a situation whereby

East-Central Europe was "instead assigned a special place in Europe's waiting room."[25] In this section, I argue that the ambiguity and insecurity created around European belonging have fuelled an exaggerated embrace of Eurocentrism among those striving for equal status in Europe, turning them against neighbouring states and regions, as well as those who are seen to be non-Europeans.

An ambiguity and insecurity around European belonging is present even in the case of East Germany, where the transition through "unification" with West Germany seemed to be almost automatic. Even though the racialized concept of Germanness directly associated with whiteness used in the process of "unification" assured East Germans of their formally equal citizenship in the new Germany, an East-West hierarchy has not been absent in this notion of (racially) "unified" Germanness.[26] White East Germans have been privileged by a notion of citizenship in Germany that until 2000 was based only on the principle of *jus sanguinis* (citizenship through descent), which automatically included them as it explicitly excluded many who had been living and working in the country for decades, even those who had been born there. While such inclusion in an otherwise exclusionary system of citizenship has constituted psychological "wages of whiteness" for former citizens of the GDR, especially in relationship to racialized groups, their relationship to white West Germans has been based on a "hierarchy of various degrees of Germanness." Hegemonic discourses in West Germany that prevailed during the Cold War and continued after "unification" have constructed East Germans as inferior and "belated" Germans in terms of the economic and political backwardness attributed to their socialist experience. Not only have certain cultural deficits based on their economic and political "backwardness" been attributed to East Germans, but also they have been isolated as being solely responsible for racism in Germany. Some of the worst aspects of Germany's "national-cultural past," specifically its authoritarian traditions and racism – the latter common in individual attitudes as well as in institutionalized and structural forms in German society – are thus conveniently externalized as an East German problem.[27]

What is more apparent in cases outside the now "unified" Germany is that, now that the Cold War is over, East Europeans are not only more open to – what have been identified by critical observers as – Orientalist judgements from Western Europe, which sees them as backward with shades of Asianness but through the IMF, EU, and NATO they are also subjects of modernizing, civilizing, and "humanitarian" missions conducted by "the West." By the end of the Cold War, socialism began to be perceived and presented as a failed system, as opposed to Cold War perceptions that saw it as a competing, alternative modernity. Whereas Eastern Europe and the Soviet Union were seen as capable of industrial and technological development during the Cold War, in the post–Cold War climate, "East-Central Europe was . . . not upgraded but 'downgraded' in the scale of development." It was seen as a "variant of the third world – and hence a space under Western tutelage."[28] It is no accident that, in this new period, modernization theory – once applied to the Third World – as well as its entire infrastructure in the form of Western organizations and consultants advising on the economy and politics, have found fertile ground in Eastern Europe. The language used for Eastern Europe in the process of tutelage is "both celebratory and patronizing," its narrative "indirectly reinforc[ing] rather than undermin[ing] the inferiorization of East European countries."[29]

In the post–Cold War environment, East Europeans experience simultaneous inclusion and exclusion, belonging in Europe and "the West," but not quite. Natasa Kovasevic characterizes the West European and American attitudes as a form of racism:

This type of racism, like racism which Orientalizes Eastern Europeans, predicates a simultaneous inclusion and exclusion: that is, the barrier to one's inclusion is no longer (on the surface, at least) one's ethnicity or race, but rather one's cultural, political and economic behavior. In this sense, inclusion is always possible since it is always possible to "tweak" one's culture or politics to merit international acceptance. On the other hand, exclusion (especially through fashionable policies such as economic sanctions or military interventions) remains a permanent feature of this still conditional inclusion.[30]

Despite all the discourse about the expansion and integration of Europe in recent decades, the reality has not been a reconsideration of the concept of "Europe" along the lines of those recently being included, but rather "an affirmation of some transcendentally pure identity of Europe in the name of which the ugly spots must be cleansed."[31]

What makes the Othering of Eastern Europe especially effective is the fact that it is not simply imposed by Western Europe, but rather that it is internalized and used by each country and region against its neighbours. For countries in Eastern Europe and the Balkans, claims to Europeanness are accompanied by attempts to push the discursive borders of Europe to their East or South:

For each nation emerging out of the Soviet Empire, the "neighbouring other" assumes the characteristics of the externalized evil; at the same time, in their quest to prove their own "Europeanness" and "modernity," the intellectuals look at the internal and neighbouring "others" in disgust.[32]

Following the disintegration of the Socialist Federal Republic of Yugoslavia, "the Balkans" have increasingly been conceptualized in a discourse which Todorova calls "Balkanism," whereby the region serves as the "repository of negative characteristics against which a positive and self-congratulatory image of the 'European' and the 'West' has been constructed."[33] What has ensued among the newly emerging states following the breakup of Yugoslavia has been the development of what Bakic-Hayden has called "nesting Orientalisms," through which a dichotomous logic of "Europe" versus the East remains intact, while a gradation internal to "the East" is introduced, ranking each country in its Europeanness and Eastness.[34] "Nesting Orientalisms" operate as a "subjectivational practice" in which all ethnic groups "not only orientalize the 'other,' but also occidentalize themselves as the West of the other."[35]

The framework in which "European expansion" is taking place "encourages the candidates not to challenge the East/West dichotomy but to align themselves with the 'right side.' It thereby feeds into Eurocentrism and xenophobia in East-Central Europe. . . ."[36] What is involved in the striving for "Europe" in Eastern Europe is a set of processes, which, I would argue, create a *precariousness* and insecurity of whiteness, simultaneously *making* and *breaking* a white status for East Europeans as an increasingly exclusivist notion of white supremacy remains the norm.

### The new bourgeoisie in the (former) Third World: Towards a transnational whiteness?

A third dimension of the destabilization of whiteness along the colour line has to do with a growing phenomenon under neo-liberal globalization of – to use Goldberg's terms – "non-whites whitened by the classed colour of money."[37] The possibility that globalism provides for multicultural diversification of the global bourgeoisie does not break down the North-South colour line completely; it just complicates it. The increased class disparities created by neo-liberal globalization means that whereas a very small sector of the bourgeoisie in the (former) Third World may move up to the ranks of a global elite, the majority of Third World peoples find themselves more deeply trapped in a North-South divide.[38] In this new era, the most important defining characteristics of new middle classes in the (former) Third World are their increased alienation from people in their own countries, and their increased identification, materially and ideologically, with a transnational elite. Even though the status of the non-white elite among the transnational bourgeoisie may be qualified as "never quite white" as they may continue to bear "the distinctive birthmarks of unaddressed because unaddressable inferiorized pasts,"[39] it is possible to argue that what makes their status akin to a form of whiteness is their relationship to their countries' people. This is a form of "whiteness" that sometimes imitates but also goes beyond the colour line. It is "embroiled with images of an affluent, Western consumer lifestyle."[40]

Even though some forms of non-European "whiteness," such as that of the elite in South America, can be partly explained by the legacy of colonialism, I would argue that it cannot simply be reduced to either history or external factors. It is also important to examine whiteness as a category of or claim to distinction, power, and superiority *within* non-European societies. It is useful to see the ways in which whiteness may not simply represent colonial victimization and psychological damage, but rather becomes an active strategy used by some groups to claim power and superiority over others in the same society. As such, whiteness would still be linked but not reduced to colonialism and post-colonialism. In his analysis of the development of white identities in Latin America, Bonnett argues that rather than seeing this development as simply a Western imposition, we should think about the ways in which whiteness is "actively interpreted and translated."[41] He writes: "Whiteness does not merely haunt contemporary Latin America like some disreputable ghost. It is also part and parcel of today's symbolic economy."[42] The specific interpretations, translations, and adaptations are determined by power relations within the post-colonial states on the one hand, and power relations between these states and the West on the other. Galen Joseph's study of the middle class in Argentina also argues that claims to whiteness are very much about contemporary attempts to locate oneself at national and international levels. "It is through middle class *portenos'* transnational imaginary (their understanding of their place in the world), as well as their national imaginary (their understanding of their relationship to others within the nation), that being white becomes meaningful."[43]

How do we explain the emergence of this new "whiteness" in non-European contexts? With globalized capitalism and the new global configuration, distinctions between the First and Third Worlds, the North and the South are being reconfigured along new lines.

Parts of the earlier Third World are today on the pathways of transnational capital and belong in the "developed" sector of the world economy. Likewise, ways of life in those parts of the First World marginalized in the new global economy are hardly distinguishable from what used to be viewed as Third World ways of life.... "North" and "South" designate not merely concrete geographic locations but also metaphorical referents: "North" denoting the pathways of transnational capital; "South" denoting the marginalized populations of the world, regardless of their location.[44]

... the globe has become jumbled up spatially as the ideology of progress is temporally: with the appearance of Third Worlds in the First World and First Worlds in the Third.[45]

In the Third World, the end of the era of import-substitution as the dominant development strategy led the national bourgeoisie to cut loose its obligatory social solidarity with other classes. Whereas development strategies based on import-substitution had forced different levels of redistribution in order to create a consumer base for industrial products, the shift to export-oriented strategies meant that even modest levels of redistribution were no longer necessary. As the Third World bourgeoisie grew stronger and emboldened by their growth through import substitution, they "looked forward to a rearrangement of alliances, with a closer relationship with the 'West' for economic gain and consumer pleasure. The erosion of the Third World state allowed this class to carry the standard of the First World."[46]

James Ferguson provides important insights into the nature of socio-economic and cultural fragmentation that has been taking place in the Third World with capitalist globalization. According to Ferguson,[47] the shift from the previous (developmentalist) modernization project to the more recent globalist one marks some radical changes in the way inequalities are seen and addressed. Acknowledging the wide variety of problems the modernization discourse presented both in theory and practice (regarding the pattern of development and the social and economic benefits it would bring), Ferguson emphasizes that the discourse was nevertheless important in the political promises it made. The developmentalism of the "modernization" project promised the socio-economic convergence of different countries and regions around the world. It assumed/promised that given time, there would be a movement everywhere from "tradition" to "modernity." This promise of convergence, however, has disappeared from contemporary discourses altogether. With the end of the promise for eventual socio-economic convergence, the concept of modernity has changed from being a *telos* to being a *status*, from a collective vision and hope for the future, to a condition of being first class:

> Now with the idea of temporal sequence removed, location in the hierarchy no longer indexes a stage of advancement, but simply a rank in a global political economic order ... ranks ... become not stages to be passed through, but nonserialized statuses, separated from each other by exclusionary walls, rather than developmental stairways. Modernity in this sense comes to appear as a standard of living, a *status*, not a telos.[48]

As it moves from *telos* to *status*, modernization becomes an exclusionary project resulting in significant social, economic, and cultural fragmentation. Ferguson suggests that "[t]he status categories of the contemporary global order . . . may even come to resemble the fixed status categories of the preindependence era, when the color bar segmented the social world into a rich, white, first-class sector and the poor, black, second-class world of the 'natives.' "[49]

As classes of people and entire nations become stuck at the lower end of the global hierarchy, unable and not expected to move up, their status comes to be seen increasingly as naturally or even racially beneath those who have achieved the status of modernity.[50] The political implications of this perception are very significant. As modernization ceases to be a promise for all, with ranks in the global order becoming "not stages to be passed through, but non-serialized statuses, separated from each other by exclusionary walls, rather than developmental stairways," "the key questions are no longer temporal ones of societal becoming (development, modernization), but spatialized ones of policing the edges of a status group."[51] The implications of Ferguson's arguments demonstrate the complexity of "race" in the present state of affairs. If one accepts Ferguson's description of the shift from the developmentalist project, it can be argued, especially with the perceived permanence of class privilege and desperation, that classes now represent different types of humanity, or even the difference between human and subhuman status. As modernity becomes a "status" under capitalist globalization, it may appear to be more "multicultural" in the sense that it might, in principle, be more open to non-Europeans. At the same time, as a very small (former) Third World elite may "whiten" itself through its participation in this modernity, the majority of people in (former) Third World nations are further "darkened" by their exclusion from new standards of capitalist modernity and prosperity both globally and nationally.

One of the most visible processes that has helped constitute the new middle classes in former Third World countries as "white" has to do with the reorganization of urban spaces in recent decades. What has been called the "citadelization" of cities has involved processes employed by the middle classes to separate themselves from the working class and marginal groups. This has been achieved by strategies including establishing gated communities; increasing participation in private as opposed to public institutions and spaces; expelling the poor from their former urban locations through gentrification, urban renewal, and the colonization of public spaces; and urban planning schemes that construct freeways to bypass slums. The separation and segregation of classes in space corresponds to a fragmentation of the city in physical and material, as well as social, administrative, political, and psychological terms. Gated communities represent the fears the middle-class occupants have of those located outside the walls, as well as the withdrawal of the middle class from the public sphere.

In addition to separating themselves from their working-class nationals and expressing their elite status, gated communities also help the middle-class inhabitants to imagine themselves as being part of the global elite. Class-segregated spaces become significant in the material and discursive construction and representation of spaces of a transnational culture, a "'global' culture of consumption." In his study of the marketing of the elite housing projects sprouting all over some of the big cities in India following liberalization of the economy in the early 1990s, Anthony King argues that these spaces help create the "complex conditions under which new 'local' as well as traveling 'global' class identities are being formed."[52]

> ... "international" and "India" are positioned as being mutually exclusive, rather than inclusive of each other. Thus, advertisements for the Manhattan apartments in Delhi suggest that "when you come home to India, you don't have to leave your international lifestyle behind." "International" here, therefore, is "other" than, or different from, India. Take, for example, "Draw the curtains and you could be in one of London's fashionable designer homes" (but not, apparently, in India). . . . [53]

As an expression of the middle-class desire to separate from the masses and join with the middle classes transnationally,[54] the so-called global city is defined in ways where concerns about aesthetics turn into "a new urban aesthetics of class purity."[55] From this perspective, the city belongs only to its wealthier inhabitants, an international business elite, and tourists:

> How do we create a pleasing living environment for the culturally diverse and mobile managers and workers associated with these global firms, so that they will desire to come and live among us for a while?
>
> The global aestheticised city is thus made beautiful to attract others rather than to make its local occupants feel at home within it. . . . More so than any of its predecessor cities the global city has no room for marginals. How are we to rid ourselves of the homeless sleeping on the city's benches? How are we to rid ourselves of those underclasses, with their high proportion of indigenous people, third-world looking (i.e., yucky-looking) migrants and descendants of migrants, who are still cramming the non-gentrified parts of the city?
>
> In the dominant modes of representation the poor become primarily like pimples, an "aesthetic nuisance." They are standing between between "us"

and the yet-to-land transcendental capital. They ought to be eradicated and removed from such a space. The aesthetics of globalization is the aesthetics of zero tolerance.[56]

What we see in current (transnational) forms of "whiteness" is a *unifying logic* at the international level, connecting the Third World bourgeoisie ever more closely with the bourgeoisie elsewhere, and a *secessionist logic* at the national level. The secessionist logic sometimes operates at the class level. In some cases, the identification with the global elite becomes so strong for the middle class that, as Sankaran Krishna comments, "one of the existential realities of being a middle class Indian is an inescapable desire to escape the rest of India."[57] Similarly, Arundhati Roy sees the Indian middle class in the neo-liberal era engaged in the "most successful secessionist struggle ever waged in India":

> Ironically, the era of the free market has led to the most successful secession-ist struggle ever waged in India – the secession of the middle and upper classes to a country of their own, somewhere up in the stratosphere where they merge with the rest of the world's elite. This Kingdom in the Sky is a complete universe in itself, hermetically sealed from the rest of India. It has its own newspapers, films, television programmes, morality plays, transport systems, malls and intellectuals.[58]

Secession is a good metaphor for Roy to discuss the fantasy of the globalized Indian middle class. Nevertheless, the term also literally applies to some of real-life political projects recently seen in South America. The referendum on regional autonomy put forward by Santa Cruz, the wealthiest region in Bolivia – which has most of the country's natural gas deposits within its bor-ders, along with industrial production and GNP – in 2008 is one example. Similarly, right-wing forces in Zulia, Venezuela's affluent western region, and in Guayas, the region known for its riches in agriculture and natural resources in Ecuador, have also been pushing for secession.[59] It is important to note that the demand for autonomy here is not based on an oppressed relationship to the rest of the country. On the contrary, it represents attempts by rich whites and mestizos to preserve race/class privilege in countries where national governments, in recent years, have started to reflect some of the grievances and demands of the Indigenous populations. Supported by the United States, these political projects represent attempts to separate from poor, racialized country people for a more effective economical and political unity with wealthy Western countries and global capital.

## Restabilizing whiteness: White supremacy in new clothes

The transformation and reconfiguration of class structures and geopolitics in the last few decades brought about by the fall of the Second and Third Worlds and the rise of neo-liberal globalism have led to cracks in "whiteness" along the colour line. The picture in the former Second World is very contradictory. On the one hand, peoples and nations in Eastern Europe have strived, with varying degrees of success, for Europeanness. On the other hand, aspirations for European status have come at the cost of Eastern European peoples experiencing forms of "Orientalism" and "Balkanism" imposed by West Europeans, their East European neighbours, and even their own country's citizens. Based on an internalization of hegemonic notions and standards of Europeanness developed in Western Europe, "Balkanism" and specific forms of "Orientalism" have not only created an ambiguity and insecurity of belonging in Europe, pitting countries, regions, and peoples against one another, but also they have helped to enable the imposition of economic and political conditions and a system of tutelage by the EU, IMF, and NATO.

The developments in the Western and former Third Worlds also present a rather complicated picture. The privileges of whiteness that the white working class has universally enjoyed in the twentieth century may be undermined both materially and ideologically through the dismantling of the welfare state and because of the political and cultural climate of neo-liberalism. Nevertheless, outside European and Euro-diasporic areas of the world, new forms of membership are emerging in the global capitalist modernity that appear as new forms of "whiteness." In different contexts, it seems that "whiteness" is more contingent on class today than it was a few decades ago. At the same time, race, in some new ways as well as traditional ones, continues to be a central organizing and legitimating principle of the economic, social, and political order. Developments since the end of the Cold War, especially noticeable in the "War on Terror," suggest that whiteness is not only being *restabilized* at national and international levels but also that it has returned with a vengeance as the result of unabashed new imperialism and new forms of racism. In this sense, the "cracks" in whiteness mentioned in the first section of this chapter complicate the picture of race globally, but by no means do they mark the end of race-thinking, or even white supremacy.

While intensified economic globalization appears to partially divorce capitalism from a necessary connection to Europe and reconfigure some of the earlier distinctions between the First and the Third Worlds, race "remains a procedure that justifies the nongeneralizability of capitalist wealth."[60] Even as global capital appears increasingly "multicultural," economic globalization continues to represent the domination of European and American values. Some scholars have emphasized the significance of multiple or alternative modernities in this era, while others suggest that the unchallenged domination of globalized capitalism since the end of the Cold War has economically and symbolically asserted and consolidated the supremacy of one way of life. Speaking of recent Chinese success in global capitalism, Arif Dirlik argues: "Ironically, the self-assertiveness of 'Orientals' under these circumstances would seem to represent not an alternative to, as they claim, but a consolidation of Eurocentric hegemony; or, more accurately, the hegemony of capital globally."[61]

Despite the fact that a few non-white people are able to cross boundaries of white privilege, we live in a world where racism along the colour line continues full force in ways that are socially, culturally, politically, economically, and ecologically consequential. In addition, "race," as defined along or *beyond* the colour line, is increasingly relevant as a logic and technology of power which separates forms of humanity and treats them differently. If we use the term "race" – to repeat Nikhil Pal Singh's definition – as "historic repertoires and cultural, spatial, and signifying systems that stigmatize and depreciate one form of humanity for the purposes of another's health, development, safety, profit and pleasure,"[62] we can argue that it continues to be of primary significance in the world.

Confirming the continuing and increasing significance of race along the colour line, there are a growing number of examples of racialized Third World bodies and lands being treated as disposable. Not only do we see a global expansion of super-exploitation for cheap labour in sweatshops and "free" trade zones (defined by some as "new slave zones"), but also we witness poor people in the Third World being used to test drugs and vaccines. Their lands, as well as Aboriginal territories in the First World, are used as sites for the production[63] or mining of dangerous chemicals, or are treated as dumping grounds for First World toxic waste.

In addition to the continuing significance of race as class privilege versus dispossession, race-thinking and racial supremacy have renewed significance in Western countries. Reinvigorated expressions of differential racism and increasingly aggressive assertions of white supremacy have, under different names, gained widespread public appeal in recent years. One example which has gained full force since the aftermath of September 11, 2001 has been anti-Arab and anti-Muslim racism. Partly based on old racial categories distinguishing between Arab versus white, a form of dark versus white, the more recent anti-Arab and anti-Muslim[64] racisms overlay these categories with geopolitical meanings and security anxieties. Powerful in civil society, as well as in state policies nationally and internationally, the rise of these forms of racism has resulted in the suspension of basic civil rights, a differential legal system, and/or suspension and differential implementation of the law for many Arabs and Muslims in the diaspora, also serving to justify wars and violent interventions.[65]

Even though current anti-Arab and anti-Muslim racism is generally attributed to the more traditional racism of neo-conservatives in national as well as foreign policy, it has been the liberal establishment and left liberals who have provided it with ideological legitimacy and enhancement. This has been clear in the support for the war in Afghanistan by liberals employing so-called feminist concerns which continue to be utilized. Articulating their position as a defence of Enlightenment values, liberals see Islam as a major threat to them. Identifying Islam with the oppression of women and homosexuals, they argue that this makes the religion not just medieval but fascistic. The new term "Islamofascism" has been a rallying cry for liberals whose version of anti-Muslim racism, like the blatantly bigoted nativism of conservatives, feeds into and justifies very similar internal policies of assimilation and militaristic policies abroad.

Another important development which has gained force, especially since the end of the Cold War, has been anti-immigrant and anti-refugee sentiments and policies in Europe, North America, and Australia. In a world where people have been displaced by global economic, political, and ecological forces, these take the shape of strict immigration policies, tight border controls, routine detention of migrants and refugees, enhanced deportation systems, demands for cultural assimilation by the state, along with increasingly nativist and racist attitudes among the white populations in these countries. The current anti-immigrant, anti-refugee climate leads towards a re-nationalizing of borders and re-nativizing of citizenship. Already underway in the immediate aftermath of the Cold War, these developments have been accelerated and justified in the heightened post–9/11 security climate. Even in the early 1990s, with the declining significance of ideological divisions and signs of an expanded union in Europe, Ali Mazrui was alarmed by the possibilities of a pan-Europeanism. Fearing that "pan-Europeanism can carry the danger of cultural chauvinism and even racism,"[66] he warned that European regional integration could lead to what he called *macroretribalization*, a form of *global apartheid* based in "an arrogant pan-Europeanism greater in ambition than anything seen since the Holy Roman Empire." He writes:

Is the white world closing ranks in Eastern Europe and the West? Will we see a more united and potentially more prosperous white world presiding over the fate of a fragmented and persistently indigent black world in the twenty-first century? Put in another way, now that apartheid in South Africa is disintegrating, is there a global apartheid in the process of formation?[67]

It is important to recognize that both the anti-Arab, anti-Muslim racisms, on the one hand, and the anti-immigrant, anti-refugee sentiments on the other, have helped significantly to reassure European and Euro-diasporic populations, whose unconditional "whiteness" has otherwise been threatened by neo-liberal policies, of their privileges of whiteness and belonging in the nation. This has been very clear from 1990s on in the politics, for example, of the more extreme nativism of Le Pen's Front National in France, which has fed on the fears and insecurities of the white "losers" of globalization, but has since spread to the political mainstream in France and in many other countries in the West.

Since 9/11, a reconfiguration of "Western" identity in civilizational terms has come to assure white people of both their unquestionable cultural and political belonging in Western countries, and their superiority over the non-Western world. With the instant popularization of Samuel Huntington's "clash of civilizations" framework in the immediate aftermath of the events of 9/11, this involved a project of "nationalizing the 'West'" and exalting what were being claimed to be Western values.[68] Political leaders as well as the corporate media in Europe, North America, and Australia articulated a "nationalism" of a transnational nature, "a *white nationalism*" confirming that *some* of their nationals belong in "Western civilization." This new notion of the nation "in effect jettisoned those of Arab and Muslim background from their place in Western nations and 'Western civilization' and made precarious the national belonging and political citizenship of many [people] of colour."[69] While some of the assumptions and claims involved in this identity are not new, their specific articulation in this period represented a heightened racism, as it involved a "confirmation, crystallization, and rigidification of the preexisting implicit boundaries of a *white* national identity and belonging."[70]

The current panorama suggests that there are processes in place which simultaneously *exclude* and *incorporate* marginal whites in whiteness. While the decline of the welfare state and the growing insecurities of global capitalism potentially turn most people into "disposable labour" (a condition previously preserved for racialized bodies), there are also successful attempts to incorporate all whites into whiteness through anti-immigrant, anti-refugee, anti-Arab, and anti-Muslim sentiments, movements, and ideologies, as well as policies on immigration and the "War on Terror." These attempts help express the wish to preserve those white privileges now being threatened by the former and also, as strong components of a hegemonic project, ensure working-class and marginalized whites' participation and support in an imperial and neo-liberal order. In some ways, this is parallel to the historical role whiteness has played in Western countries. Nevertheless, in a time of increased global integration, as well as increased militarization, securitization, and visions for an infinite "War on Terror," it threatens to sow the seeds of a far more repressive and violent future.

## Notes

1 Some of the analysis in this chapter develops points taken up in two of my other papers: "Contesting or Affirming 'Europe'? European Enlargement, Aspirations for 'Europeanness' and New Identities in the Margins of Europe," *Journal of Contemporary European Studies* 18,2 (2010); and "Annexing the Language of Class: Culture Talk, White Imaginaries of the Middle Class and the (Geo)Political Economy of Neoliberalism," submitted for *Theorizing Anti-Racism*, forthcoming, edited by Abigail Bakan and Enakshi Dua.

2 Nikhil Pal Singh, *Black Is a Country: Race and the Unfinished Struggle for Democracy* (Cambridge, MA: Harvard University Press, 2004), 223.

3 Alastair Bonnett, "How the British Working Class Became White: The Symbolic (Re)formation of Racialized Capitalism," *Journal of Historical Sociology* 11,3 (1998), 316–40.

4 Mike Davis, *Planet of Slums* (London: Verso Books, 2006).

5 Manning Marable, "Globalization and Racialization" *ZNet* (August 13, 2004), ⟨http://www.zmag.or/content/print_article.cfm?itemID=6034&sectionID=30⟩, accessed May 20, 2006.

6 Loic Wacquant, "From Mass Slavery to Mass Incarceration: Rethinking the 'Race Question' in the US," *New Left Review* 13 (2002), 41–60.

7 See Angela Davis, *Are Prisons Obsolete?* (New York: Seven Stories Press, 2003) and *Abolition Democracy: Beyond Prisons, Torture and Empire* (New York: Seven Stories Press, 2005). Also see Julia Sudbury, *Global Lockdown: Race, Gender and the Prison-Industrial Complex* (London: Routledge, 2005).

8 Kenan Malik argues that the original use of the term was much different from the later, popular uses. He cites Gunnar Myrdal for coining the term in 1963 to emphasize the dangers of de-industrialization. Kenan Malik, *The Meaning of Race* (New York: New York University Press, 1996), 73.

9 Cited in Margaret Weir, "From Equal Opportunity to 'the New Social Contract,'" in *Racism, the City and the State*, ed. Malcolm Cross and Michael Keith (London: Routledge, 1993), 100.

10 Charles W. Mills, *From Class to Race: Essays in White Marxism and Black Radicalism* (Lanham, MD: Rowman and Littlefield, 2003), 124.

11 Linda Gordon argues that it is actually the fuzziness of the term that gives it power and widespread appeal, as it encapsulates a wide variety of anxieties in the U.S. Linda Gordon, "The 'Underclass' and the U.S. Welfare State," *The Socialist Register* 31 (1995), 163–87.

12 David Theo Goldberg, *Racist Culture* (Cambridge, MA: Blackwell Publishing, 1993), 172; emphasis added.

13 Cited in Malik, *The Meaning of Race*, 199.

14 Ibid., 200; emphasis added.

15 Beverley Skeggs, *Class, Self and Culture* (London: Routledge, 2004), 91.

16 Beverley Skeggs, "The Re-Branding of Class: Propertising Culture," in *Rethinking Class: Culture, Identities, Lifestyles*, ed. Fiona Devine et al. (New York: Palgrave Macmillan, 2005), 67.

17 Skeggs, *Class, Self and Culture*, 117.

18 Skeggs, "The Re-Branding of Class," 49.

19 Ibid., 50.

20 Chris Haylett, "Illegitimate Subjects? Abject Whites, Neoliberal Modernization, and Middle-Class Multiculturalism," *Environment and Planning D: Society and Space* 19,3 (2001), 352.

21 Ibid., 364.

22 Ibid., 365.

23 Merje Kuus, "Europe's Eastern Expansion and the Reinscription of Otherness in East-Central Europe," *Progress in Human Geography* 28,4 (2004), 472–89.

24 Neumann cited in Kuus, "Europe's Eastern Expansion," 475.

25 Merje Kuus, *Geopolitics Reframed: Security and Identity in Europe's Eastern Enlargement* (New York: Palgrave Macmillan, 2007), 27.

26 Juliane Edler, "Towards a Historical Materialist Approach to Racism in Post-'Unification' Germany," *Socialist Studies* 3,1 (2007), 27–48.

27 Ibid.

28 Kuus, "Europe's Eastern Expansion," 475.

29 Kuus, *Geopolitics Reframed*, 28–9.

30 Natasa Kovacevic, "Orientalizing Post-Communism: Europe's 'Wild East' in Literature and Film," *Reconstruction: Studies in Contemporary Culture* 8,4 (2008), 33, ⟨http://reconstruction.eserver.org/084/kovacevic.sthml⟩, accessed March 22, 2010.

31 Ibid., 32.

32 Laszlo Kurti, "Globalisation and the Discourse of Otherness in the 'New' Eastern and Central Europe," in *The Politics of Multiculturalism in the New Europe*, ed. Tariq Modood and Pnina Werbner (London: Zed Books, 1997), 41.

33 Maria Nikolaeva Todorova, *Imagining the Balkans* (New York: Oxford University Press, 1997), 188.

34 Milica Bakic-Hayden, "Nesting Orientalisms: The Case of Former Yugoslavia," *Slavic Review* 54,4 (1995), 917–31.

35 Ibid., 919.

36 Kuus, "Europe's Eastern Expansion," 484.

37 David Theo Goldberg, *Racial States* (Cambridge: Blackwell Publishing, 2002), 222.

38 For a rather apocalyptic vision of the polarization of global wealth and Third World class disparities, see Davis, *Planet of Slums*.

39 Goldberg, *Racial States*, 222.

40 Alastair Bonnett, *The Idea of the West: Culture, Politics, and History* (New York: Palgrave Macmillan, 2004), 34.

41 Alastair Bonnett, "A White World? Whiteness and the Meaning of Modernity in Latin America and Japan," in *Working through Whiteness: International Perspectives*, ed. Cynthia Lavine-Rasky (Albany: State University of New York Press, 2002), 72.

42 Ibid., 85.

43 Galen Joseph, "Taking Race Seriously: Whiteness in Argentina's National and Transnational Imaginary," *Identities* 7,3 (2000), 337.

44 Arif Dirlik, "The Postcolonial Aura: Third World Criticism in the Age of Global Capitalism," in *Dangerous Liaisons: Gender, Nation and Postcolonial Perspectives*, ed. Anne McClintock, Aanis Muffit, and Ella Shohat (Minneapolis: University of Minnesota Press, 1997), 518.

45 Ibid., 520.

46 Vijay Prashad, *The Darker Nations: A People's History of the Third World* (New York: New Press, 2007), 217–18.

47 James Ferguson, "Decomposing Modernity: History and Hierarchy after Development," in *Postcolonial Studies and Beyond*, ed. Ania Loomba et al. (Durham, NC: Duke University Press, 2005), 166–81.

48 Ibid., 176.

49 Ibid., 175.

50 Ibid., 177.

51 Ibid., 176, 179.

52 Anthony King, "Speaking from the Margins: 'Postmodernism,' Transnationalism, and the Imagining of Contemporary Indian Urbanity," in *Globalization and the Margins*, ed. Richard Grant and Rennie Short (New York: Palgrave Macmillan, 2002), 87.

53 Ibid., 83.

54 What may seem ironic in the case of these "cosmopolitan" aspirations is the fact that they sometimes exist side by side with the politics of nativism and ethnicism on the part of the same actors. Similar to neo-conservatism in the West, right-wing populisms can articulate capitalist and (economic) globalist interests with ethnicist, racist, and even fundamentalist positions. It is now well established, for example, that in India much of the political support for the Hindu fundamentalist party BJP has come from the global(izing) middle class. Likewise, in Turkey there has been a significant growth in recent decades of a conservative Muslim bourgeoisie which adheres to an Islamist nativism and populism – of being ordinary, common people ideologically – but elitist in its lifestyle. Some of the most radical neo-liberal reforms in the economy have been achieved under the government of the Islamist party AKP.

Even though the neo-liberal class elitism and populist nativism of the middle classes may appear contradictory, they are not necessarily so. As Prashad has argued, with the "assassination of the Third World Project" and the emptying of nationalism from its social and economic objectives, cultural nationalism has been the only kind of nationalism left. With the demise of the Third World, Prashad argues: "Dominant classes in these states adopted two postures, and sometimes both: an eagerness to be untethered from their societies and/or linked to their population through ascribed identities of faith and race. The domestic elites were always a weak link for the national liberation agenda." Prashad, *The Darker Nations*.

55 Leela Fernandes, "The Politics of Forgetting: Class Politics, State Power and the Restructuring of Urban Space in India," *Urban Studies* 41,12 (2004), 2420–421.

56 Ghassan Hage, *Against Paranoid Nationalism: Searching for Hope in a Shrinking Society* (Annandale, NSW: Pluto Press Australia, 2003), 19–20.

57 Sankaran Krishna, "The Bomb, Biography and the Indian Middle Class," *Economic and Political Weekly* 41,23 (2006), 2327.

58 Arundhati Roy, "Listening to Grasshoppers: On Genocide, Denial and Celebration," *Communalism Watch* (January 26, 2008), ⟨http://communalism.blogspot.com/2008/01/arundhati-roy-on-genocide-denial-and.html⟩, accessed March 22, 2010.

59 Nikolas Kozloff, "Meet South America's New Secessionists: From a Texan Venezuelan to an Ecuadorian Giuliani," *Counterpunch* (May 30, 2008), ⟨http://www.counterpunch.org/kozloff05302008.html⟩, accessed March 22, 2010.

60 Jodi Melamed, "The Spirit of Neoliberalism: From Racial Liberalism to Neoliberal Multiculturalism," *Social Text* 24,4 89 (2006), 2.

61 Dirlik, "The Postcolonial Aura," 122.

62 Singh, *Black Is a Country*, 223.

63 At the time of the writing of this chapter, people in Bhopal, India, and their allies marked the twenty-fifth anniversary of the chemical disaster caused by Union Carbide in 1984. Following a settlement in 1989, which minimally compensated only some of the survivors and victims, Union Carbide still has not taken responsibility to clean up the contamination. As a result, a quarter century after the disaster, the soil and the water at the site and the surrounding region remains soaked in toxic substances and continues to create new victims. See Randeep Ramesh, "Bhopal Water Still Toxic 25 Years After Deadly Gas Leak, Study Finds," *Guardian* (London), December 1, 2009, ⟨http://www.guardian.co.uk/world/2009/dec/01/bhopal-chemical-studies-toxic-levels⟩, accessed March 22, 2010; and Indra Sinha, "Bhopal: 25 Years of Poison," *Guardian* (London), December 3, 2009, ⟨http://www.guardian.co.uk/environment/2009/dec/04/bhopal-25-years-indra-sinha⟩, accessed March 22, 2010. The original disaster, along with the continuing injustice and neglect, remain stark examples of the treatment of the Third World as disposable.

64 At the time of the writing of this chapter, Switzerland had a referendum, approved by 57.5% of its voters, banning the construction of new minarets from Muslim religious sites.

65 Liz Fekete, *A Suitable Enemy: Racism, Migration and Islamophobia in Europe* (London: Pluto Press, 2009); Sherene H. Razack, *Casting Out: The Eviction of Muslims from Western Law and Politics* (Toronto: University of Toronto Press, 2008).

66 Ali Mazrui, "Global Apartheid? Race and Religion in the New World Order," in *The Gulf War and the New World Order: International Relations of the Middle East*, ed. Tareq Y. Ismael and Jacqueline S. Ismael (Gainesville: University Press of Florida, 1994), 528.

67 Ibid., 521.

68 Sunera Thobani, *Exalted Subjects: Studies in the Making of Race and Nation in Canada* (Toronto: University of Toronto Press, 2007), 225.

69 Sedef Arat-Koç, "The Disciplinary Boundaries of Canadian Identity after September 11: Civilizational Identity, Multiculturalism, and the Challenge of Anti-Imperialist Feminism," *Social Justice* 32,4 (2005), 34.

70 Ibid., 33.

# 8 : Questioning efforts that seek to "do good": Insights from transnational solidarity activism and socially responsible tourism

## Gada Mahrouse

HOW DO WE ANALYZE RACIALIZED POWER in social justice interventions? How might social justice interventions transcend the constraints of liberalism or, to borrow Charles Mills's term, "racial liberalism"?[1] In this chapter, I attempt to respond to these questions by applying a critical race lens to two current yet disparate examples of social justice initiatives. First, exploring the contemporary phenomenon of transnational[2] direct action solidarity, I focus on the volunteer recruiting practices of one feminist organization in Palestine to examine some of the erroneous ways in which racialized differences are often understood and dealt with by such organizations. I then shift attention from radical direct action activism to consumer-based approaches to social justice, with an examination of two organizations currently promoting "ethical" or socially responsible tourism. Specifically, I argue that many well-meaning social justice efforts and interventions are incredibly rich sites for exploring racialized privilege and whiteness, because they reveal the extent to which white hegemony and the liberal paradigm impede changes that might otherwise shift existing power relations. I conclude with a reflection on what can be gained pedagogically from focusing critical attention on various practices that seek to "do good."

There are three converging motivations for the focus of this chapter's discussion. The first comes from the ongoing need to consider what scholars of colonial histories have variously shown – that imperial and colonial domination has consistently been legitimized and framed in terms of benevolence and as being for the greater good.[3] Certainly, this pattern continues today, where "helping" often becomes a vehicle for neo-colonialism.[4] The second motivation is the desire to build upon some of the discussions that took place at the ninth annual RACE conference in Montreal in 2009. The objective of organizers and contributors was a feminist and anti-racist interrogation of various practices that are intended to remedy some of the problems and conflicts in the world, including those employed by peace and development

NGOs, humanitarian organizations, and state responses to past injustices.[5] The theme of this conference came out of the recognition that although much scholarship has celebrated the work of various well-meaning organizations and interventions, much less attention has been paid to critically examining their effects. In response, the conference sought to "explore the ramifications of such interventions with respect to the possible ways in which they serve and reinforce existing power structures and relations."[6]

The third and overarching motivation for the focus of this chapter is a long-standing interest in anti-racism pedagogies and a critique of the widely used approaches that exist. In particular, this critique centres upon approaches that typically address questions of racialized injustice by focusing on extreme forms of blatant racism and are based on a conception of power in which awareness, personal responsibility, and active engagement are viewed as the means for social change. As I have argued elsewhere, underlying these approaches is the assumption that when exposed to inspirational ideas or writings, students are more likely to become empowered social justice actors who will challenge or resist systems of domination.[7] I contend that the liberal underpinnings of these approaches in fact serve primarily to further empower those who are already privileged. Attempting to respond to the shortcomings of such approaches, then, I argue for a reverse method of teaching Western students about racialized injustices. Specifically, I draw on examples of direct action solidarity activism and "ethical/responsible" tourism to demonstrate that many well-meaning practices can offer important insights into how racialized systems of power are reproduced.

The themes explored in this chapter draw from the works of feminist scholars who have developed critical theoretical and methodological frameworks for examining global and local responsibility. In particular, I am indebted to a small but growing body of critical feminist scholarship which has tirelessly shown how liberalism poses great challenges for social justice. This research has sought to theorize racial power in ways that consider North-South relations of global power, and has paid particular attention to the ways in which appeals for social justice are limited and shaped by racialized, gendered, and national identities and understandings. These feminist scholars include Sara Ahmed, Sedef Arat-Koç, Inderpal Grewal, Caren Kaplan, Sherene Razack, Ella Shohat, Andrea Smith, Sunera Thobani, Haunani Kay Trask, and Adrienne Wing, to name a few.[8] As these scholars argue, calls for solidarity and equality often conceal the inequalities between differently racialized groups, and social justice interventions abroad (re)constitute white/Westerners as benevolent, liberal subjects.[9]

The theoretical understanding of racialized power that underlies this discussion is largely informed by the ideas political philosopher Charles Mills puts forth on liberalism and the racial contract, or what he refers to as "racial liberalism."[10] Explaining that the egalitarian ideology of liberalism has unquestioningly become the hegemonic political outlook of the modern age, Mills draws attention to its racialized underpinnings. He points out that the ubiquity and attractiveness of liberalism is its broad appeal to *fairness and equality* – principles that are difficult to argue against.[11] What Mills persuasively argues is that under liberalism, the ideas of fairness and equality are intrinsically *unfair* and *unequal* because as a political theory it largely overlooks the fundamental issue of racial equality. Showing how blatant forms of racism have "underpinned the liberal framework from the outset," Mills highlights that both Locke and Kant, the two philosophers who are seen as central to the liberal tradition, both limited property rights, self-ownership, and personhood to white men. He goes on to point out:

> Locke invested in African slavery, justified native American expropriation, and helped write the Carolina constitution of 1669, which gave masters absolute power over their slaves. Kant, the most important ethicist of the modern period and the famous theorist of personhood and respect, turns out to be one of the founders of modern scientific racism, and thus a pioneering theorist of subpersonhood and disrespect. . . . [12]

While one might assume that these incongruities between the theories and practices of the founding fathers of liberalism are merely reflective of the accepted values of their particular times, Mills argues that such blatant paradoxes continue today. For instance, he points out that while there are lively debates within contemporary political philosophy (i.e., over left-wing versus right-wing liberalism, or contractarian liberalism versus communitarianism), the field continues to ignore the ways in which racial subordination is rationalized by liberalism. Offering the example of the five major works of prominent liberal philosopher John Rawls (which includes *A Theory of Justice*, a book now canonized as the most important work in twentieth-century political philosophy), Mills asks us to consider the implications of Rawls's almost complete marginalization of the central issue of racial inequality. In over one thousand pages of text, sentences on race and racism appear on only a half-dozen pages. This example enables Mills to make his claim about liberalism's ironic yet incessant disregard of questions of racial inequality. Of course, the philosophical arguments Mills puts forth are far more complex than this simple observation.[13] Nevertheless, the notable absence of the very concept of race in Rawls's work begs an important question: justice for whom? In short, Mills asserts that within liberalism "justice and equal protection [can be] effectively denied even while being triumphantly proclaimed."[14]

Drawing on the works of the above-mentioned critical feminist scholars, as well as Mills's notion of racial liberalism, I will present further evidence of the utter inadequacy of the liberal framework and demonstrate that it continues to frame justice efforts, even those which appear to be operating out of more radical politics.

## "Inclusion" and "diversity" in solidarity efforts in Palestine: A case study

To study racialized power in social justice interventions, one compelling site is accompaniment and witnessing (sometimes referred to as "human shield") activism, which involves people from the West travelling to conflict zones to provide a supportive and protective international presence to those living under the threat of violence. The racialized dimensions of this kind of direct action activism is particularly salient because, as a strategy, it employs "whiteness" and the status inscribed upon the bodies of citizens of Western countries.[15] Using a critical race lens, I have examined several aspects of this activism elsewhere, including descriptions of how Canadians who have participated in it negotiate their racialized positioning in their media and awareness-raising educational work, as well as the ways in which race, gender, class, and sexuality interlock to produce nationalist discourses which (re)position Canadians as peaceful and benevolent global citizens.[16] While each of those aspects revealed some of the contradictions in such practices, for the purpose of my argument here, I will focus on one example that illustrates some of the more insidious ways in which profound paradoxes of liberalism can arise in such transnational social justice efforts.

The focus of my example is a formal volunteer recruitment effort made by a direct action solidarity group called the International Women's Peace Service (IWPS), whose mandate is to "provide accompaniment and intervene non-violently to try to prevent human rights abuses." This group, which is stationed in Palestine, has established a long-term presence in the village of Haris in the West Bank where, since 2002, members on three-month rotations provide support and protection to the villagers. IWPS is a women-only group that operates on feminist principles. Recognizing that certain groups of women are under-represented in their membership, they proactively seek "to strengthen organisational diversity by recruiting team members and volunteers from among *women of colour* and from the *two-thirds world*."[17] In their 2005 application pack, they explain this perceived gap as follows:

Women of poor & working class backgrounds from all corners of the world including African, Central & Latin American, Asian and first nation/indigenous women are underrepresented in IWPS to date . . . we need to encourage women who have the backgrounds and skills that *will make us truly a diverse international group of women*. We need to be proactive about assessing our make up and developing and applying an outreach plan to address gaps. We also need to actively support the women who we recruit. We need all T[eam] M[ember]s' commitment to this to help to make our organization *truly inclusive and reflective of the global community*.[18]

To achieve a diverse membership, they offer financial support in the form of a scholarship to cover some of the travel costs to Palestine. Importantly, their materials give no indication of how differently racialized bodies might be used in their campaigns. Instead, one is left to assume that the diverse membership would be working side by side in all capacities of the activism, including on the front lines, thereby sending the message that women from all parts of the world are united in their support of Palestinians.

The well-meaning intentions behind this recruitment policy and diversity attempt are evident. It is an earnest and concrete response to criticism lodged by some who have pointed out that "on the global level, the feminist movement has been dominated by U.S. and other western feminists" who have excluded or essentialized "the perspectives and needs of women of color and Third World women."[19] This effort to recruit under-represented women is also likely emerging from what Marion Young refers to as "a politics of recognition," whereby those working for social justice and against the individualism of liberalism understand that special treatment is sometimes required for certain groups.[20] IWPS's policy, then, is a clear example of how "Western feminists are now attempting to include women of color and women from other countries and cultures as part of their intellectual and activist movement."[21] As a public relations strategy, the display of differently racialized women working together in "interracial harmony" must also be appreciated as a way of modelling the ultimate vision of the movement.[22] Furthermore, this type of inclusiveness can also be productive because it can help feminist activists "see their own ethnocentricity and understand their privileged position as compared to that of Third World women and women of color."[23]

Given the particular aims of IWPS, their recruitment initiative bears further scrutiny. Specifically, as I will argue, when a critical race analysis is used to consider this gesture, particularly the racialized understandings that underpin this policy and the possible motivations behind it, one can see that the IWPS's outreach efforts to bring in under-represented women in fact *reinforces* the liberal notions of multiculturalism, despite the fact that it appears in the radical context of direct action activism. It is important to state, however, that in singling out the IWPS, the purpose is not to scapegoat this particular organization nor to obscure the fact that IWPS continues to provide much-needed support to Palestinians, including participating in demonstrations and opposition to the Apartheid Wall, helping to remove roadblocks, and accompanying ambulances. Indeed, the issues raised here are put forth to encourage the self-reflection that characterizes most members of groups like IWPS and as such, is meant to provide an example that can be instructive for considering the pitfalls of liberalism within global solidarity work. I want to therefore make clear that although I focus on IWPS here, the approach they take to recruitment is common in other solidarity social justice organizations.

To contemplate the racialized effects of the IWPS's attempt at inclusivity and diversity, some insights can first be drawn from the 1964 Freedom Summer campaign of the American civil rights movement. Like the "international presence" activism undertaken by the IWPS and other groups with similar goals, the Freedom Summer campaign also deployed a strategy of using differently racialized bodies. Historians of the civil rights movement explain that explicit efforts to bring white people into the movement were initially made not only to gain publicity but also because it was believed that the presence of white Northerners would reduce the violence against Black people.[24] It was widely understood that the successes of the campaign depended on the fact that the white recruits would have particular roles to play as allies in the movement such as assisting in setting up and running community centres and "Freedom Schools," working on the "White Folks" Project, and registering voters.[25] It was believed that the white recruits could use their skills and privilege more effectively in such roles, but more importantly, limiting the involvement of the white recruits to particular roles and projects was meant to ensure that the Black activists would remain as the decision makers and leaders of the movement. Also instructive is the fact that despite these attempts to ensure that the movement was not overtaken by the white recruits, interracial tensions between the white and Black students eventually overtook the campaign. Reflecting on the cross-racial tensions that emerged, Carmichael and Hamilton, leaders of what became the Black Power movement, identify what they believe to be some of the major fallacies of such alliances.[26] First, they posit that members of different racial groups cannot share common interests. Second, they state effective coalitions cannot be formed across socio-economic class differences. Third, they challenge the assumption that coalitions "are or can be sustained on a moral, friendly, sentimental basis, or on appeals to conscience."[27] Of course, this very brief sketch only outlines a few aspects of what was a complex and multi-faceted movement. Nevertheless, these points reveal the pragmatic ways in which racialized positioning can be used in solidarity campaigns, as well as the challenges that arise in working across asymmetrical relations of power.

To further contemplate the racialized effects of attempts at inclusivity and diversity, it is important to bear in mind that the specific type of direct action "international presence" solidarity work undertaken by IWPS – witnessing and accompaniment – is explicitly based on a visible, embodied form of whiteness. As literature on similar efforts elsewhere reveals, volunteers from South American, Asian, and African countries, and those who are visibly people of colour are not only less effective but also face more danger and are often mistreated by the authorities either because they are mistaken for "locals" or simply because they are regarded as more expendable than those who have white skin.[28] The hosting communities are aware of these dynamics and therefore make purposeful attempts to recruit activists who are visibly white because they are the ones who could lend a degree of security.[29] Indeed, in terms of efficacy, the mandate of providing an "international presence" should be understood as a euphemism for a "Western/white presence," at least on the visible front lines of their direct actions. This being the case, one can see that it is more effective that the IWPS volunteers who will be demonstrating on the front lines are citizens of a powerful Western country *and* have white skin. Thus, the IWPS's conflation of "women of colour" who are presumably from white/Western countries, and women from the global South, whom they refer to as "two-thirds women," also demands consideration. In the context of this transnational solidarity activism this is a profoundly important distinction, since the weight of the activism obviously relies on citizenship from a powerful Western country and the hosting community is less likely to benefit from citizens of countries in the global South. Yet, with their well-meaning efforts to be inclusive and representative, the IWPS appears to have lost sight of this pragmatism. Furthermore, since white/Westerners are far more effective and safe in this activism than Westerners of colour, IWPS's efforts to recruit women of colour from the West also seem misguided. As the number of killings and injuries to white Western solidarity activists in Palestine illustrate, even unambiguously white bodies are not always immune to violent attacks by Israeli security forces when they align themselves too closely with Palestinians.[30]

Given that even those with white skin can be dispossessed of their privilege and targeted in such charged political settings, one can see how the absence of the physical markers of whiteness and "Westernness" would render people of colour and those from developing countries less effective and more vulnerable to attack. The IWPS's gesture of actively recruiting and facilitating the participation of under-represented women is an example of calls for inclusion by "making room" or "creating space," which are made without historicizing the relations of exchange that they are embedded in.[31] Ironically, in trying to be fair and attempting to avoid the liberal pitfall of ignoring racialized differences, the recruitment efforts of this organization nevertheless obscured the differences, and inadvertently ignored them.

This examination of IWPS's recruitment policy also raises questions about what might prompt some groups to strive for "inclusion" and "diversity" in contexts where it could diminish the efficacy of their activism instead of strengthening it. In other words, what might be the motivation behind this effort, given that its support and protection work would be compromised by the inclusion of women who are not racialized as Western or white? I propose that such efforts may emerge out of the desire of members to falsely imagine themselves as equal to those they are trying to assist. In addition, the commitment to diversifying the organization helps the Western members of such groups feel like they are working within a "global sisterhood" in ways that repeat the patterns of their second wave feminist predecessors.[32] Ahmed's exploration of desire for intimacy with the Other offers important insights into this false sense of solidarity. Writing about Western feminists' attempts to work closely alongside Other women, she argues that proximity (either physical or the fantasy of being close) is not a means of transgression, but a technique "which allows the reassertion of the agency of the dominant subject."[33] In this sense, what Ahmed wants us to consider about gestures like the IWPS's efforts to invite Other women to participate in transnational solidarity activism is how "the story remains organised around" those who are trying to overcome differences. Ahmed also cautions that a desire for intimacy is very closely tied to a liberal vision of the white self as always open to others.

Thus, in certain geopolitical contexts such as Palestine, attempts to recruit under-represented women suggest that discourses of diversity and inclusion within liberalism have become so normalized and depoliticized they are now being performed in contexts where it is no longer effective or appropriate. This reality presents a good example of what Thobani has identified as a recurring contradiction in contemporary Western feminism, where on the one hand there are repeated warnings against the assumption of a universally shared human condition, and on the other hand universality is repeatedly reproduced within it.[34] An alternative approach, one that which operates on the principle of what some have described as a *situated* practice, would demand that IWPS think about their gestures of diversity *in relation to* the specificity of the conflict in which they involve themselves, and could indicate that this kind of recruitment defeats IWPS's basic purposes.[35] This approach might also suggest generating alternative types of scholarships, such as funding for Palestinian women who may not have the means to access education or employment. Furthermore, a situated practice might encourage the IWPS to instead put their energies into recruiting white Western women for the front lines of their direct actions in Palestine. This is not to suggest that women who are not racialized as white and Western cannot be assets to organizations like the IWPS. Indeed, some of the founding and most active members of IWPS and other politically influential solidarity groups in Palestine have been Palestinian, Arab-American, and Israeli women. The point is not to discount their work or the effects of their presence. It is merely to highlight that, by and large, new recruits, especially those who may not be experienced in this activism, be made to understand that given the ways in which their bodies are read, they would have different solidarity roles to play. Perhaps they could work behind the scenes and provide effective assistance from outside of Palestine.

*[handwritten margin note: Diff. Solid. roles]*

## The paradoxes of ethical/responsible tourism

A very compelling manifestation of doing good that has emerged in recent years can be found in the realm of tourism. Since socially conscious people from the "First World" are increasingly uncomfortable with the idea of participating in conventional forms of tourism, various NGOs are now promoting socially responsible options variously known as "ethical," "reality," "fair," or "justice" tourism.[36] Yet, given its undeniably exploitative and often devastating effects, the paradoxical coupling of tourism with social justice has attracted curiosity and some criticism in ways that offer glimpses into the complex, racialized dynamics that arise from such forms of travel. For example, a January 2007 travel feature in *The Globe and Mail* was sardonically titled "On the Left, Notice the Poverty."[37] In another report, the perspective of a Mexican whose town is frequented by Western activists who want to visit the Zapatista regions is offered, indicating that some of the "locals" are uneasy with these tours.[38] Cynically referring to the Westerners as "Zapatourists," the Mexican observer is quoted as saying that they "pacify their own guilty consciences on our [Mexican] soil."[39] Other reports hint at the marketing of mysticism, exoticism, and authenticity, as in an example that describes Western tourists taking small boats to "speak to an older woman whom the locals called a genuine Amazon shaman."[40] While some academics are raising important critical questions on these forms of ethical/justice tourism, others suggest that they are hopeful and praiseworthy.[41]

A fundamental difference can be found among various ethical/responsible tourism groups. Some recognize the exploitative nature of tourism and attempt to limit and soften its detrimental effects, while others assert that these more responsible approaches not only provide a less invasive form of tourism but also the means through which global inequality can be overturned.[42] As an article on ethical travel in the progressive *Utne Reader* magazine states, "proponents of ethical travel believe that continuing to travel the globe is not only necessary, it's vitally important."[43] In what follows, I will explore some of the ways in which the approaches of two specific organizations promote ethical and responsible tourism. The two organizations I will examine are Tourism Concern and Global Exchange. My approach to examining them is in line with that of Lisle, who explains that "the current consensus over ethical tourism (i.e. that it is the solution to all our problems) can only be maintained to the extent that it silences the problems, difficulties and consequences that ethical tourism itself produces."[44] Thus, in keeping with my goal of interrogating the racialized power in practices that seek to do good, my discussion aims to question the ethical and social justice claims made by such initiatives.

### Tourism Concern

Tourism Concern is "an independent, non-industry based, U.K. charity" organization with the goal of fighting exploitation in tourism through educational campaigning. Its website states that it aims to ensure "that tourism always benefits local people."[45] To this end, it offers tourists information on the ways in which the tourism industry violates the human rights of people in the global South. Some of the important specific campaigns that Tourism Concern has undertaken include working with survivors of the Asian tsunami to help ensure they won't be displaced to make way for resorts, raising awareness on how tourism to Burma provides vital financial support to the brutal military dictatorship, and campaigning for the rights of porters in Nepal. Their website also includes a section entitled "Travel Dilemmas" in which provocative questions are posed to readers, such as: "Should you take a holiday in a country governed by an authoritarian regime? Is it OK to give to begging children? Slum tourism or voyeurism?" Clearly impressive in its aims and endorsed by some well-respected authorities on global justice, there can be little doubt that the work of Tourism Concern is contributing to raising awareness and more equitable and critical forms of tourism.

Upon a closer view, however, some questions about Tourism Concern's liberal underpinnings and its vision of social justice can be instructive. For instance, the above-mentioned discussion on the "slum tourism or voyeurism" dilemma begins with a commentary in which Joao Vergara, a Tourism Concern consultant and volunteer on a project in the *favelas* (slums) of Rio de Janeiro, remarks on how tourism is benefiting people in the slums and how "the community likes hosting tourists as they can show how proud they are of their home," adding that, in time, "the benefits could be larger, with more people being involved by, for example, hosting tourists in their own houses."[46] The only response to Vergara's piece is made by someone named da Rocinha, a self-declared "proud resident" of the *favela* whose main concern about having slum tours is that they be done with a person who lives in the community. What is absent from the way this "dilemma" is tackled are several pressing questions and contentious themes and practices that are of concern for critical feminist, post-colonial, and anti-racist activists and scholars. Most notably, this discussion fundamentally fails to address the effects of positioning the world's poor and marginalized as tourist attractions. More troubling still, there is no mention of why such poverty exists in the first place, or of the complicity of the ethical tourist's consumption and lifestyle that contributes to this poverty.

Tourism Concern also produces an ethical guidebook that is available for purchase: *The Ethical Travel Guide: Your Passport to Exciting Alternative Holidays*, which promotes practices such as "off the beaten track adventures."[47] Yet when one considers that going to more remote places, even to spread the tourist dollar, may actually cause or exacerbate the environmental, cultural, and social problems that tourism produces, one has to question the claim that such practices could be defined as "more" ethical. Moreover, to be listed in this directory as an "ethical" tour operator, an individual simply has to fill out a questionnaire in ways that meet the standards set by Tourism Concern (for example, by indicating that they hire local women). These methods raise the question of how stringently the standards set by Tourism Concern can actually be monitored. It is not difficult to imagine business-savvy tour operators and hotel owners falsely representing themselves as more ethical than their competition in order to attract the socially conscious readers of this guidebook.

Finally, a cursory view of Tourism Concern's website suggests that one of its main concerns is to ameliorate the conditions of tourism on host communities in ways that will "feel good" for tourists. Put differently, the social justice they envision is one that requires that the comfort levels of Western tourists remain intact. This is most evident in one of the tabs on its home page that contains the heading "avoid guilt trips." It lists ten ways in which "everyone can be a better tourist." The list is comprised of the tired and familiar "dos and don'ts" approach to awareness-raising about cultural differences – many of which are so common that nowadays they can be found on mainstream tourist websites as well. For example, they include statements like "think about what sort of clothing is appropriate for both men and women," "ask before taking pictures of people," and "talk to local people." This web page goes on to assure the would-be ethical tourist that "by taking any, some or all of these actions you are personally fighting tourism exploitation." In spite of all the important awareness-raising work they do, Tourism Concern's solution-driven approach offers Westerners a way to have "a better holiday" not only by alleviating their guilt but also by allowing them to believe that, in taking their holiday, they are doing good for others. As one traveller in the *Ethical Travel Guide* states, "knowing that you are helping to support a vulnerable community makes [tourism] even better."[48] Thus, in the typical racial liberalism tradition, the individual's right to travel is not only reinforced through this kind of organization but also made virtuous. More importantly, the "individual" with this right is the person who has the money, the official papers, and the time. The fact that not all individuals have this right is conveniently overlooked.

### Global Exchange

Like Tourism Concern, a U.S.-based non-governmental organization called Global Exchange declares that "meaningful, socially responsible travel can, and does, change the world."[49] Global Exchange does not just campaign and raise awareness as Tourism Concern does. In fact, it organizes and offers educational "reality tours" as a form of social justice activism. In recent years, it has offered tours to approximately thirty different destinations, mostly countries in the global South. Typically, these package tours attract white middle-class people, mainly from the U.S., last between ten and twelve days, and consist of visiting various local communities to see and learn about the social conditions which people live in as a means of raising awareness about global power imbalances. Global Exchange's Reality Tours emphasize social movements to stress the resilience and resourcefulness of the local people. Their materials also indicate that they promote a critical view of power structures, as is evident in one of their publications they distribute to tourists, which states: "As visitors, we must be conscious of and sensitive to not only the power relations existing amongst us and the people we engage abroad, but also those existing amongst us and our fellow travellers."[50]

While Global Exchange's Reality Tours share several common features with other forms of responsible tourism (for example, they require participants to abide by a code of conduct similar to that of Tourism Concern), they clearly operate out of more politicized objectives than some other responsible tourism NGOs, and as a result are seen by some as offering one of the most impressive models of ethical travel. For example, while Higgins-

Desbiolles concedes that various forms of alternative tourism have been co-opted by the mainstream tourism industry, she posits Global Exchange as an example of "justice" tourism that provides a *real* alternative.[51]

Despite all the praise they receive, when examined through a critical lens, these reality tours also raise several compelling questions about North-South relations of power, especially about the "exchange" and educational opportunities they provide, as well as the affective and meaning-making processes they enable. For example, such a lens would enable a theorization of the particular tensions that arise when the tourists' ability to travel demarcates them as among the world's affluent visiting some of the world's poorest, and yet these encounters are framed as *reciprocity* through various discourses of exchange that work to conceal the asymmetrical power relations. Furthermore, it would reveal that the underlying educational premise of these tours – an approach known as "contact hypothesis" – is one that has been disputed both in critical tourism studies and by many critical educators.[52] As the research of Raymond and Hall has shown, such encounters can potentially reinforce, rather than reduce, stereotypes. To illustrate their claim that ethical tourism can result in the development of what they refer to as "lotto logic" among participants, Raymond and Hall offer the following quote made by a volunteer who went to South Africa. When this individual saw the low standard of living of South African children, he remarked that "it kind of makes you appreciate how lucky we are at Christmas."[53] In other words, what was gained from this encounter amounted to a sense of having good fortune compared to the Other, and being grateful for the ability to consume. Furthermore, Raymond and Hall point out that even where cross-cultural appreciation does occur at an individual level, this does not necessarily lead to changes in broader perceptions of nationalities or cultures. Indeed, this study suggests that contact with local communities as a means of bridging differences and contributing towards understanding does little to shift power structures.

More interesting still are the affective and meaning-making dimensions of reality tours. Elsewhere, I have analyzed the experiences and perspectives of a group of women who participated on a Global Exchange reality tour.[54] Examining their ambivalent understandings of privilege, their satisfaction with the experience, and the fact that their comfort levels remained intact, I concluded that the reality tour served, ultimately, to secure feelings of innocence, redemption, and benevolence. Uncovering some discourses of morality that emerged through their anti-racist intentions, I argued that the reality tour encounter shaped white subjectivity in ways that failed to attend to the racialized structures in which they were embedded – notably, liberal discourses such as those pertaining to human rights. Underpinning such discursive formations of morality is the liberal imperative to seek justice for all, an imperative which is replete with denials of the salience of race and racism. I also suggested that through such tourism encounters, paradigms of Orientalist thinking continue to reproduce themselves and to shape the ways dominant groups (i.e., white Westerners) understand themselves and their role in the world, including the world inhabited by the Other. As such, my analysis cautioned that certain displays of so-called ethical/responsible tourist practices cannot only displace social responsibility but can also reinstate the very power relations they seek to address.

Indeed, my analysis of this preliminary research has revealed a dynamic similar to that which has been discussed in research on other forms of ethical or well-intentioned global travel, such as Lisle's analysis of ethical tours, which has revealed that power relations are not sidestepped in ethical tourism encounters, no matter how "respectful" the tourist tries to be.[55] Lisle explains that "ethical tourism is not simply an innocent form of 'doing good,' but rather operates through a complex moral economy in which virtue and pleasure are always interlinked."[56] Similarly, Heron's work on Canadian women development workers in Africa also demonstrates that good intentions and collaborative efforts obscure power relations insofar as they falsely imply that a "common ground" is being shared.[57] While my findings come to parallel conclusions, what is striking about the appearance of these dynamics in Reality Tourism is that that such claims to innocence are more readily available than ever. Whereas in Heron's study, the development workers established themselves both as superior and as innocent gradually through lengthy stays and through long-term commitments to international development, my research shows that a similar sense of superiority and innocence can now be secured after just ten days on a Reality Tour. In other words, these tours afford Westerners a quick and easy feel-good way not only to reconcile their discomforts but also to reconstitute themselves as ethical and moral beings.

In sum, the proliferation of ethical/responsible tourism options must make us heed a warning with respect to racialized power. As Lisle puts it, "perhaps we should all book 'responsible' holidays, pursue ecotourism and volunteer to protect the rainforest – but we should *not* make the mistake of thinking that these activities make us more virtuous or ethical than anyone else."[58]

## Conclusion: Race, liberalism, and pitfalls of social justice interventions: pedagogical implications

In this chapter, I have presented a discussion of racialized power dynamics in social justice interventions in ways that interrogate their complexities and contradictions. I have argued that a key first step to exploring racialized privilege in social justice interventions is to look for and identify the ways in which liberalism may frame various efforts and initiatives. This demands that careful attention be paid to context and history. As well, it requires contemplation of the ways in which notions of equality and difference are mobilized to consider whose rights are in fact being protected and upheld. Most importantly, race must be understood as an insidious conceptual and political structure, and not as an event.

While many educators are likely to use the work of organizations such as IWPS, Global Exchange, and Tourism Concern as inspirational exemplars of social justice, I have taken the approach of examining their shortcomings. Similarly, while most critical educators might feel heartened when their students are incited to become actively involved in social justice activism, I prefer to caution my students to be vigilant about what injustices their participation may inadvertently reinforce. Indeed, instead of showing students all that can be achieved through social justice efforts, I contend that it is better to show them how real change fails to take place as a result of certain initiatives. This is not to discourage them, but to help them to see with some candour just how hollow many claims to social justice can be. Perhaps most importantly, students need to notice how our involvement with social justice activism obscures our complicity in current power imbalances and allows us to conceive of ourselves as innocent. As Lauren Berlant points out, "in the liberal society that sanctions individuality as sovereign, we like our positive emotions to feel well intentioned and we like our good intentions to constitute the meaning of our acts."[59] It is in asking such questions that I believe some of the less obvious aspects of how racialized power operates might be revealed.

While I have focused here on just two specific sites, many other possibilities and opportunities to critically analyze the racialized aspects of various social justice interventions abound. For example, instead of focusing on how war is formulated in and operates through blatantly racist understandings (a fact that is difficult *not* to know) a more instructive approach would be to throw into question the subversive/reproductive potential of current *anti-militarism* efforts. Through such an approach, many important insights on how everyday militarism is perpetuated can be gleaned by examining sites where it is being actively resisted.[60] This might reveal to students how both militarism and humanitarianism often paradoxically share the same racialized conceptual terrain, and inspire them to consider the implications of this reality.[61] Another salient example for such an approach is the Hurricane Katrina disaster. Since most people cannot dispute the fact that the lack of response to those who suffered the most devastating effects of this hurricane were extremely racialized, it might prove more fruitful to teach about how so many of the Katrina relief efforts recentred whiteness.[62] The taken-for-granted autonomy and goodness of NGOS of all types require further critical thought as well. As some authors have argued, there is an important distinction between the subcontractual role of NGOS in the provisionn of social services and social justice.[63] Moreover, as Andrea Smith points out, one must contemplate how the non-profit system impacts on the practice and imagination of the political left, and the political space for autonomous grass-roots movement-building in the arena of social justice.[64]

By critically examining some concrete examples of doing good, I have proposed and mapped out a path of inquiry for studying racialized power, privilege, and social injustice. The goal is to enable an understanding of various forms of benevolent engagement as a complex and ongoing process, one that is inextricably bound within the confines of liberalism and white supremacy. While the 2009 RACE conference presented a tremendous start to engaging these issues more broadly, many more opportunities are needed. It is through such opportunities to reflect on these practices that a solid understanding of the ways in which racialized relations of power shape and impede resistance movements can be established.

## Notes

Thanks to Nirmala Bains for her valuable research assistance and insights, and to Suzanne Lenon, Aziz Choudry, and the anthology's editors for helpful comments and feedback.

1 Charles Mills, "Racial Liberalism," *PMLA* 123,5 (2008), 1380–97.
2 My use of the term "transnational" in this chapter refers to the physical movements of people across borders of nation-states.
3 Gayatri Spivak explains that the much-invoked figure of the oppressed subject (or subaltern) is used to legitimize interventions like development. See Gayatri Chakravorty Spivak, "Can the Subaltern Speak?" in *The Post-Colonial Studies Reader*, ed. Bill Ashcroft, Gareth Griffiths, and Helen Tiffin (London: Routledge: 2006), 28–37. Frantz Fanon has also explained that the success of colonialism rests in part in its ability to employ brutal violence and force under the guise of a principled "non-violence" position. See Frantz Fanon, *The Wretched of the Earth* (New York: Grove Weidenfeld, 1963). Another example of this can be found in the work of Edward Said, who pointed out that in his 1910 lecture in the British House of Commons Arthur Balfour justified the necessity for British occupation of Egypt as being for the sake of the Egyptians, and for the sake of Europe at large. See Edward W. Said, *Orientalism* (New York: Random House, 1978).
4 See Sedef Arat-Koç, "Hot Potato: Imperial Wars or Benevolent Interventions? Reflections on 'Global Feminism' Post–September 11th," *Atlantis: A Women's Studies Journal* 26,2 (2002), 433–44. See also Lila Abu-Lughod, "Do Muslim Women Really

Need Saving? Anthropological Reflections on Cultural Relativism and Its Others," in *Feminist Frontiers*, 7th ed., ed. Verta Taylor, Nancy Whittier, and Leila Rupp (Boston: McGraw-Hill, 2007), 484–93; and Sherene H. Razack, *Dark Threats and White Knights: The Somalia Affair, Peacekeeping, and the New Imperialism* (Toronto: University of Toronto Press, 2004).

5 The problem that was identified in the call for papers for the 2009 RACE conference was as follows: "The politics, cultures and economies of doing good seem to have gained a redemptive, sanctioned and empowering status, which has elevated actions and actors above critical scrutiny." This is the approach many nations and humanitarian organizations take, rather than focusing on any of the myriad conditions of state-sanctioned, blatantly racist violence taking place in the world. The increasing criminalization, surveillance, and incarceration of people of colour, the alarming homicide rate of Aboriginal women in Canada, the hunger and abject poverty emerging out of glaringly racialized, globalized economics, and, of course, the racist "War on Terror" and ongoing occupations of Iraq, Afghanistan, and Palestine, are but a few examples of the issues this "do good" approach is supposed to address. The following questions were identified as possible issues to be addressed at the conference: What is defined as "doing good," and how is it tied to constructions of benevolent others? Who is positioned and empowered to "do good"? How is "doing good" historically embedded, and what are some of its foreseen and unforeseen consequences? What does an anti-racist and anti-colonial lens reveal about past and present humanitarian actions and interventions, and how might it inform present and future practice(s)? What are the relations between humanitarianism and imperialism? How can these relations be exposed and meaningfully addressed? RACE (Researchers and Academics of Colour for Equity/ Equality), "The Politics, Cultures, and Economies of Doing Good," *Annual Conference Programme* (Montreal: Concordia and McGill Universities, 2009).

6 The conference call listed a broad range of contemporary examples of "do-goodism" that could benefit from a critical race feminist analysis. These included numerous examples of global interventions, such as advocacy and solidarity campaigns, rescue missions, international development and aid, as well as various state and private initiatives and philanthropic structures in the North American context. One powerful conference presentation on the latter was the keynote lecture given by Andrea Smith entitled "Captured by the State: The Anti-Violence Movement and the Non-Profit Industrial Complex." Drawing from her previous work experiences as a non-profit government-funded rape crisis counsellor in the U.S., Smith discussed the non-profit industrial complex as a system of relationships between state social services, charitable foundations, and social justice organizations that results in the control of political movements. Another authoritative analysis was presented by Joanne Di Nova from Ryerson University, who focused on the June 2008 Canadian government apology for the "Indian Residential Schools." Di Nova incisively pointed out that these apologies do not really address the source of the destructive policies that spawned them, which is ongoing colonization. Furthermore, such official apologies lead to self-congratulation and reaffirmation of the national self-image. The apology signals a closure – the "problem" of Aboriginals is then regarded as being solved.

Consequently, the government is less likely to feel responsible for and committed to policies and programs that are meant to empower First Nations communities. RACE, *Annual Conference Programme*.

7 See Gada Mahrouse, "Producing Peaceful Citizens through a Lesson on the FTAA Quebec Summit Protests," *Canadian Journal of Education* 29,2 (2006), 436–53.

8 Some of these scholars work under the banners of "global critical race feminism," "transnational feminism," "Indigenous feminism," and "anti-racist feminism," or any combinations thereof.

9 As I explain elsewhere, to get at all of the complex factors that shape this white/ Western racialized positioning, I combine the terms "white" and "Western" to point how they intertwine, conflate, and stand in for one another. The slash or virgule (/) as it is used here between the words "white/Western" will most often serve to emphasize the close relationship between the two ideas. See Gada Mahrouse, "Race-Conscious Transnational Activists with Cameras: Mediators of Compassion," *International Journal of Cultural Studies* 11,1 (2008), 87–105. Many of these debates have centred on how the various feminist movements use "human rights" discourses. For instance, see Sherene H. Razack, *Looking White People in the Eye: Gender, Race, and Culture in Courtrooms and Classrooms* (Toronto: University of Toronto Press, 1998); Sara Ahmed, *Strange Encounters: Embodied Others in Post-Coloniality* (New York: Routledge, 2000); Wendy Hesford and Wendy Kozol, *Just Advocacy? Women's Human Rights, Transnational Feminisms, and the Politics of Representation* (New Brunswick, NJ: Rutgers University Press, 2005); and Inderpal Grewal, "On the New Global Feminism and the Family of Nations: Dilemmas of Transnational Feminist Practice," in *Talking Visions: Multicultural Feminism in a Transnational Age*, ed. Ella Shohat (Cambridge, MA: MIT Press, 1998), 501–30.

10 According to Mills, liberalism refers to the anti-feudal, egalitarian ideology of individual rights and freedoms that emerged in the seventeenth and eighteenth centuries to oppose absolutism and ascriptive hierarchy. Mills, "Racial Liberalism," 1380.

11 Here, Mills is primarily referring to the social contract theory stimulated by Rawls's theory of justice, otherwise known as contractarian (or deontological) liberalism. Moreover, he explains that while there are myriad debates about and within liberalism (i.e., the right- or left-wing versions), liberalism itself is rarely challenged. Mills, "Racial Liberalism," 1380.

12 Ibid.

13 For instance, he calls for the adoption of a domination contract framework, and a discussion of Rawls's notion of justice as fairness. Ibid.

14 Ibid., 1381.

15 As I have explained elsewhere, my use of the term "whiteness" is meant to capture a relational discursive positioning which privileges and sustains the global dominance of imperial subjects. The notion of whiteness used in this essay also encompasses nation and therefore does not mean skin colour per se, but rather is formulated through the understanding that social identities are fluid, constructed and produced through knowledge, and that white privilege and power are post-colonial conditions. This conception also recognizes that like all social categories, the boundaries of whiteness shift over time and place and that white subjects are con-

stituted in diasporic, hybrid, and transnational identities and affiliations. See Mahrouse, "Race-Conscious Transnational Activists." See also Inderpal Grewal and Caren Kaplan, "Warrior Marks: Global Feminism's Neo-Colonial Discourse in a Multicultural Context," *Camera Obscura* 39 (1996), 4–33.

16 For this research, I examined the publications of solidarity projects and conducted in-depth interviews with Canadians who have participated in direct action solidarity in various war/conflict zones. Fifteen interviews were conducted between March and May 2005. See Gada Mahrouse, "Transnational Activists, News Media Representations, and Racialized 'Politics of Life': The Christian Peacemaker Team Kidnapping in Iraq," *Citizenship Studies* 13,4 (2009), 311–31.

17 International Women's Peace Service, "Application Pack for IWPS Volunteers in the West Bank" (N.p.: International Women's Peace Service, 2005), 4; emphasis added. The term "two-thirds world" is meant to reflect the quality of life led by peoples and communities around the world, while moving away from the misleading geographical and ideological binaries that the terms North/South or Third/First World connote. The IWPS website has since been modified, and they are no longer using these terms. For more about these terms see Chandra T. Mohanty, *Feminism without Borders: Decolonizing Theory, Practicing Solidarity* (Durham, NC: Duke University Press, 2003), 227.

18 IWPS, "Application Pack," 2–3; emphasis added.

19 Antoinette Sedillo Lopez, "Comparative Analysis of Women's Issues: Toward a Contextualized Methodology," in *Global Critical Race Feminisms*, ed. Adrien Katherine Wing and Angela Y. Davis (New York: New York University Press, 2000), 68.

20 Iris Marion Young, *Justice and the Politics of Difference* (Princeton: Princeton University Press, 1990).

21 Lopez, "Comparative Analysis of Women's Issues," 68.

22 William T.M. Riches, *The Civil Rights Movement: Struggle and Resistance*, 2nd ed. (New York: Palgrave Macmillan, 2004); Becky Thompson, *A Promise and a Way of Life* (Minneapolis: University of Minnesota Press, 2001).

23 Lopez, "Comparative Analysis of Women's Issues," 68.

24 Emily Stoper, *The Student Nonviolent Coordinating Committee: The Growth of Radicalism in a Civil Rights Organization* (New York: Carlson Publishing, 1989); Bruce Dierenfield, *The Civil Rights Movement* (New York: Pearson Longman, 2004).

25 See Len Holt, *The Summer That Didn't End: The Story of the Mississippi Civil Rights Project of 1964* (New York: Da Capo Press, 1992); and Riches, *The Civil Rights Movement*.

26 Stokely Carmichael and Charles Hamilton, *Black Power: The Politics of Liberation in America* (New York: Random House, 1967).

27 Ibid., 75.

28 Focusing on Peace Brigades International, for example, Mahony and Eguren point out that "the supposed immunity and protective power of the volunteers is based on physical characteristics such as skin colour and national identity." See Liam Mahony and Luis Enrique Eguren, *Unarmed Bodyguards: International Accompaniment for the Protection of Human Rights* (Hartford, CT: Kumarian Press, 1997), 251.

29 It is important to note that the attention paid to racialized experiences presented in these texts are exceptional because in most literature on transitional solidarity activism, explicit references to race are either largely absent or the racialized differences between the activists and those they assist are glossed over.

30 The famous case of Rachel Corrie exemplifies this dynamic. For more on this, see Malini Johar Scheuller, *Locating Race: Global Sites of Post-Colonial Citizenship* (Albany: State University of New York Press, 2009).

31 Caren Kaplan, "The Politics of Location as Transnational Feminist Practice," in *Scattered Hegemonies: Postmodernity and Transnational Feminist Practices*, ed. Inderpal Grewal and Caren Kaplan (Minnesota: University of Minnesota Press, 1994), 138.

32 bell hooks, "Sisterhood: Political Solidarity between Women," in *Dangerous Liaisons: Gender, Nation, and Postcolonial Perspectives*, ed. Anne McClintock, Aamir Mufti, and Ella Shohat (Minneapolis: University of Minnesota Press, 1997), 396–411; Adrienne Rich, "Notes Toward a Politics of Location," in *Feminist Postcolonial Theory: A Reader*, ed. Reina Lewis and Sara Mills (London: Routledge, 2003), 29–42.

33 Ahmed, *Strange Encounters*, 124.

34 Thobani examines feminist texts that oppose the War on Terror to illustrate the insidious ways in which such texts reposition whiteness as innocent of imperialist histories and present complicities. Using the example of acclaimed post-structuralist feminist Judith Butler's book *Precarious Life*, Thobani draws attention to the fact that the text is primarily a discussion of shared vulnerability and the common experience of mourning. In her attempt to implore her readers to interrogate military practices, Butler equates the vulnerability of the U.S. which, as Thobani points out, is "the most powerful political community on the planet" with the vulnerability of the vastly unequal societies that the superpower is invading and occupying. Despite the fact that Butler cautions against the assumption of a universally shared human condition, her analysis repeatedly and explicitly reproduces it. Furthermore, Butler's "human" subject is generalized to such a degree that a discussion of power relations between white and non-white subjects can be evaded. See Sunera Thobani, "White Wars: Western Feminisms and the 'War on Terror,'" *Feminist Theory* 8,2 (2007), 169–85.

35 See Nahla Abdo and Ronit Lentin, "Writing Dislocation, Writing the Self: Bringing (Back) the Political into Gendered Israeli-Palestinian Dialoguing," in *Women and the Politics of Military Confrontation: Palestinian and Israeli Gendered Narratives of Dislocation*, ed. Nahla Abdo and Ronit Lentin (New York: Berghahn Books, 2002), 1–33. See also Ella Shohat, "Area Studies, Gender Studies, and the Cartographies of Knowledge," *Social Text* 20,3 (2002), 67–78; Mohanty, *Feminism without Borders*; and Grewal and Kaplan, "Warrior Marks."

36 While many similar forms of alternative tourism, such as volunteer and ecotourism certainly share some overlapping goals, the term "socially responsible" tourism will refer specifically to short-term trips (averaging ten to fourteen days) which are primarily intended as educational holidays, as opposed to actively participating in the communities visited (which is the case with some "solidarity" or "volunteer" tourism projects). The increased awareness of the detrimental effects

of tourism can be attributed, in part, to widely circulated texts such as Jamaica Kincaid's "A Small Place," which reveals the contrasts between the experiences of vacationers and the realities of the people whose lives the tourism impact. Jamaica Kincaid, *A Small Place* (New York: Plume, 1989). For a summary of different forms of "alternative tourism" and their shortcomings, see Freya Higgins-Desbiolles, "Justice Tourism and Alternative Globalisation," *Journal of Sustainable Tourism* 16,3 (2008), 345–64.

37 Shawn Blore, "On the Left, Notice the Poverty," *The Globe and Mail* (Toronto), January 20, 2007, ⟨http://www.theglobeandmail.com/life/article75216.ece⟩, accessed March 21, 2010.

38 Charles Montgomery, "Revolutionary Tourism," *The Vancouver Sun*, March 10, 2001. See ⟨http://www.charlesmontgomery.ca/tourism.html⟩.

39 Ibid.

40 Mike Comerford, "A Dose of Reality in Ecuador: Shunning Sun and Fun for Social Activism," *Daily Herald* (Chicago), May 21, 2006, Business Section.

41 Freya Higgins-Desbiolles, "More Than an 'Industry': The Forgotten Power of Tourism as a Social Force," *Tourism Management* 27,6 (2006), 1192–208; Deborah McLaren, *Rethinking Tourism and Ecotravel,* 2nd ed. (Bloomfield, CT: Kumarian Press, 2003); Regina Scheyvens, "Poverty Tourism," *Development Bulletin* 55 (2001), 18–20.

42 McLaren, *Rethinking Tourism.*

43 Laine Bergeson, "A Just Vacation," *Utne Reader* 137 (2006), 88.

44 Debbie Lisle, "Joyless Cosmopolitans: The Moral Economy of Ethical Tourism" (paper presented at the ISA's 49th Annual Convention: Bridging Multiple Divides, San Francisco, CA, March 26, 2008), 4.

45 This quote and all subsequent references to the Tourism Concern website in this section were found at ⟨http://www.tourismconcern.org.uk⟩, accessed on October 19, 2009.

46 Ibid.

47 Polley Pattullo and Orely Minelli, *The Ethical Travel Guide: Your Passport to Exciting Alternative Holidays* (London: Earthscan Publications, 2009).

48 Ibid., 52.

49 An American-based non-governmental organization (NGO) called "Global Exchange" is the longest standing and leading North American operator of reality tours, offering thirty-six different destinations, all but three of which are to countries in the global South. See ⟨http://www.globalexchange.org⟩, accessed March 21, 2010.

50 Reality Tour Delegate welcome letter. In 2007, Global Exchange sent this generic letter as part of the orientation package for people who signed up for one of their reality tours.

51 At the same time, the fact that the reality tours make money for Global Exchange raises issues about what some have called the marketing or commodification of resistance. See Clifford Bob, *The Marketing of Rebellion: Insurgents, Media, and International Activism* (New York: Cambridge University Press, 2005).

52 In this sense, reality tours share several commonalities with multicultural and citi-

zenship education, which seek to promote and encourage respect for difference and understandings of the rights of others. Yet literature that offers critical analyses of the challenges and shortcomings of these approaches to education suggest there is little evidence that exposure to difference and the development of personal connections will result in real social change. Indeed, some educators have critiqued the vague and elusive notions of increased personal understanding and the acceptance of difference as overly simplistic approaches to pressing global problems, and that such approaches in fact perpetuate and obscure relations of power.

53 Eliza Marguerite Raymond and C. Michael Hall, "The Development of Cross-Cultural (Mis)understanding through Volunteer Tourism," *Journal of Sustainable Tourism* 16,5 (2010), 537.

54 Gada Mahrouse, "Feel Good Tourism: The Ethical Option for Socially-Conscious Westerners," *ACME: An International E-Journal of Critical Geographies*, Special Issue: Gender, Power and Transcultural Relations (forthcoming).

55 Lisle, "Joyless Cosmopolitans," 10.

56 Ibid.

57 Barbara Heron, *Desire for Development: Whiteness, Gender and the Helping Imperative* (Waterloo, ON: Wilfrid Laurier University Press, 2008).

58 Lisle, "Joyless Cosmopolitans," 17–18.

59 Lauren Berlant, "Compassion (and Withholding)," in *Compassion: The Culture and Politics of an Emotion*, ed. L. Berlant (New York: Routledge, 2004), 13.

60 A useful entry point into such a discussion comes through the chapter "Writing Dislocation" by Abdo and Lentin. Writing about Jewish and Palestinian women's alliances in protesting the Israeli occupation of Palestine, they grapple with how feminist "peace" projects are embedded within nationalist investments. A more recent articulation of this idea can be found in Angela Y. Davis, "A Vocabulary for Feminist Praxis: On War and Radical Critique," in *Feminism and War: Confronting U.S. Imperialism*, ed. Robin Riley, Chandra Mohanty, and Minne Bruce Pratt (London: Zed Books, 2008), 19–26.

61 See the conclusion in Razack, *Dark Threats and White Knights*.

62 One text on this subject is "To Render Ourselves Visible." Among other things, it examines the phenomenon of gentrification spurred by white volunteers. See Alisa Bierria, Mayaba Liebenthal, and INCITE! Women of Color Against Violence, "To Render Ourselves Visible: Women of Colour Organizing and Hurricane Katrina," in *What Lies Beneath: Katrina, Race, and the State of the Nation*, ed. South End Press Collective (Cambridge, MA: South End Press, 2007), 31–47.

63 The writings of Aziz Choudry and Sangeeta Kamat on this issue are especially instructive. See Aziz Choudry, "Transnational Activist Coalition Politics and the De/Colonization of Pedagogies of Mobilization: Learning from Anti-Neoliberal Indigenous Movement Articulations," *International Education* (2007), 97–112; and Sangeeta Kamat, "The Privatisation of Public Interest: Theorizing NGO Discourse in a Neoliberal Era," *Review of International Political Economy* 11,1 (2004), 155–76.

64 Smith, "Captured by the State."

# Bibliography

Abdo, Nahla, and Ronit Lentin. "Writing Dislocation, Writing the Self: Bringing (Back) the Political into Gendered Israeli-Palestinian Dialoguing." In *Women and the Politics of Military Confrontation: Palestinian and Israeli Gendered Narratives of Dislocation,* edited by Nahla Abdo and Ronit Lentin, 1–33. New York: Berghahn Books, 2002.

Abella, Rosalie Silberman. *Equality in Employment: The Report of the Royal Commission on Equality in Employment.* Ottawa: Supply and Services Canada, 1984.

Abu-Lughod, Lila. "Do Muslim Women Really Need Saving? Anthropological Reflections on Cultural Relativism and Its Others." In *Feminist Frontiers,* 7th ed., edited by Verta Taylor, Nancy Whittier, and Leila J. Rupp, 484–93. Boston: McGraw Hill, 2007.

_____. "Do Muslim Women Really Need Saving? Anthropological Reflections on Cultural Relativism and Its Others." *American Anthropologist* 104, 3 (2002), 783–90.

Acoose, Janice. "A Revisiting of Maria Campbell's *Halfbreed.*" In *Looking at the Words of Our People: First Nations Analysis of Literature,* edited by Jeanette C. Armstrong, 138–50. Penticton, BC: Theytus Books, 1993.

Agamben, Giorgio. *State of Exception.* Translated by Kevin Attell. Chicago: University of Chicago Press, 2005.

_____. *Homo Sacer: Sovereign Power and Bare Life.* Translated by Daniel Heller-Roazen. Stanford, CA: Stanford University Press, 1998.

Aguirre, Adalberto. "Academic Storytelling: A Critical Race Theory Story of Affirmative Action." *Sociological Perspectives* 43,2 (2000), 319–39.

Ahmed, Sara. " 'You End Up Doing the Document Rather than Doing the Doing': Diversity, Race Equality and the Politics of Documentation." *Ethnic and Racial Studies* 30,4 (2007), 590–609.

_____. "This Other and Other Others." *Economy and Society* 31,4 (2002), 558–72.

_____. *Strange Encounters: Embodied Others in Post-Coloniality.* London: Routledge, 2000.

_____. "(Meta)fictions." In *Differences that Matter: Feminist Theory and Postmodernism,* 142–65. Cambridge: Cambridge University Press, 1998.

_____. "The Language of Diversity." *Ethnic and Racial Studies* 30,2 (2007), 235–56.

Aiken, Sharryn J. "From Slavery to Expulsion: Racism, Canadian Immigration Law and the Unfulfilled Promise of Modern Constitutionalism." In *Interrogating*

*Race and Racism,* edited by Vijay Agnew, 55–111. Toronto: University of Toronto Press, 2007.

————. "Of Gods and Monsters: National Security and Canadian Refugee Policy." *Revue québécoise de droit international* 14,2 (2003), 1–51.

Alfred, Taiaiake, and Jeff Corntassel. "Being Indigenous: Resurgences Against Contemporary Colonialism." In *Politics of Identity IX,* edited by Richard Bellamy. Oxford: Government and Opposition Ltd., 2005.

Altamirano-Jiménez, Isabel. "The Politics of Tradition: Aboriginal Nationalism and Women. Mexico and Canada in a Comparative Perspective." PhD diss., University of Alberta, 2006.

Amnesty International. "Stolen Sisters: Discrimination and Violence Against Indigenous Women in Canada." ⟨http://www.amnesty.ca/campaigns/sisters_overview.php⟩. Accessed March 10, 2010.

————. "Stop Violence Against Indigenous Women." ⟨http://www.amnesty.ca/campaigns/svaw_indigenous_women.php⟩. Accessed March 10, 2010.

Amos, Valerie, and Pratibha Parmar. "Challenging Imperial Feminism." *Feminist Review,* 17 (1984), 3–19.

Anthias, Floya, and Nira Yuval-Davis. *Racialized Boundaries: Race, Nation, Gender, Colour and Class and the Anti-Racist Struggle.* London: Routledge, 1992.

Appiah, Anthony K., and Amy Gutmann. *Color Conscious: The Political Morality of Race.* Princeton: Princeton University Press, 1996.

Arat-Koç, Sedef. "Contesting or Affirming 'Europe'? European Enlargement, Aspirations for 'Europeanness' and New Identities in the Margins of Europe." *Journal of Contemporary European Studies* 18,2 (2010).

————. "The Disciplinary Boundaries of Canadian Identity after September 11: Civilizational Identity, Multiculturalism, and the Challenge of Anti-Imperialist Feminism." *Social Justice* 32,4 (2005), 32–49.

————. "Hot Potato: Imperial Wars or Benevolent Interventions? Reflections on 'Global Feminism' Post–September 11th." *Atlantis: A Women's Studies Journal* 26,2 (2002), 433–44.

————. "Gender and Race in 'Non-discriminatory' Immigration Policies in Canada: 1960s to the Present." In *Scratching the Surface: Canadian Antiracist Feminist Thought,* edited by Enakshi Dua and Angela Robertson, 207–33. Toronto: Women's Press, 1999.

————. "The Politics of Family and Immigration in the Subordination of Domestic Workers in Canada." In *Gender in the 1990s: Images, Realities, and Issues,* edited by E.D. Nelson and Barrie Robinson, 413–42. Toronto: Nelson Publishers, 1995.

Archuleta, Elizabeth. " 'I Give You Back': Indigenous Women Writing to Survive." *Studies in American Indian Literatures* 18,4 (2006), 88–114.

Ardener, Shirley, ed. *Defining Females: The Nature of Women in Society.* New York: Wiley, 1978.

Arendt, Hannah. *The Origins of Totalitarianism.* New York: Harcourt Brace Jovanovich, 1973.

————. "Race Thinking before Racism." *The Review of Politics* 6,1 (1944), 36–73.

Armstrong, Jeannette, ed. *Looking at the Words of Our People: First Nations Analysis of Literature.* Penticton, BC: Theytus Books, 1993.

Armstrong, Jeannette, and Lally Grauer, eds. *Native Poetry in Canada: A Contemporary Anthology*. Peterborough, ON: Broadview Press, 2001.

Armstrong, Sally. *Veiled Threat: The Hidden Power of the Women of Afghanistan*. Toronto: Penguin Canada, 2003.

————. "Shrouded in Secrecy." *Chatelaine* (May 2001), 131.

————. "Veiled Threat: Afghanistan's Women under Taliban Rule." *Homemaker's* (1997), 16–29.

Aylward, Carol A. *Canadian Critical Race Theory: Racism and the Law*. Halifax: Fernwood, 1999.

Bahdi, Reem. "No Exit: Racial Profiling and Canada's War Against Terrorism." *Osgoode Hall Law Journal* 41,2/3 (2003), 293–317.

Bakic-Hayden, Milica. "Nesting Orientalisms: The Case of Former Yugoslavia." *Slavic Review* 54,4 (1995), 917–31.

Bannerji, Himani. *The Dark Side of the Nation: Essays on Multiculturalism, Nationalism and Gender*. Toronto: Canadian Scholars' Press, 2000.

————. *Thinking Through: Essays on Feminism, Marxism and Anti-Racism*. Toronto: Women's Press, 1995.

————. *Returning the Gaze: Essays on Racism, Feminism and Politics*. Toronto: Sister Vision Press, 1993.

————. "Introducing Racism: Notes Towards an Anti-Racist Feminism." *Resources for Feminist Research* 16,1 (1987), 10–12.

Barkan, Elazar, and Ronald Bush, eds. *Prehistories of the Future: The Primitive Project and the Culture of Modernism*. Palo Alto, CA: Stanford University Press, 1995.

Barthes, Roland. *Mythologies*. Translated by Annette Lavers. London: Paladin Press, 1973.

Baum, Bruce. *The Rise and Fall of the Caucasian Race: A Political History of Racial Identity*. New York: New York University Press, 2006.

Bauman, Zygmunt. *Society under Siege*. Cambridge: Polity Press, 2002.

————. *Postmodern Ethics*. Oxford: Blackwell, 1993.

Becker, Howard. "Whose Side Are We On?" *Social Problems* 15 (1967), 240–47.

Bell, Derrick. "Property Rights in Whiteness: Their Legal Legacy, Their Economic Costs." In *Critical Race Theory: The Cutting Edge*, edited by Richard Delgado, 71–79. Philadelphia: Temple University Press, 1995.

Bell, Lee Anne. "Sincere Fictions: The Pedagogical Challenges of Preparing White Teachers for Multicultural Classrooms." *Equity and Excellence in Education* 35,3 (2003), 236–44.

————. "Telling Tales: What Stories Can Tell Us about Racism." *Race Ethnicity and Education* 6,1 (2003), 3–28.

Bergeson, Laine. "A Just Vacation – It's Not If Travellers Have Fun, It's How." *Utne – Minneapolis* 137 (2006), 88–89.

Berlant, Lauren. "Compassion (and Withholding)." In *Compassion: The Culture and Politics of an Emotion*, edited by Lauren Berlant, 1–13. New York: Routledge, 2004.

Bhattacharyya, Gargi, John Gabriel, and Stephen Small. *Race and Power: Global Racism in the Twenty-First Century*. London: Routledge, 2002.

Bierria, Alisa, Mayaba Liebenthal, and Incite! Women of Color Against Violence. "To Render Ourselves Visible: Women of Color Organizing and Hurricane Katrina." In *What Lies Beneath: Katrina, Race, and the State of the Nation*, edited by The South End Press Collective, 31–47. Cambridge, MA: South End Press, 2007.

Bird, Elizabeth S., and Robert W. Dardenne. "Myth, Chronicle, and Story: Exploring the Narrative Qualities of News." In *Mass Communication as Culture: Myth and Narrative in Television and the Press*, edited by James Carey, 67–87. Beverly Hills: Sage, 1988.

Bird Rose, Deborah. "Land Rights and Deep Colonising: The Erasure of Women." *Aboriginal Law Bulletin* 3,85 (1996), 6–14.

Block, Irwin. "CanWest Chief Attacks 'Cancer' in the Media. Anti-Israel Bias 'Destroying Credibility.' Fundamental Precepts of Honest Reporting Have Been Abandoned, Israel Asper Says." *The Gazette* (Montreal), October 31, 2002, A3.

Bogo, Didier. "Security and Immigration: Towards a Critique of the Governmentality of Unease." *Alternatives: Global, Local, Political* 27 (2002), 63–92.

Bonnett, Alastair. *The Idea of the West: Culture, Politics and History*. New York: Palgrave Macmillan, 2004.

———. "A White World? Whiteness and the Meaning of Modernity in Latin America and Japan." In *Working through Whiteness: International Perspectives*, edited by Cynthia Lavine-Rasky, 69–105. Albany: State University of New York Press, 2002.

———. *White Identities: An Historical and International Introduction*. London: Longman, 2000.

———. "How the British Working Class Became White: The Symbolic (Re)formation of Racialized Capitalism." *Journal of Historical Sociology* 11,3 (1998), 316–40.

Bourdieu, Pierre. "Language and Symbolic Power." In *The Discourse Reader*, edited by Adam Jaworski and Nikolas Coupland, 502–13. London: Routledge, 1999.

Brand, Dionne. *Bread Out of Stone: Recollection, Sex, Recognitions, Race, Dreaming, Politics*. Toronto: Vintage Canada, 1998.

Brand, Dionne, and Krisantha Sri Bhaggiyadatta. *Rivers Have Sources, Trees Have Roots: Speaking Racism*. Toronto: Cross-Cultural Communications, 1986.

Bremner, Lindsay. "Border/Skin." In *Against the Wall*, edited by Michael Sorkin, 122–37. New York: The New Press, 2005.

Brigham, Golden. "The Lessons of 'Indigenous' Women for Theory and Activism in Feminist Anthropology." *Voices: A Publication of the Association for Feminist Anthropology* 5 (2001), 1–8.

Brodie, Janine. "Canada's 3-D's: The Rise and Decline of the Gender-Based Policy Capacity." In *Remapping Gender in the New Global Order*, edited by Marjorie Griffin-Cohen and Janine Brodie, 166–84. London: Routledge, 2007.

Brodie, Janine, and Isabella Bakker. *Where Are the Women? Gender Equity, Budgets and Canadian Public Policy*. Ottawa: Canadian Centre for Policy Alternatives, 2008.

Bullock, Katherine H., and Gul Joya Jafri. "Media (Mis)Representations: Muslim Women in the Canadian Nation." *Canadian Woman Studies* 20,2 (2000), 35–40.

Burton, Antoinette M. "The White Woman's Burden: British Feminists and the 'Indian Woman,' 1865–1915." In *Western Women and Imperialism: Complic-*

*ity and Resistance*, edited by Nupur Chaudhuri and Margaret Strobel, 137–57. Bloomington: Indiana University Press, 1992.

Burwell, Catherine. "Reading Lolita in Times of War: Women's Book Clubs and the Politics of Reception." *Intercultural Education* 18,4 (2007), 281–96.

Butcher, Jim. *The Moralization of Tourism: Sun, Sand . . . and Saving the World?* New York: Routledge, 2003.

Butler, Judith. *Precarious Life: The Powers of Mourning and Violence.* London: Verso Books, 2004.

Byers, Michael. "Afghanistan: The Wrong Mission for Canada." *The Tyee,* October 6, 2006. ⟨http://thetyee.ca/Views/2006/10/06/Afghanistan⟩. Accessed November 27, 2007.

Calhoun, Cheshire. "Responsibility and Reproach." *Ethics* 99,2 (1989), 389–406.

Calliste, Agnes, and George Dei, eds. *Anti-Racist Feminism.* Halifax: Fernwood, 2000.

Campbell, Maria. *Halfbreed.* Toronto: McClelland and Stewart, 1973.

Canadian Association of University Teachers. "A Partial Picture: The Representation of Equity-Seeking Groups in Canada's Universities and Colleges." *CAUT Equity Review* 1 (November 2007), 1–6.

Canada Border Services Agency. "Fact Sheet: Security Certificates" (April 2005). ⟨http://www.cbsa-asfc.gc.ca/newsroom/factsheets/2005/certificat-e.html⟩. Accessed March 18, 2006.

Canadian Corrections Association. *Indians and the Law.* Ottawa: Department of Indian Affairs, 1967.

Canadian Council for Refugees. "Refugees and Security" (March 2001, updated February 2003). ⟨http://www.ccrweb.ca/security.pdf⟩. Accessed March 18, 2006.

Cañas, Sandra. "The Little Mosque on the Prairie: Examining (Multi) Cultural Spaces of Nation and Religion." *Cultural Dynamics* 20,3 (2008), 195–211.

Carmichael, Stokely, and Charles V. Hamilton. *Black Power: The Politics of Liberation in America.* New York: Random House, 1967.

Carr, Paul R., and Darren E. Lund, eds. *The Great White North? Exploring Whiteness, Privilege and Identity in Education.* Rotterdam, NLD: Sense Publishers, 2007.

Carty, Linda, and Dionne Brand. "Visible Minority Women: A Creation of the Colonial State." In *Returning the Gaze: Essays on Racism, Feminism and Politics,* edited by Himani Bannerji, 207–22. Toronto: Sister Vision Press, 1993.

Chesler, Phyllis. *The New Anti-Semitism: The Current Crisis and What We Must Do About It.* San Francisco: Jossey-Bass, 2003.

Choudry, Aziz. "Transnational Activist Coalition Politics and the De/Colonization of Pedagogies of Mobilization: Learning from Anti-Neoliberal Indigenous Movement Articulations." *International Education* (2007), 97–112.

Chunn, Dorothy E., Susan B. Boyd, and Hester Lessard, eds. *Reaction and Resistance: Feminism, Law and Social Change.* Vancouver: UBC Press, 2007.

Cloud, Dana L. " 'To Veil the Threat of Terror': Afghan Women and the 'Clash of Civilizations' in the Imagery of the U.S. War on Terror." *Quarterly Journal of Speech* 90,3 (2004), 285–306.

Comerford, Mike. "A Dose of Reality in Ecuador Shunning Sun and Fun for Social Activism." *Daily Herald* (Chicago), May 21, 2006, Business Section.

Connor, Helen. "Reclamation of Cultural Identity for Maori Women: A Response to 'Prisonisation.'" In *Bitter Sweet: Indigenous Women in the Pacific*, edited by Alyson Jones, Phyllis Herda, and Tamasailau M. Suaalii, 125–36. Otago, NZ: University of Otago Press, 2000.

Conte, Christine. "Ladies, Livestock, Land and Lucre: Women's Networks and Social Status on the Western Navajo Reservation." *American Indian Quarterly* 6 (1982), 105–24.

Cooke, Miriam. "Saving Brown Women." *Signs: Journal of Women in Culture and Society* 28,1 (2002), 468–70.

Cornell, Drucilla. *Beyond Accommodation: Ethical Feminism, Deconstruction and the Law*. London: Routledge, 1991.

Cravatte, Celine, and Nadege Chabloz. "Enchantment and Solidarity: Which Dream Does 'Fair Tourism' Sell?" *Tourist Studies* 8 (2008), 231–47.

Crenshaw, Kimberlé, Neil Gotanda, Gary Peller, and Kendall Thomas, eds. *Critical Race Theory: The Key Writings that Formed the Movement*. New York: New Press, 1995.

Culleton, Beatrice. *In Search of April Raintree*. Winnipeg: Pemmican Publications, 1983.

Dabashi, Hamid, ed. *Dreams of a Nation*. London: Verso Books, 2006.

Damm, Kateri. "Speaking Native Realities in Maria Campbell's *Halfbreed* and Beatrice Culleton's *In Search of April Raintree*." In *Looking at the Words of Our People: First Nations Analysis of Literature*, edited by Jeannette Armstrong, 93–114. Penticton, BC: Theytus Books, 1993.

Davis, Angela Y. "A Vocabulary for Feminist Praxis: On War and Radical Critique." In *Feminism and War: Confronting U.S. Imperialism*, edited by Robin L. Riley, Chandra Talpade Mohanty, and Minnie Bruce Pratt, 19–26. London: Zed Books, 2008.

_____. *Abolition Democracy: Beyond Prisons, Torture and Empire*. New York: Seven Stories Press, 2005.

_____. *Are Prisons Obsolete?* New York: Seven Stories Press, 2003.

Davis, Mike. *Planet of Slums*. London: Verso Books, 2006.

Dean, Mitchell. *Governmentality: Power and Rule in Modern Society*. London: Sage, 1999.

Delgado, Richard. "Storytelling Oppositionists and Others: A Plea for Narrative." *Michigan Law Review* 87 (1989), 2411–441.

_____, ed. *Critical Race Theory: The Cutting Edge*. Philadelphia: Temple University Press, 1995.

_____. *Critical Whiteness Studies: Looking Behind the Mirror*. Philadelphia: Temple University Press, 1997.

Delgado, Richard, and Jean Stefancic. *Critical Race Theory: An Introduction*. New York: New York University Press, 2001.

Dierenfield, Bruce J. *The Civil Rights Movement*. New York: Pearson Longman, 2004.

Dirlik, Arif. "Place-Based Imagination: Globalism and the Politics of Place." In *Places and Politics in the Age of Globalization*, edited by Roxann Prazniak and Arif Dirlik, 15–51. Lanham, MD: Rowman and Littlefield, 2001.

_____. "The Postcolonial Aura: Third World Criticism in the Age of Global Capitalism." In *Dangerous Liaisons: Gender, Nation, and Postcolonial Perspectives*, edited by Anne McClintock, Aamir Mufti, and Ella Shohat, 501–28. Minneapolis: University of Minnesota Press, 1997.

Disch, Lisa. "More Truth than Fact: Storytelling as Critical Understanding in the Writing of Hannah Arendt." *Political Theory* 21,4 (1993), 665–94.

Dixon, Travis L., Christina L. Azocar, and Michael Casas. "The Portrayal of Race and Crime on Television Network News." *Journal of Broadcasting & Electronic Media* 47,4 (2003), 498–523.

Dixon, Travis L., and Daniel Linz. "Television News, Prejudicial Pretrial Publicity, and the Depiction of Race." *Journal of Broadcasting & Electronic Media* 46,1 (2002), 112–36.

———. "Overrepresentation and Underrepresentation of African Americans and Latinos as Lawbreakers on Television News." *Journal of Communication* 50,2 (2000), 131–54.

———. "Race and the Misrepresentation of Victimization on Local Television News." *Communication Quarterly* 27,5 (2000), 547–73.

Dossa, Shiraz. "Lethal Muslims: White-Trashing Islam and the Arabs." *Journal of Muslim Minority Affairs* 28,2 (2008), 225–36.

Dua, Enakshi. "On the Effectiveness of Anti-Racist Policies in Canadian Universities: Issues of Implementation of Policies by Senior Administration." In *Racism in the Canadian University: Demanding Social Justice, Inclusion, and Equity*, edited by Frances Henry and Carol Tator, 160–95. Toronto: University of Toronto Press, 2009.

Dua, Enakshi, and Angela Robertson, eds. *Scratching the Surface: Canadian Anti-Racist Feminist Thought*. Toronto: Women's Press, 1999.

Edler, Juliane. "Towards a Historical Materialist Approach to Racism in Post-'Unification' Germany." *Socialist Studies* 3,1 (2007), 27–48.

Eisenstein, Zillah. *Against Empire: Feminisms, Racism and the West*. London: Zed Books, 2004.

Engle, Karen. "Constructing Good Aliens and Good Citizens: Legitimizing the War on Terror(ism)." *University of Colorado Law Review* (2004), 59–114.

Entman, Robert M. "Modern Racism and the Image of Blacks in Local Television News." *Critical Studies in Mass Communication* 7,4 (1990), 332–45.

Epstein, Barbara. "What Happened to the Women's Movement?" *Monthly Review* 53,1 (2001), 1–13.

Ewick, Patricia, and Susan S. Silbey. "Subversive Stories and Hegemonic Tales: Toward a Sociology of Narrative." *Law and Society Review* 29 (1995), 197–226.

Eze, Emmanuel Chukwudi. *Achieving Our Humanity: The Idea of the Postracial Future*. New York: Routledge, 2001.

Fahmy, Shahira. "Picturing Afghan Women: A Content Analysis of AP Wire Photographs during the Taliban Regime and after the Fall of the Taliban Regime." *Gazette: The International Journal for Communication Studies* 66,2 (2004), 91–112.

Faludi, Susan. *Backlash: The Undeclared War Against American Women*. New York: Crown Publishers, 1991.

Fanon, Frantz. *Black Skin, White Masks*. London: Pluto Press, 1986.

———. "Concerning Violence." In *The Wretched of the Earth*, 35–106. New York: Grove Weidenfeld, 1963.

Fassin, Didier. "Humanitarianism as a Politics of Life." *Public Culture* 19,3 (2007), 499–520.

Fekete, Liz. *A Suitable Enemy: Racism, Migration and Islamophobia in Europe.* London: Pluto Press, 2009.

Feminist Majority Foundation. "Eleanor Smeal Urges President to Fulfill Promise to Afghan Women." *Feminist Daily News* (Washington), May 22, 2002. ⟨http://feminist.org/news/newsbyte/uswirestory.asp?id=6544⟩. Accessed June 6, 2002.

Fennell, David A., and David C. Malloy. *Codes of Ethics in Tourism: Practice, Theory, Synthesis.* Toronto: Channel View Publications, 2007.

Ferguson, James. "Decomposing Modernity: History and Hierarchy after Development." In *Postcolonial Studies and Beyond*, edited by Ania Loomba et al., 166–81. Durham, NC: Duke University Press, 2005.

Ferguson, Niall. Interview by Lawrence A. Tish, "The War of the World: Conversation with Niall Ferguson." Institute for International Studies, University of California, Berkeley, 2006. ⟨http://globetrotter.berkeley.edu/people6/Ferguson/ferguson06-con5.html⟩. Accessed March 10, 2010.

Fernandes, Leela. "The Politics of Forgetting: Class Politics, State Power and the Restructuring of Urban Space in India." *Urban Studies* 41,12 (2004), 2415–430.

Fernandez, Sonya. "The Crusade over the Bodies of Women." *Patterns of Prejudice* 43,3/4 (2009), 269–86.

Fine, Michelle. *Disruptive Voices: The Possibilities of Feminist Research.* Ann Arbor: University of Michigan Press, 1992.

Fiske, John. *Media Matters: Race and Gender in U.S. Politics.* Rev. ed. Minneapolis: University of Minnesota Press, 1996.

Fleras, Augie, and Jean Lock Kunz. *Media and Minorities: Representing Diversity in a Multicultural Canada.* Toronto: Thompson Educational Publishing, 2001.

Foucault, Michel. "Governmentality." Translated by Rosi Braidotti and revised by Colin Gordon. In *The Foucault Effect: Studies in Governmentality*, edited by Graham Burchell, Colin Gordon, and Peter Miller, 87–104. Chicago: University of Chicago Press, 1991.

————. "Of Other Spaces." *Diacritics* 16,1 (1986), 22–27.

————. "Governmentality." *Ideology and Consciousness* 6 (1986), 5–21.

————. "The Subject and Power." In *Michel Foucault: Beyond Structuralism and Hermeneutics*, edited by Hubert Dreyfus and Paul Rabinow, 208–26. Chicago: University of Chicago Press, 1983.

————. *Power/Knowledge: Selected Interviews and Other Writings.* New York: Pantheon Books, 1980.

Frankenberg, Ruth, ed. *Displacing Whiteness: Essays in Social and Cultural Criticism.* Durham, NC: Duke University Press, 1997.

————. *White Women, Race Matters: The Social Construction of Whiteness.* Minneapolis: University of Minnesota Press, 1993.

Franks, Mary Anne. "Obscene Undersides: Women and Evil between the Taliban and the United States." *Hypatia: A Journal of Feminist Philosophy* 18,1 (2003), 135–56.

Freire, Paulo. *Pedagogy of the Oppressed.* New York: Continuum, 1998.

Gabriel, John. *Whitewash: Racialized Politics and the Media.* London: Routledge, 1998.

Ghafour, H. "Beauticians Without Borders Teach Basics to Afghan Women." *The Globe and Mail* (Toronto), February 24, 2004, A1.

Goddard, John. "Why Ottawa Saw an 'Imposter' in Mohamud Case." *Toronto Star*, September 30, 2009, A1, A19.

————. "Consular File Shows How Case Was Spun." *Toronto Star*, October 2, 2009, GT1, GT4.

Goldberg, David Theo. *The Threat of Race: Reflections on Racial Neoliberalism.* Malden, MA: Wiley Blackwell, 2009.

————. "Racial Europeanization." *Ethnic and Racial Studies* 29,2 (2006), 331–64.

————. *The Racial State.* Cambridge, MA: Blackwell Publishing, 2002.

————. *Racist Culture: Philosophy and the Politics of Meaning.* Cambridge, MA: Blackwell Publishing, 1993.

Gordon, Linda. "The 'Underclass' and the U.S. Welfare State." *The Socialist Register* 31 (1995), 163–87.

Goulding, Warren. *Just Another Indian: A Serial Killer and Canada's Indifference.* Calgary: Fifth House Publishers, 2001.

Green, Joyce, ed. *Making Space for Indigenous Feminism.* Halifax: Fernwood, 2007.

Greenberger, Allen J. *The British Image of India: A Study in the Literature of Imperialism 1880–1960.* London: Oxford University Press, 1969.

Grewal, Inderpal. "On the New Global Feminism and the Family of Nations: Dilemmas of Transnational Feminist Practice." In *Talking Visions: Multicultural Feminism in a Transnational Age*, edited by Ella Shohat, 501–30. Cambridge, MA: MIT Press, 1998.

Grewal, Inderpal, and Caren Kaplan. "Warrior Marks: Global Feminism's Neo-Colonial Discourse in a Multicultural Context." *Camera Obscura* 39 (1996), 4–33.

Hackett, Robert A., Richard Gruneau, Donald Gutstein, Timothy A. Gibson, and NewsWatch Canada. *The Missing News: Filters and Blind Spots in Canada's Press.* Ottawa: Canadian Centre for Policy Alternatives and Toronto: Garamond Press, 2000.

Hage, Ghassan. *Against Paranoid Nationalism: Searching for Hope in a Shrinking Society.* Annandale, NSW: Pluto Press Australia, 2003.

Hagedorn, Jessica. "Asian Women in Film: No Joy, No Luck." In *Facing Difference: Race, Gender, and Mass Media*, edited by Shirley Biagi and Marilyn Kern-Foxworth, 32–37. Thousand Oaks, CA: Pine Forge Press, 1997.

Hall, Stuart. "Race: The Floating Signifier (Transcript)." Media Education Foundation, 1997. ⟨http://www.mediaed.org/assets/products/407/transcript_407 .pdf⟩. Accessed October 7, 2009.

————, ed. *Representation: Cultural Representation and Signifying Practices.* London: Sage and The Open University, 1997.

————. "The Whites of Their Eyes: Racist Ideologies and the Media." In *The Media Reader*, edited by Manuel Alvarado and John O. Thompson, 9–23. London: British Film Institute, 1990.

Hall, Stuart, Chas Critcher, Tony Jefferson, and Brian Roberts. *Policing the Crisis: Mugging, the State and Law and Order.* London: MacMillan Press, 1978.

Harjo, Joy, and Gloria Bird. *Reinventing the Enemy's Language: Contemporary Native Women's Writing of North America*. New York: W.W. Norton, 1997.

Haylett, Chris. 2001. "Illegitimate Subjects? Abject Whites, Neoliberal Modernization, and Middle-Class Multiculturalism." *Environment and Planning D: Society and Space* 19,3 (2001), 351–70.

Heinrich, Jeff. "Politics 101: The Art of Staying Calm in the Event of Obnoxious Questioning." *The Gazette* (Montreal), September 13, 2008, A15.

Henry, Frances, and Carol Tator, eds. *Racism in the Canadian University: Demanding Social Justice, Inclusion, and Equity*. Toronto: University of Toronto Press, 2009.

_____. *Discourses of Domination: Racial Bias in the Canadian English-Language Press*. Toronto: University of Toronto Press, 2002.

Henry, Frances, Carol Tator, Winston Mattis, and Tim Rees. *The Colour of Democracy: Racism in Canadian Society*. 2nd ed. Toronto: Harcourt Brace, 2000.

Herman, Edward S., and Robert Waterman McChesney. *The Global Media: The New Missionaries of Corporate Capitalism*. Washington: Cassell, 1997.

Heron, Barbara. *Desire for Development: Whiteness, Gender and the Helping Imperative*. Waterloo, ON: Wilfrid Laurier University Press, 2008.

Hesford, Wendy S., and Wendy Kozol. *Just Advocacy? Women's Human Rights, Transnational Feminisms, and the Politics of Representation*. New Brunswick, NJ: Rutgers University Press, 2005.

Higgins-Desbiolles, Freya. "Justice Tourism and Alternative Globalisation." *Journal of Sustainable Tourism* 16,3 (2008), 345–64 .

_____. "More Than an 'Industry': The Forgotten Power of Tourism as a Social Force." *Tourism Management* 27,6 (2006), 1192–208.

Hirschkind, C., and S. Mahmood. "Feminism, the Taliban and the Politics of Counterinsurgency." *Anthropological Quarterly* 75,2 (2008), 339–54.

*Hollywood Harems*. Written and directed by Tania Kamal-Eldin. 25 min. New York: Women Make Movies, 1999. VHS/DVD.

Holt, Len. *The Summer That Didn't End: The Story of the Mississippi Civil Rights Project of 1964*. New York: Da Capo Press, 1992.

hooks, bell. *Ain't I A Woman: Black Women and Feminism*. Boston: South End Press, 1999.

_____. "Sisterhood: Political Solidarity between Women." In *Dangerous Liaisons: Gender, Nation, and Postcolonial Perspectives*, edited by Anne McClintock, Aamir Mufti, and Ella Shohat, 396–411. Minneapolis: University of Minnesota Press, 1997.

_____. *Talking Back: Thinking Feminist, Thinking Black*. Boston: South End Press, 1989.

Ignatiev, Noel. *How the Irish Became White*. New York: Routledge, 1996.

Indra, Doreen. "The Invisible Mosaic: Women, Ethnicity and the Vancouver Press, 1905–1976." In *The Mass Media and Canadian Diversity*, edited by Stephen E. Nancoo and Robert Sterling Nancoo, 92–108. Mississauga, ON: Canadian Educators' Press, 1997.

_____. "The Invisible Mosaic: Women, Ethnicity and the Vancouver Press, 1905–1976." *Canadian Ethnic Studies* 13 (1981), 63–74.

International Women's Peace Service. "Application Pack for IWPS Volunteers in the West Bank." N.p.: International Women's Peace Service, 2005.

Jaimes-Guerrero, M. Annette. "Patriarchal Colonialism and Indigenism: Implications for Native Feminist Spirituality and Native Womanism." *Hypatia* 18,2 (2003), 58–69.

JanMohamed, Abdul R. "The Economy of Manichean Allegory: The Function of Racial Difference in Colonial Literature." *Critical Inquiry* 12,1 (1985), 59–87.

Jamarkani, Amira. "Narrating Baghdad: Representing the Truth of War in Popular Non-Fiction." *Critical Arts: A South-North Journal of Cultural and Media Studies* 2,1 (2007), 32–46.

Jiwani, Yasmin. "Soft Power – Policing the Border through Canadian TV Crime Drama." In *The Political Economy of Media and Power*, edited by Jeffery Klaehn, 275–93. New York: Peter Lang, 2010.

_____. "Helpless Maidens and Chivalrous Knights: Afghan Women in the Canadian Press." *University of Toronto Quarterly* 78,2 (2009), 728–44.

_____. " 'Culture' Depends on Who's Defining It." *The Vancouver Sun*, August 8, 2007, Op-Ed Page.

_____. *Discourses of Denial: Mediations of Race, Gender and Violence.* Vancouver: UBC Press, 2006.

_____. "War Talk – Engendering Terror: Race, Gender and Representation in Canadian Print Media." *International Journal of Media & Cultural Politics* 1,1 (2005), 15–21.

_____. "The Eurasian Female Hero(ine): Sydney Fox as the Relic Hunter." *Journal of Popular Film & Television* 32,4 (2005), 182–91.

_____. "The Great White North Encounters September 11: Race, Gender, and Nation in Canada's National Daily, *The Globe and Mail.*" *Social Justice* 32,4 (2005), 50–68.

_____. "The Exotic, the Erotic and the Dangerous: South Asian Women in Popular Film." *Canadian Woman Studies* 13,1 (1992), 42–46.

Jiwani, Yasmin, and Young, Mary Lynn. "Missing and Murdered Women: Reproducing Marginality in News Discourse." *Canadian Journal of Communication* 31,4 (2006), 895–917.

Joseph, Galen. "Taking Race Seriously: Whiteness in Argentina's National and Transnational Imaginary." *Identities* 7,3 (2000), 333–71.

Jung, Courtney. "The Politics of Indigenous Identity: Neo-Liberalism, Cultural Rights and the Mexican Zapatists." *Social Research* 7,2 (2003), 433–62.

Kamat, Sangeeta. "The Privatization of Public Interest: Theorizing NGO Discourse in a Neoliberal Era." *Review of International Political Economy* 11,1 (2004), 155–76.

Kaplan, Caren. "The Politics of Location as Transnational Feminist Practice." In *Scattered Hegemonies: Postmodernity and Transnational Feminist Practices*, edited by Inderpal Grewal and Caren Kaplan, 37–52. Minnesota: University of Minnesota Press, 1994.

Karim, Karim H. *Islamic Peril.* Montreal: Black Rose Books, 2000.

Kelley, Ninette, and Michael Trebilcock. *The Making of the Mosaic: A History of Canadian Immigration Policy.* Toronto: University of Toronto Press, 2000.

Kerr, Derek. "Beheading the King and Enthroning the Market: A Critique of Foucauldian Governmentality." *Science & Society* 63,2 (1999), 173–202.

Khan, Shahnaz. "Between Here and There: Feminist Solidarity and Afghan Women." *Genders Online* 33 (2001). ⟨http://www.genders.org/g33/g33_kahn .html⟩. Accessed June 15, 2003, and June 1, 2004.

Kincaid, Jamaica. *A Small Place.* New York: Plume, 1989.

King, Anthony D. "Speaking from the Margins: 'Postmodernism,' Transnationalism, and the Imagining of Contemporary Indian Urbanity." In *Globalization and the Margins,* edited by Richard Grant and Rennie Short, 72–90. New York: Palgrave Macmillan, 2002.

Kingsbury, Benedict. " 'Indigenous Peoples' as an International Legal Concept." In *Indigenous Peoples of Asia,* edited by R. H. Barnes et al., 13–34. Ann Arbor, MI: University of Michigan Association for Asian Studies, 1995.

Kline, Marlee. "Complicating the Ideology of Motherhood: Child Welfare Law and First Nations Women." In *Open Boundaries: A Canadian Women's Studies Reader,* edited by B. Crow and L. Gotell, 189–99. Toronto: Prentice Hill, 2005.

Kobayashi, Audrey. "Now You See Them, How You See Them: Women of Colour in Canadian Academia." In *Feminist Issues: Selected Papers from the WIN Symposia 2000–2001,* edited by S. Heald, 44–54. Ottawa: Humanities and Social Science Federation of Canada, 2002.

Kovacevic, Natasa. "Orientalizing Post-Communism: Europe's 'Wild East' in Literature and Film." *Reconstruction: Studies in Contemporary Culture* 8,4 (2008), 33. ⟨http://reconstruction.eserver.org/084/kovacevic.sthml⟩. Accessed March 22, 2010.

Kozloff, Nikolas. "Meet South America's New Secessionists: From a Texan Venezuelan to an Ecuadorian Giuliani." *Counterpunch* (May 30, 2008). ⟨http://www.counterpunch.org/kozloff05302008.html⟩. Accessed March 22, 2010.

Krishna, Sankaran. "The Bomb, Biography and the Indian Middle Class." *Economic and Political Weekly* 41,23 (2006), 2327–331.

————. "Race, Amnesia and the Education of International Relations." *Alternatives: Global, Local, Political* 26,4 (2001), 401–24.

Kunz, Jean Lock, and Augie Fleras. "Visible Minority Women in Mainstream Advertising: Distorted Mirror or Looking Glass?" *Atlantis: A Women's Studies Journal* 22,2 (1998), 27–38.

Kuokkanen, Rauna. "Sámi Women, Autonomy, and Decolonization in the Age of Globalization." *Act 4: Finnish Sapmi* (2006), 1–37.

Kurti, Laszlo. "Globalisation and the Discourse of Otherness in the 'New' Eastern and Central Europe." In *The Politics of Multiculturalism in the New Europe,* edited by Tariq Modood and Pnina Werbner, 29–53. London: Zed Books, 1997.

Kuus, Merje. *Geopolitics Reframed: Security and Identity in Europe's Eastern Enlargement.* New York: Palgrave Macmillan, 2007.

————. "Europe's Eastern Expansion and the Reinscription of Otherness in East-Central Europe." *Progress in Human Geography* 28,4 (2004), 472–89.

Lalvani, Suren. "Consuming the Exotic Other." *Critical Studies in Mass Communication* 12,3 (1995), 263–86.

Larocque, Emma. "My Home Town Northern Canada South Africa." In *Native Poetry in Canada: A Contemporary Anthology,* edited by Jeannette C. Armstrong and Lally Grauer, 154–59. Peterborough, ON: Broadview Press, 2001.

Lawrence, Bonita, and Kim Anderson. "Introduction to 'Indigenous Women': The State of Our Nations." *Atlantis: A Women's Studies Journal* 29 (2005), 1–6.

Lawson, Victoria, Richa Nagar, et al. "Locating Globalization: Feminist (Re)readings of the Subjects and Spaces of Globalization." *Economic Geography* 78 (2002), 257–84.

Lazreg, Marnia. "The Perils of Writing as a Woman on Women in Algeria." *Feminist Studies* 14,1 (1988), 81–107.

Lenk, Helle-Mai. "The Case of Émilie Ouimet: News Discourse on Hijab and the Construction of Québécois National Identity." In *Anti-Racist Feminism*, edited by Agnes Calliste and George Dei, 73–88. Halifax: Fernwood, 2000.

Lévi-Strauss, Claude. *The Savage Mind*. Chicago: University of Chicago Press, 1966.

———. "The Effectiveness of Symbols." In *Structural Anthropology*, translated by C. Jacobson and B. G. Schoepf, 186–205. New York: Basic Books, 1963.

Lewis, Reina. *Gendering Orientalism, Race, Femininity and Representation*. New York: Routledge, 1996.

Li, Peter S. "Unneighbourly Houses or Unwelcome Chinese: The Social Construction of Race in the Battle over 'Monster Homes' in Vancouver, Canada." *International Journal of Comparative Race and Ethnic Relations* 1,1 (1994), 14–33.

Lindberg, Tracey. "What Do You Call an Indian Woman with a Law Degree? Nine Aboriginal Women at the University of Saskatchewan College of Law Speak Out." *Canadian Journal of Women and the Law* 9,2 (1996), 301–35.

Lisle, Debbie. "Joyless Cosmopolitans: The Moral Economy of Ethical Tourism." In *Cultural Political Economy*, edited by Jacqueline Best and Matthew Paterson, 139–58. New York: Routledge, 2009.

Lopez, Antoinette Sedillo. "Comparative Analysis of Women's Issues: Toward a Contextualized Methodology." In *Global Critical Race Feminisms*, edited by Adrien Katherine Wing and Angela Y. Davis, 67–80. New York: New York University Press, 2000.

Lorde, Audre. *Sister Outsider: Essays and Speeches*. Trumansburg, NY: Crossing Press, 1984.

Louw, Eric P. "The 'War against Terrorism': A Public Relations Challenge for the Pentagon." *Gazette: The International Journal for Communication Studies* 65,3 (2003), 211–30.

Lowe, Lisa. *Critical Terrains: French and British Orientalisms*. Ithaca, NY: Cornell University Press, 1994.

Lubiano, Wahneema. "Black Ladies, Welfare Queens, and State Minstrels: Ideological War by Narrative Means." In *Race-ing Justice, En-gendering Power: Essays on Anita Hill, Clarence Thomas, and the Construction of Social Reality*, edited by Toni Morrison, 323–61. New York: Pantheon Books, 1992.

Macdonald, Myra. "Muslim Women and the Veil: Problems of Image and Voice in Media Representations." *Feminist Media Studies* 6,1 (2006), 7–23.

MacIvor, Sharon. "A Social Policy Agenda for First Nations Women." In *Critical Choices, Turbulent Times*, edited by Frank Tester, Chris McNiven, and Robert Case, 100–107. Vancouver: University of British Columbia School of Social Work, 1996.

MacLean, John. *Canadian Savage Folk: The Native Tribes of Canada*. Toronto: William Briggs, 1896.

Mahony, Liam, and Luis Enrique Eguren. *Unarmed Bodyguards: International Accompaniment for the Protection of Human Rights*. Hartford, CT: Kumarian Press, 1997.

Mahrouse, Gada. "Feel Good Tourism: The Ethical Option for Socially-Conscious Westerners." *ACME: An International E-Journal of Critical Geographies*, Special Issue: Gender, Power and Transcultural Relations. Forthcoming.

———. "Transnational Activists, News Media Representations, and Racialized

'Politics of Life': The Christian Peacemaker Team Kidnapping in Iraq." *Citizenship Studies* 13,4 (2009), 311–31.

―――. "Race-Conscious Transnational Activists with Cameras: Mediators of Compassion." *International Journal of Cultural Studies* 11,1 (2008), 87–105.

―――. "Producing Peaceful Citizens through a Lesson on the FTAA Quebec Summit Protests." *Canadian Journal of Education*, Special Issue: Democracy and Education 29,2 (2006), 436–53.

Mahtani, Minelle. "Representing Minorities: Canadian Media and Minority Identities." *Canadian Ethnic Studies* 33,3 (2001), 93–133.

Malik, Kenan. *The Meaning of Race: Race, History and Culture in Western Society.* New York: New York University Press, 1996.

Mani, Lata. *Contentious Traditions: The Debate on Sati in India.* Berkeley: University of California Press, 1998.

Manji, Irshad. *The Trouble with Islam: A Wake-Up Call for Honesty and Change.* Toronto: Random House, 2003.

Marable, Manning. "Globalization and Racialization." *Znet* (August 13, 2004). ⟨http://www.zcommunications.org/globalization-and-racialization-by-manning-marable⟩. Accessed May 20, 2006.

Maracle, Lee. *I Am Woman: A Native Perspective on Sociology and Feminism.* Vancouver: Press Gang Publishers, 1996.

Marx, Anthony. "Race Making and the Nation-State." *World Politics* 48,2 (1996), 180–208.

Mathieu, Sarah-Jane. "North of the Colour Line: Sleeping Car Porters and the Battle Against Jim Crow on Canadian Rails, 1880–1920." *Labour/Le Travail* (2001). ⟨http://www.historycooperative.org/journals/llt/47/02mathie.html⟩. Accessed March 10, 2010.

Matsuda, Mari, Charles R. Lawrence III, Richard Delgado, and Kimberlè Williams Crenshaw. *Words that Wound: Critical Race Theory, Assaultive Speech, and the First Amendment.* Boulder, CO: Westview Press, 1993.

Mayer, Lorraine F. "A Return to Reciprocity." *Hypatia* 22,3 (2007), 22–42.

Mazrui, Ali. "Global Apartheid? Race and Religion in the New World Order." In *The Gulf War and the New World Order: International Relations of the Middle East*, edited by Tareq Y. Ismael and Jacqueline S. Ismael, 521–35. Gainesville: University Press of Florida, 1994.

McBratney, John. "Images of Indian Women in Rudyard Kipling: A Case of Doubling Discourse." *Inscriptions* 3,4 (1988), 47–57.

McClintock, Anne. *Imperial Leather, Race, Gender and Sexuality in the Colonial Contest.* New York: Routledge, 1995.

McLaren, Deborah. *Rethinking Tourism and Ecotravel.* 2nd ed. Bloomfield, CT: Kumarian Press, 2003.

Melamed, Jodi. "The Spirit of Neoliberalism: From Racial Liberalism to Neoliberal Multiculturalism." *Social Text* 24,4 89 (2006), 1–24.

Messor-Davidow, Ellen. *Disciplining Feminism: From Social Activism to Academic Discourse.* Durham, NC: Duke University Press, 2002.

Michaels, Eric. "For a Cultural Future: Frances Jupurrurla Makes TV at Yuendumu." *Art and Criticism Monograph Series* 3 (1987), 1–80.

Miller, John, and Kimberly Prince. *The Imperfect Mirror, Analysis of Minority Picture and News in Six Canadian Newspapers.* Toronto: Ryerson Polytechnic University School of Journalism, 1994.

Mills, Charles W. "Racial Liberalism." *PMLA* 123,5 (2008), 1380–97.

————. *From Class to Race: Essays in White Marxism and Black Radicalism.* Lanham, MD: Rowman and Littlefield, 2003.

Moghadam, Valentine. "Afghan Women and Transnational Feminism." *Middle East Women's Studies Review* 16,3/4 (2001), 1–12.

Mohanram, Rhadika. "The Construction of Place: Maori Feminism and Nationalism in Aotearoa/New Zealand." *NWSA* 8,1 (1996), 50–69.

Mohanty, Chandra Talpade. *Feminism without Borders: Decolonizing Theory, Practicing Solidarity.* Durham, NC: Duke University Press, 2003

————. "Cartographies of Struggle: Third World Women and the Politics of Feminism." In *Third World Women and the Politics of Feminism,* edited by Chandra Talpade Mohanty, Ann Russo, and Lourdes Torres, 1–47. Bloomington: Indiana University Press, 1991.

————. "Under Western Eyes: Feminist Scholarship and Colonial Discourses." In *Third World Women and the Politics of Feminism,* edited by Chandra Talpade Mohanty, Ann Russo, and Lourdes Torres, 53–80. Bloomington: Indiana University Press, 1991. First published in *Feminist Review* 30 (1988), 61–88.

Montgomery, Charles. "Revolutionary Tourism." *The Vancouver Sun,* March 10, 2001. ⟨http://www.charlesmontgomery.ca/tourism.html⟩.

Monture-Angus, Patricia. *Thunder in My Soul: A Mohawk Woman Speaks.* Halifax: Fernwood, 1995.

Monture, Patricia. " 'Doing Academia Differently': Confronting 'Whiteness' in the University." In *Racism in the Canadian University: Demanding Social Justice, Inclusion and Equity,* edited by Frances Henry and Carol Tator, 76–105. Toronto: University of Toronto Press, 2009.

Monture, Patricia, and Patricia D. McGuire, eds. *First Voices: An Aboriginal Women's Reader.* Toronto: Inanna Publications, 2009.

Morales, Aurora Levins. *Medicine Stories: History, Culture and the Politics of Integrity.* Cambridge, MA: South End Press, 1998.

Moreton-Robinson, Aileen. "Troubling Business: Difference and Whiteness within Feminism." *Australian Feminist Studies* 15,33 (2000), 343–52.

Morrison, Toni. "The Official Story: Dead Man Golfing." In *Birth of a Nation'hood: Gaze, Script, and Spectacle in the O.J. Simpson Case,* edited by Toni Morrison and Claudia Brodsky Lacour, vi–xxviii. New York: Pantheon Books, 1997.

Muscati, Sina Ali. "Arab/Muslim 'Otherness': The Role of Racial Constructions in the Gulf War and the Continuing Crisis with Iraq." *Journal of Muslim Minority Affairs* 22,1 (2002), 131–48.

Nahanee, Anne Teresa. "Indian Women, Sex Equality, and the Charter." In *Women and the Canadian State,* edited by Caroline Andrew, 89–103. Montreal: McGill-Queen's University Press, 1997.

Napoleon, Val. "Extinction by Number: Colonialism Made Easy." *Canadian Journal of Law and Society* 16,1 (2001), 113–45.

Narayan, Uma. *Dislocating Cultures: Identities, Traditions and Third World Feminism.* London: Routledge, 1997.

Nayak, Meghana. "Orientalism and 'Saving' U.S. State Identity after 9/11." *International Journal of Feminist Politics* 8,1 (2006), 42–61.

Newdick, Vivian. "The Indigenous Woman as Victim of Her Own Culture in Neo-Liberal Mexico." *Cultural Dynamics* 17,1 (2005), 73–92.

Ng, Roxana. *The Politics of Community Services: Immigrant Women, Class, and State.* 2nd ed. Halifax: Fernwood, 1996.

Ng, Roxana, Joyce Scane, and Pat Staton. *Anti-Racism, Feminism, and Critical Approaches to Education.* Westport, CT: Bergin and Garvey, 1995.

Noelle-Karimi, Christine. "History Lessons: In Afghanistan's Decades of Confrontations with Modernity, Women Have Always Been the Focus of Conflict." *The Women's Review of Books* 19,7 (2002), 1, 3–4.

Nye, Joseph S. Jr., and William A. Owens. "America's Information Edge." *Foreign Affairs* 75,2 (1996), 20–36.

Oliver, Mary Beth. "African American Men as 'Criminal and Dangerous': Implications of Media Portrayals of Crime on the 'Criminalization' of African American Men." *Journal of African American Studies* 7,2 (2003), 3–18.

Patai, Daphne, and Noretta Koertege. *Professing Feminism: Cautionary Tales from the Strange World of Women's Studies.* New York: Basic Books, 1994.

Pattullo, Polly, and Orely Minelli. *The Ethical Travel Guide: Your Passport to Exciting Alternative Holidays.* London: Earthscan Publications, 2009.

Pearson, Patricia. "See No Evil, No More." *The Globe and Mail* (Toronto), April 19, 2003, A19.

Philips, M. Nourbese. *Frontiers: Essays and Writings in Racism and Culture.* Stratford, ON: Mercury Press, 1993.

Prashad, Vijay. *The Darker Nations: A People's History of the Third World.* New York: New Press, 2007.

Ramesh, Randeep. "Bhopal Water Still Toxic 25 Years After Deadly Gas Leak, Study Finds." *Guardian* (London), December 1, 2009. ⟨http://www.guardian.co.uk/world/2009/dec/01/bhopal-chemical-studies-toxic-levels⟩. Accessed March 22, 2010.

Ramirez, Reyna. "Race, Tribal Nation, and Gender: A Native Feminist Approach to Belonging." *Meridians: Feminism, Race, Transnationalism* 7,2 (2007), 22–40.

Ramos, Alcita. *Indigenism.* Madison: University of Wisconsin Press, 1998.

Rankin, L. Pauline, and Jill Vickers. "Women's Movements and State Feminism: Integrating Diversity into Public Policy." In *Feminisms and Womanisms: A Women's Studies Reader,* edited by Althea Prince and Susan Silva-Wayne, 43–51. Toronto: Women's Press, 2004.

Rawls, John. *A Theory of Justice.* Rev. ed. Cambridge, MA: Belknap Press of Harvard University Press, 2003.

Ray, Beth. *Bitters in the Honey: Tales of Hope and Disappointment across Divides of Race and Time.* Fayetteville: University of Arkansas Press, 1999.

Raymond, Eliza Marguerite, and C. Michael Hall. "The Development of Cross-Cultural (Mis)understanding through Volunteer Tourism." *Journal of Sustainable Tourism,* 16,5 (2010), 530–43.

Razack, Sherene H. *Casting Out: The Eviction of Muslims from Western Law and Politics.* Toronto: University of Toronto Press, 2008.

————. "Geopolitics, Culture Clash and Gender After 911." *Social Justice Review* 32,4 (2005), 11–32.

————. "Imperilled Muslim Women, Dangerous Muslim Men and Civilised Europeans: Legal and Social Responses to Forced Marriages." *Feminist Legal Studies* 12,2 (2004), 129–74.

_____. *Dark Threats and White Knights: The Somalia Affair, Peacekeeping, and the New Imperialism*. Toronto: University of Toronto Press, 2004.

_____, ed. *Race, Space, and the Law: Unmapping White Settler Society*. Toronto: Between the Lines, 2002.

_____. "Gendered Racial Violence and Spatialized Justice: The Murder of Pamela George." *Canadian Journal of Law and Society* 15,2 (2000), 91–130.

_____. "Simple Logic: The Identity Documents Rule and the Fantasy of a Nation Besieged and Betrayed." *Journal of Law and Social Policy* 15 (2000), 181–211.

_____. *Looking White People in the Eye: Gender, Race, and Culture in Courtrooms and Classrooms*. Toronto: University of Toronto Press, 1998.

_____. "Race, Space, and Prostitution: The Making of the Bourgeois Subject." *Canadian Journal of Women and the Law* 10,2 (1998), 338–76.

_____. "Storytelling for Social Change." In *Returning the Gaze: Essays on Racism, Feminism and Politics*, edited by Himani Bannerji, 83–100. Toronto: Sister Vision Press, 1993.

Reed, Betsy, ed. *Nothing Sacred: Women Respond to Religious Fundamentalism and Terror*. New York: National Books, 2002.

Rich, Adrienne. "Notes Toward a Politics of Location." In *Feminist Postcolonial Theory: A Reader*, edited by Reina Lewis and Sara Mills, 29–42. London: Routledge, 2003.

Richardson, Laurel. *Fields of Play: Constructing an Academic Life*. New Brunswick, NJ: Rutgers University Press, 1997.

_____. "Narrative and Sociology." *Journal of Contemporary Ethnography* 19 (1990), 116–35.

Riches, William Terence Martin. *The Civil Rights Movement: Struggle and Resistance*. 2nd ed. New York: Palgrave Macmillan, 2004.

Riley, Robin L., Chandra Talpade Mohanty, and Minnie Bruce Pratt, eds. *Feminism and War: Confronting U.S. Imperialism*. London: Zed Books, 2008.

Robinson, Gertrude J. *Gender, Journalism, and Equity: Canadian, U.S., and European Perspectives*. Cresskill, NJ: Hampton Press, 2005.

Rose, Nikolas. *Powers of Freedom: Reframing Political Thought*. Cambridge: Cambridge University Press, 1999.

Ross, Karen. "Selling Women (Down the River): Gendered Relations and the Political Economy of Broadcast News." In *Sex & Money: Feminism and Political Economy in the Media*, edited by Eileen Meehan and Ellen Riordan, 112–29. Minneapolis: University of Minnesota Press, 2002.

Routledge, Paul. "Critical Geopolitics and Terrains of Resistance." *Political Geography* 15,6/7 (1996), 509–31.

Roy, Arundhati. "Listening to Grasshoppers: On Genocide, Denial and Celebration." *Communalism Watch* (January 26, 2008). ⟨http://communalism .blogspot.com/2008/01/arundhati-roy-on-genocide-denial-and.html⟩. Accessed March 22, 2010.

Russo, Ann. "The Feminist Majority Foundation's Campaign to Stop Gender Apartheid." *International Feminist Journal of Politics* 8,4 (2006), 557–80.

Said, Edward. *Covering Islam: How the Media and Experts Determine How We See the Rest of the World*. New York: Pantheon Books, 1981.

_____. *Orientalism*. New York: Random House, 1978.

Samuel, Edith, and Njoki Wane. " 'Unsettling Relations': Racism and Sexism Expe-

rienced by Faculty of Color in a Predominantly White Canadian University."
*The Journal of Negro Education* 74,1 (2005), 76–87.

Scheyvens, Regina. "Poverty Tourism." *Development Bulletin* 55 (2001), 18–20.

Schochet, Gordon. "Tradition as Politics and the Politics of Tradition." In *Question of Tradition*, edited by Mark Salber Phillips and Gordon Schochet. Toronto: University of Toronto Press, 2004.

Schröder, Ingo W. "The Political Economy of Tribalism in North America: Neo-Tribal Capitalism?" *Anthropological Theory* 3,4 (2003), 335–56.

Schueller, Malini Johar. *Locating Race: Global Sites of Post-Colonial Citizenship.* Albany: State University of New York Press, 2009.

Scott, James C. *Domination and the Arts of Resistance: Hidden Transcripts.* New Haven: Yale University Press, 1990.

Scott, Joan Wallach, ed. *Women's Studies on the Edge.* Durham, NC: Duke University Press, 2008.

————. *The Politics of the Veil.* Princeton: Princeton University Press, 2007.

Secor, Anna J. " 'An Unrecognizable Condition Has Arrived': Law, Violence and the State of Exception in Turkey." In *Violent Geographies: Fear, Terror and Political Violence*, edited by Derek Gregory and Allan Pred, 37–54. New York: Routledge, 2007.

Shade, Leslie Regan, and Michael Lithgow. "The Cultures of Democracy: How Ownership and Public Participation Shape Canada's Media Systems." In *Mediascapes: New Patterns in Canadian Communication*, 3rd ed., edited by Leslie Regan Shade, 200–20. Toronto: Nelson Publishers, 2010.

Shaheen, Jack G. *Reel Bad Arabs: How Hollywood Vilifies a People.* New York: Olive Branch Press, 2001.

Sharify-Funk, Meena. "Representing Canadian Muslims: Media, Muslim Advocacy Organizations, and Gender in the Ontario Shari'ah Debate." *Global Media Journal, Canadian Edition* 2,2 (2009), 73–89.

Sharma, Nandita. *Home Economics: Nationalism and the Making of "Migrant Workers" in Canada.* Toronto: University of Toronto Press, 2006.

Shohat, Ella. "Area Studies, Gender Studies, and the Cartographies of Knowledge." *Social Text* 20,3 (2002), 67–78.

Shohat, Ella, and Robert Stam. *Unthinking Eurocentrism, Multiculturalism and the Media.* London: Routledge, 1994.

Siegfried, André. *The Race Question in Canada.* London: Eveleigh Nash, 1907.

Silvera, Makeda, ed. *The Other Woman: Women of Colour in Contemporary Canadian Literature.* Toronto: Sister Vision Press, 1995.

————. *Silenced: Caribbean Domestic Workers Talk with Makeda Silvera.* 2nd ed. Toronto: Sister Vision Press, 1989; Toronto: Williams Wallace Publishers, 1983.

Silverblatt, Irene M. *Modern Inquisitions: Peru and the Colonial Origins of the Civilized World.* Durham, NC: Duke University Press, 2005.

Simpson, J.S. "Easy Talk, White Talk, Back Talk: Some Reflections on the Meaning of Our Words." *Journal of Contemporary Ethnography* 25 (1996), 372–89.

Singh, Nikhil Pal. *Black Is a Country: Race and the Unfinished Struggle for Democracy.* Cambridge, MA: Harvard University Press, 2004.

Sinha, Indra. "Bhopal: 25 Years of Poison" *Guardian* (London), December 3, 2009. ⟨http://www.guardian.co.uk/environment/2009/dec/04/bhopal-25-years-indra-sinha⟩. Accessed March 22, 2010.

Skeggs, Beverley. "The Re-Branding of Class: Propertising Culture." In *Rethinking Class: Culture, Identities, Lifestyles,* edited by Fiona Devine et al., 46–68. New York: Palgrave Macmillan, 2005.

————. *Class, Self and Culture.* London: Routledge, 2004.

Smeal, Eleanor. "Eleanor Smeal Urges President to Fulfill Promise to Afghan Women," *Feminist Daily News* (Washington), May 22, 2002. ⟨http://feminist .org/news/newsbyte/uswirestory.asp?id=6544⟩. Accessed June 6, 2002.

Smith, Andrea. "Introduction." *The Revolution Will Not Be Funded: Beyond the Non-profit Industrial Complex,* ed. Incite! Women of Color Against Violence. Cambridge, MA: South End Press, 2007.

————. "Heteropatriarchy and the Three Pillars of White Supremacy: Rethinking Women of Color Organizing." In *The Color of Violence: The Incite! Anthology,* edited by Incite! Women of Color Against Violence, 63–73. Cambridge, MA: South End Press, 2006.

Smith, Linda Tuhiwai. *Decolonizing Methodologies: Research and Indigenous Peoples.* London: Zed Books, 1999.

Smith, Malinda S., ed. *Securing Africa: Post-9/11 Discourses on Terrorism.* Aldershot, UK: Ashgate Publishing, 2010.

————. "Racism and Motivated Ignorance." *The Ardent: Anti-Racism and Decolonization Review* 1,1 (2008), vi–vii.

Smolash, Wendy Naava. "Mark of Cain(ada): Racialized Security Discourse in Canada's National Newspapers." *University of Toronto Quarterly* 78,2 (2009), 745–63.

Spivak, Gayatri Chakravorty. "Can the Subaltern Speak?" In *The Post-Colonial Studies Reader,* edited by Bill Ashcroft, Gareth Griffiths, and Helen Tiffin, 28–37. London: Routledge, 2006.

————. "Response to 'The Difference Within: Feminism and Critical Theory.'" In *The Difference Within: Feminism and Critical Theory,* edited by Elizabeth Meese and Alice Parker, 208–220. Philadelphia: John Benjamins Publishing, 1989.

St. Denis, Verna. "Feminism Is for Everybody: Aboriginal Women, Feminism and Diversity." In *Making Space for Indigenous Feminism,* edited by Joyce Green, 33–52. Halifax: Fernwood, 2007.

Stabile, Carole A., and Deepa Kumar. "Unveiling Imperialism: Media, Gender and the War on Afghanistan." *Media, Culture & Society* 27,5 (2005), 765–82.

Stasiulis, Daiva. "Relational Positionalities of Nationalisms, Racisms and Feminisms." In *Between Woman and Nation: Nationalisms, Transnational Feminisms, and the State,* edited by Caren Kaplan, Norma Alarcón, and Minoo Moallem, 182–218. Durham, NC: Duke University Press, 1999.

Steuter, Erin, and Deborah Wills. *At War with Metaphor, Media, Propaganda, and Racism in the War on Terror.* Lanham, MD: Lexington Books, 2008.

Stolba, C. "Feminists Go To War. The Women's Quarterly, Independent Women's Forum" (2002). ⟨http://www.iwf.org/pubs/twq/Winter2002i.shtml⟩. Accessed June 16, 2002.

Stone-Mediatore, Shari. "Chandra Mohanty and the Revaluing of 'Experience.'" In *Decentering the Center: Philosophy for a Multicultural, Postcolonial and Feminist World,* edited by Uma Narayan and Sandra Harding, 110–27. Bloomington: Indiana University Press, 2000.

Stoper, Emily. *The Student Nonviolent Coordinating Committee: The Growth of*

*Radicalism in a Civil Rights Organization*. New York: Carlson Publishing, 1989.

Sudbury, Julia. *Global Lockdown: Race, Gender and the Prison-Industrial Complex*. London: Routledge, 2005.

Taiaiake, Alfred. *Peace, Power, Righteousness: An Indigenous Manifesto*. Oxford: Oxford University Press, 1999.

Task Force on Federally Sentenced Women. *Creating Choices: The Report of the Task Force on Federally Sentenced Women*. Ottawa: Correctional Service of Canada, 1990.

Thobani, Sunera. "Gender and Empire: Veilomentaries and the War on Terror." In *Global Communications: Toward a Transcultural Political Economy*, edited by Paula Chakravartty and Yuezhi Zhao, 219–42. Lanham, MD: Rowman and Littlefield, 2008.

————. "White Wars: Western Feminisms and the 'War on Terror.'" *Feminist Theory* 8,2 (2007), 169–85.

————. *Exalted Subjects: Studies in the Making of Race and Nation in Canada*. Toronto: University of Toronto Press, 2007.

————. "War Frenzy." *Atlantis: A Women's Studies Journal* 27,1 (2002), 5–11.

Thompson, Becky. *A Promise and a Way of Life*. Minneapolis: University of Minnesota Press, 2001.

Todd, Sharon. "Veiling the 'Other,' Unveiling Our 'Selves': Reading Media Images of the Hijab Psychoanalytically to Move beyond Tolerance." *Canadian Journal of Education* 23,4 (1998), 438–51.

Todorova, Maria Nikolaeva. *Imagining the Balkans*. New York: Oxford University Press, 1997.

Treviño, A. Javier, Michelle Harris, and Derron Wallace. "What's So Critical about Critical Race Theory?" *Contemporary Justice Review* 11,1 (2008), 7–10.

Trinh, Minh-ha T. *Woman, Native, Other*. Bloomington: Indiana University Press, 1989.

Tsing, Anna. *The Realm of the Diamond Queen*. Princeton: Princeton University Press, 1993.

Turton, David, ed. *War and Ethnicity: Global Connections and Local Violence*. Rochester, NY: University of Rochester Press, 1997.

Udel, Lisa. "Revision and Resistance." *Frontier: A Journal of Women Studies* 22,2 (2001), 43–62.

Van Maanen, John. *Tales of the Field: On Writing Ethnography*. Chicago: University of Chicago Press, 1998.

Vivian, Bradford. "The Veil and the Visible." *Western Journal of Communication* 63,2 (1999), 115–39.

Voegelin, Eric. *Race and State*. Edited by Klaus Vondung. Translated by Ruth Hein. Baton Rouge: Louisiana State University Press, 1933.

Wacquant, Loic. "From Mass Slavery to Mass Incarceration: Rethinking the 'Race Question' in the US." *New Left Review* 13 (2002), 41–60.

Wane, Njoki, Riyad Ahmed Shahjahan, and Anne Wagner. "Walking the Talk: Decolonizing the Politics of Equity of Knowledge and Charting the Course for an Inclusive Curriculum in Higher Education." *Canadian Journal of Development Studies* 25,3 (2005), 499–510.

Weber, Cynthia. "Not Without My Sister(s): Imagining a Moral American in Kandahar." *International Feminist Journal of Politics* 7,3 (2005), 358–76.

Weber, Clare M. *Visions of Solidarity: U.S. Peace Activists in Nicaragua from War to Women's Activism and Globalization.* New York: Lexington Books, 2006.

Weir, Margaret. "From Equal Opportunity to 'the New Social Contract.' " In *Racism, the City and the State*, edited by Malcolm Cross and Michael Keith, 93–107. London: Routledge, 1993.

Werbner, Pnina. "Islamophobia: Incitement to Religious Hatred – Legislating a New Fear?" *Anthropology Today* 21,1 (2005), 5–9.

West, Cornel. "A Genealogy of Modern Racism." In *Race Critical Theories*, edited by Philomena Essed and David Theo Goldberg, 90–111. Malden, MA: Blackwell Publishers, 2002.

Wilkinson, Lynn R. "Hannah Arendt on Isak Dinesen: Between Storytelling and Theory." *Comparative Literature* 56,1 (2004), 77–98.

Williams, Patricia J. *Open House: Of Family, Friends, Food, Piano Lessons, and the Search for a Room of My Own.* New York: Farrar, Straus and Giroux, 2004.

———. *The Alchemy of Race and Rights: Diary of a Law Professor.* Cambridge, MA: Harvard University Press, 1992.

———. "The Emperor's New Clothes." In *Seeing a Color-blind Future: The Paradox of Race*, 3–16. New York: Farrar, Straus and Giroux, 1998.

Wiltenburg, Joy. "True Crime: The Origins of Modern Sensationalism." *American Historical Review* 109,5 (2004), 1377–404.

Wing, Adrien Katherine, ed. *Critical Race Feminism: A Reader.* 2nd ed. New York: New York University Press, 2003.

———. *Global Critical Race Feminism.* New York: New York University Press, 2000.

Winter, James. *Media Think.* Montreal: Black Rose Books, 2002.

———. *Democracy's Oxygen: How Corporations Control the News.* Montreal: Black Rose Books, 1997.

Wuthnow, Julie. "Deleuze in the Postcolonial: On Nomads and Indigenous Politics." *Feminist Theory* 3,2 (2002), 183–200.

Yeğenoğlu, Meyda. *Colonial Fantasies: Towards a Feminist Reading of Orientalism.* Cambridge: Cambridge University Press, 1998.

Young, Iris Marion. *Justice and the Politics of Difference.* Princeton: Princeton University Press, 1990.

Young-Bruehl, Elizabeth. "Hannah Arendt's Storytelling." *Social Research* 44,1 (1977), 183–90.

Zacharias, Usha. "Legitimizing Empire: Racial and Gender Politics of the War on Terrorism." *Social Justice* 30,2 (2003), 123–32.

Zine, Jasmin. "Unsettling the Nation: Gender, Race and Muslim Cultural Politics in Canada." *Studies in Ethnicity and Nationalism* 9,1 (2009), 146–93.

———. "Muslim Women and the Politics of Representation." *American Journal of Islamic Social Sciences* 19,4 (2002), 1–23.

Zine, Jasmin, Lisa K. Taylor, and Hilary E. Davis. "An Interview with Zarqa Nawaz." *Intercultural Education* 18,4 (2007), 379–82.

# Contributors

· · · · · · · · · · · · · · · · · · · · · · · · · · · · · · · · · · ·

**Isabel Altamirano-Jiménez** is an assistant professor in the Department of Political Science and Faculty of Native Studies at the University of Alberta. Her publications include "Nunavut: Whose Homeland, Whose Voices?" (2008) and "Indigenous Peoples and the Topography of Gender in Mexico and Canada" (2007).

**Sedef Arat-Koç** is an associate professor in the Department of Politics and Public Administration at Ryerson University. Her publications include "A Cultural Turn in Politics: Bourgeois Class Identity and White-Turk Discourses" (2007) and "Whose Transnationalism? Canada, 'Clash of Civilization' Discourse, and Arab and Muslim Canadians" (2006).

**Yasmin Jiwani** is an associate professor in the Department of Communications Studies at Concordia University and author of *Discourses of Denial: Mediations of Race, Gender and Violence* (2006) and co-editor of *Girlhood: Redefining the Limits* (2006).

**Gada Mahrouse** is an assistant professor at the Simone de Beauvoir Institute in the Faculty of Arts at Concordia University. She is the author of "Transnational Activists, News Media Representations, and Racialized 'Politics of Life'" (2009) and "Race-Conscious, Transnational Activists with Cameras" (2008).

**Patricia A. Monture** is a professor in the Department of Sociology at the University of Saskatchewan and the author of many books, including co-editor of *First Voices: An Aboriginal Women's Reader* (2009) and *Thunder in My Soul: A Mohawk Woman Speaks* (1995).

**Sherene H. Razack** is a professor in the Department of Sociology and Equity Studies in Education at OISE/University of Toronto. She is the author of numerous books, including *Casting Out: The Eviction of Muslims from Western Law and Politics* (2008) and *Looking White People in the Eye: Gender, Race, and Culture in Courtrooms and Classrooms* (1998).

**Malinda S. Smith** is an associate professor in the Department of Political Science at the University of Alberta. She is the editor of three books, including

213

*Securing Africa: Post-9/11 Discourses on Terrorism* (2010) and *Beyond the "African Tragedy": Discourses on Development and the Global Economy* (2006).

**Sunera Thobani** is an associate professor in Women's and Gender Studies in the Faculty of Arts and the director of the Centre for Studies in Race, Autobiography, Gender and Age (RAGA) at the University of British Columbia. She is the author of *Exalted Subjects: Studies in the Making of Race and Nation in Canada* (2007).

# Index

abandonment, 87–104; of Muslims, 7; role of state in, 10
Abdo, Nahla, xii
Abella, Rosalie, 40
ablism, 32
Aboriginal. *See* Indigenous
abortion, access to, 127
Abu-Lughod, Lila, 67
academic freedom, 44
academy: conduct in, 44–45; corporatization in, 39; equity in, 38–40; gender and whiteness in, 37–55; women hired in, 40. *See also* universities
Achakzai, Sitara, 71
accompaniment activism, 172, 175
Acoose, Janice: *Looking at the Words of Our People*, 1
activism, transnational solidarity, 169–84
affirmative action, 46
Afghanistan: Canadian soldiers in, 85n73; destruction of national sovereignty in, 134; invasion of, 7–8, 64, 128, 129–41, 163, 185n5; opposition to invasion in, 132–41; peacekeeping in, 76; refugees from, 88; Soviets in, 98; support for invasion in, 129–32; veil as legitimization for intervention in, 66; veiling in, 65
Afghan society, representations of as ultrapatriarchal, 71
Afghan women: born in Afghanistan vs. foreign-born, 72; diasporic, 72; "freeing" of, 7; media representation of, 68–73; oppressed, vs. Western women, 65; oppression of, 66–67; "saving" of, 138; transition of from victims to survivors, 68
Agamben, Giorgio, 90, 91, 96
agency: denial of, 127; Indigenous women's, 120; Western vs. non-Western understandings of, 121
Ahmed, Sara, 37, 46, 54, 170, 176

Aiken, Sharryn, 93–94, 98
AKP (Adalet ve Kalkınma Partisi), 167n54
Alfred, Taiaiake, 113
Algerian people, 97
al Qaeda, 138–39, 141
Amiel, Barbara, 142n3
amnesia, 10
Amnesty International, 6
ANC (African National Congress), 96
Anthias, Floya, 64
anti-Arab racism, 162–64
anti-capitalism, prison abolition and, 150
anti-colonialism, x, xvi, 130, 140; feminist critique of, 1, 3; praxis of, 9
anti-discrimination, 46
anti-feminist politics, 127
anti-globalization, 130
anti-immigrant sentiment, 7, 149, 163–64
anti-imperialism, 129, 130; prison abolition and, 150
anti-Muslim racism, 162–64
anti-Pinochet organizations, 99
anti-racism, x, xiv, xvi, 3, 50, 53, 129, 130, 140, 169; feminism and, 2, 8, 48; pedagogies of, 170; prison abolition and, 150
anti-refugee sentiment, 7, 149, 163–64
anti-Semitism, 130–32; vs. anti-Zionism, 132
anti-terrorism, 7
anti-violence movement, 127
apartheid: gender, 137–41; global, 163
Apartheid Wall, 174
Arabs, media portrayal of, 60, 63
Arafat, Yasser, 98
Arar, Maher, 89, 90, 104
Arat-Koç, Sedef, xiii, xv, 66–67, 170
Ardener, Shirley: *Defining Females*, 116
Arendt, Hannah, xvi, 43, 54, 90, 92; *The Origins of Totalitarianism*, xiv–xv
Argentina, middle class in, 156
Aristide, Jean-Bertrand, 148
Armstrong, Jeanette, xii

Armstrong, Sally, 69; *Daughters of Afghanistan*, 129
Asian CritLit, 9
Asper, "Izzy," 60
assimilation, 10, 62, 115
audit academy, 47
authenticity, 116, 122; marketing of, 177
autonomy, Indigenous, 112, 120

Bakic-Hayden, Milica, 155
Balfour, Arthur, 184n3
Balkanism, 155, 161
Balkans, 154–55
Bannerji, Himani, xiii, 6, 41, 48, 49, 50; "Introducing Racism: Notes Towards an Anti-Racist Feminism," 48–49; *Returning the Gaze*, 2, 3
Barthes, Roland, 82n39
Bauman, Zygmunt, 62, 90, 92–93, 94, 103
Beauticians Without Borders, 68
benevolence, 169, 172. *See also* "do-goodism"
Berlant, Lauren, 183
Bernard, Wanda Thomas, xiii
Bhopal (India), 168n63
Bill C-86 (Amendments to the *Immigration and Refugee Protection Act*), 87, 93
Binns, Barbara, xi
BJP (Bharatiya Janata Party), 167n54
Black males, crime and, 61, 63
Black Power movement, 174
Black women, as "welfare queens," 63
Bogo, Didier, 95, 97
Bolivia, 160
Bonnett, Alastair, 156
*Border, The*, 75
bourgeoisie, transnational, 148, 155–60
Brand, Dionne, 49
branding exercises, 46
Brazil, Indigenous politics in, 112
"browning": of spaces, 33; of transnational bourgeoisie, 148
bureaucracy, race and, 87–104
Burma, 178
burqa, 59, 68, 72, 75, 77; as standing for all Afghan women, 66. *See also* veiling
Bush (George W.) Administration, 129–30, 132–33, 138, 140
Butler, Judith: *Precarious Life*, 132–37, 141, 188n34
Byers, Michael, 86n88

Calhoun, Cheshire, 41–42
Calliste, Agnes, xi, 3, 23

Campbell, Maria: *Halfbreed*, 1
Canada: condemnation of by UN, 6; criticism of as white settler society, 1; as partner in occupation of Afghanistan, 8; as peacekeeper, 7–8, 76; as tolerant and multicultural, 76; troops in Afghanistan, 129
Canadian Association of University Teachers (CAUT), 38, 40, 52
Canadian Corrections Association, 26
Canadian Council for Refugees (CCR), 93, 97, 98, 104n5
Canadian national subject, constitution of, 4
Canadian Security Intelligence Service (CSIS), 91, 93–96, 98
capitalism: consumer, 68; resistance to, xv; violence and, 138
capitalist globalism, (geo)political economy of, 147–65
Carmichael, Stokely, 174
Catholic Church, 144n20
centralization, Indigeneity and, 113
Chesler, Phyllis, 142n3; *The New Anti-Semitism*, 129–32, 141
Chief Electoral Officer, 76
child care, 6
child custody rights, 127
child welfare system, 5, 26
Chilean people, 99
China, 162
Choudry, Aziz, xvi, 190n63
Choy, Wayson, xii
"citadelization," 158
"citizen," unpacking of category of, 4
citizenship, 5, 6, 75; equality of, 46; "ethnic," 6; inclusion of people of colour into, 7; liberalization of policies of, 6; market, 46, 48; Muslims and, 7; re-nativizing of, 163; social, 48
*Citizenship Guide*, ix, xvi
civil rights, erosion of, 132
civil rights movement, 46, 47, 138, 174
"clash of civilizations," ix, xiii, 7, 130, 164
class, 3, 4, 32, 111, 150; inequality, 114, 148; nationalist discourses and, 172; race and, 148, 162; racialization of, 3; segregation of, 158–59; whiteness and, 149
class relations, reconfiguration, 149–52
Cloud, Dana, 67
"coalition of the willing," 66
Cold War, 152–54, 161
collective, survival of, 117

collective identity, 119
collective memory, 112
colonialism, 1, 29, 61, 62, 64, 114, 131, 156, 169; gender and, 2, 114–15; legitimization of, 61; Muslim women and, 67; reproduction of, 117; resistance to, xv; settler, 1–2, 4; sexual violence and, 2, 4
coloniality, 8
colonial oppression, 25
colonial tropes, 60
colour: people of, 5, 7, 87; scholars of, 26; women of, 2, 4, 5, 6, 9, 49, 111, 118, 127, 173, 175
colour-blindness: liberal, 147; myth of, 37, 48
colour line, racism based on, 147–65
common sense, Gramscian notion of, 41
communitarianism, 171
concentration camp, 93; security delay as, 93–103
Connor, Helen, 114
conquest of Americas, 135, 138
"contact hypothesis," 181
containment, 76
Contractor, Nazneen, 85n83
convergence: socio-economic, 157; spaces of, 112
Cooke, Miriam, 67
Corntassel, Jeff, 113
corporate concentration, 60
corporate corruption, 138
corporate logic, 46
corporatization of academy, 39
Correctional Service of Canada, 34n6
Corrie, Rachel, 188n30
Coulter, Anne, 142n3
counternarratives, 41
crime, Black males and, 61
criminal justice system, Indigenous women in, 24–26; overrepresentation of Indigenous people in, 26, 30
critical legal theory, 9
critical race feminism, 1–16, 44
critical race scholarship, x–xiii, 131, 173
critical race theory, 9, 11, 135, 148, 169, 173
critical tourism studies, 181
critical whiteness studies, 10–11
crusades, 67
CSIS. See Canadian Security Intelligence Service
Culleton, Beatrice: In Search of April Raintree, 2
cultural capital, denial of, 150

cultural continuity, 113
cultural deficits, 153
cultural difference, 7; veiled Muslim women and, 76
cultural identity, 111
culturalism, 67
cultural practices, Indigenous, 5
culture: death by, 76; death of, 76; disciplining of, 76
culture-talk, xiv

Dabashi, Hamid, 136–37
Death of a Princess, The, 71
decolonization, 24, 27, 111, 116, 119–21
deconstruction, 37
"degenerate" spaces, 28; vs. "respectable" spaces, 29
Dei, George, 23
deliberative democracy, 50
demonic figures, archetypal, 62–63
Department of Immigration, 93
Department of Public Safety and Emergency Preparedness, 101
Department of Public Security, 93
deprivation, economic and moral, 152
Dhruvarajan, Vanaja, xi
difference, naturalization of, 61
Di Nova, Joanne, 185n6
Dirlik, Arif, 162
disabilities, persons with, 43; academic feminism and, 52; decline in representation of, 51; discrimination against, 40; improved conditions for, 46; marginalization of, 37; women with, 127
disciplinary institutions, 45
disciplinary legitimacy, 42
disciplinary power, 47
discipline, 42, 45; punishment and, 45
disciplining, 42; of culture, 76
discrimination, 40, 47; against disabled persons, 40; gender, 114, 120; reverse, 51; systemic, 46
disenfranchisement, political, 150
dispossession, 4, 5, 10
diversity: from equity to, 44–48; gender equity vs., 39; language of, 46; as management, 46; as praxis, 47; in solidarity efforts in Palestine, 172–77
diversity management, 47
diversity-talk, 47
Divine, David, xiii
"do-goodism," 169–84
domestic workers: Black, 3; from Philippines, 6

dominance, as normative frame of reference, 60
Dossa, Shiraz, 75
"double marginal," 118
doubling discourses, 59–79
Drakich, Janice
Dua, Enakshi, xii, xiii, 31, 53
duplicity, 88, 89
Dutrizac, Benoît, 77–78

Eastern Europe: as Other, 152, 154; post-socialist, 152–55
East Germany, 153; "backwardness," 153; unification with West Germany, 153
East/West binary: Europe and, 152–53, 155; rejection of, 138, 139, 141
Ebrahim, Mahejabeen, 53
Ecuador, 160
education, access to, 5, 6, 10
education system, 25; as racist and colonial, 26; as "unrealistic and paternalistic," 26
Egypt: British occupation of, 184n3
Eisenstein, Zillah: Against Empire, 137–41
embodiment, 121
emergency measures, 91
Emes, Claudia, 53
empire, four-stage gendered logic of, 67
employment: access to, 5, 6, 10; roadblocks to, 102
employment equity, 40, 48; opposition to, 50
Employment Equity Act, 55n5
entrepreneurship, micro-business, 68
epistemologies, Indigenous, 121
equity: in academy, 38–40; diversity and, 44–48; employment, 40, 48, 50; gender, 37, 39, 40, 42, 51, 54; gender equity and, 49, 52; as social justice, 45; telling tales about, 40–44
equity fatigue/failure, 46
"equity hires," 29, 30; scholars who benefit from, 31
equity issues, vs. women's issues, 40
equity officers, 31
equity practices, 37
equity praxis, 37
equity-talk, 45; as artful dodging, 48–53; disjuncture between practice and, 44, 48, 52
Eritrean people, 97
essentialism, 120, 121, 173
essentialized identity, 116
ethical tourism, 169; paradoxes of,

177–82. See also socially responsible tourism
Ethiopia, Mengistu regime in, 99
Ethiopian people, 97
"ethnic" citizenship, 6
ethnicism, politics of, 167n54
ethnicity, 13, 111
Eurocentrism, 153, 155
Europeanness, 152
European settlers, 5
European Union (EU), 152, 153, 161
exception, spaces of, 91–93, 95–97
exceptionalism, 61
exclusion, 76, 120, 147, 148, 173
exclusionary discourses, 51
exnomination, 60
exoticism, marketing of, 177
expansion, European, 154–55
experience, as knowledge, 30–33
export-oriented strategies, 157
expulsion, of Muslims, 7

Fahmy, Shahira, 68
fair tourism, 177
"family class," 6
Fanon, Frantz, 62, 135, 184n3
Farley, Anthony, xiii
favelas, in Rio de Janeiro, 178–79
"feminazis," 127
feminism: academic, 52; "alternate," 139; anti-colonial, 3; anti-racist, 2, 8, 48; bureaucratization of, 127; conflict between women and men and, 115; critical race, 9–10; criticism of among Indigenous peoples, 115; disagreements in, 127, 176; exclusionary, 140; as external to Indigenous peoples, 117; hegemonic, 53; "hijacking" of, 138; imperial, 71, 140; Indigenous, 111, 116–22; Indigenous women and, 8, 9, 111–22; institutionalization of, 127; invisibilization within, 48; nationalism and, 111–22; non-white, 49; post-colonial, 111; professionalization of, 127; radical potential, dilution of, 127; and support for invasion of Afghanistan, 129–32; transformational potential, exhausting of, 127; Western, War on Terror and, 127–42; as Western phenomenon, 139; white, 54, 127–42; white women as "real" subject of, 127
Feminist Majority Foundation, 129
feminist politics, death of, 127
feminist praxis, 54

feminist theory, 37, 111
Ferguson, James, 157–58
Fernandez, Sonya, 78
fetish, women of colour as, 3
First Nations, ix; violence against, xiii
First World, vs. Third World, 156
Fiske, John, 60
"folk devils," 62–63, 75
forced marriage, 75
Foreign Domestic Movement Program, 6
forgetting, systematic, 10
Foucault, Michel, 37, 39, 44–45, 94; *Society Must Be Defended*, xvi
fragmentation, economic and cultural, 157–58
Freedom Summer campaign, 174
free trade zones, 162
French–English conflict, 78
Freud, Sigmund, 135
Front National (France), 164

gated communities, 158–59
Gayle, Nogha, xi
*Gazette, The*, 78
gender, 3, 4; colonialism and, 2; discrimination, 114, 118, 120; inequality, 114; nationalist discourses and, 172; nationhood and, 117; race and, in Canadian media, 59–79; race and, in university, 23–34; racialization of, 3; as relational, 75, 111; relations of in pre-colonized vs. colonized societies, 122; as social construction that orders and constrains, 9; subjugation through, 78; War on Terror and, 7; whiteness and, in the academy, 37–55
gender apartheid, 137–41
gender binary, 139
gender domination, 119
gendered hate, 29
gendered violence, 29
gender equity, 37, 39, 40, 42, 51, 54; from equity to, 49, 52
gender oppression, 139–40
gender roles, 119
gentrification, 158, 190n62
geography: feminist, 120; global, 120
George, Pamela, 4, 28–29
Germanness, racialization of, 153
Germany: authoritarianism in, 153; racism in, 153; unification of, 153. *See also* East Germany; West Germany
ghettoes, American, 150
glass ceiling, 40

global: local vs., 112; and local responsibility, 170
global apartheid, 163
global city, 159
global economy, restructuring of, 5
Global Exchange, 180–82, 183
globalism, capitalist, 147–65
globalization, 67; neo-liberal, xv, 147, 148, 155, 161
global power, North-South relations of, 170
"global sisterhood," 140, 176
*Globe and Mail, The*, 177; "Behind the Veil," 68–73; representation of Afghan women in, 68–73
Goldberg, David Theo, xv, 92, 131, 151, 155
Gosine, Andil, xiii
Goven, Suleyman, 94–97, 99, 103
governmentality, 39, 44–45; neo-liberal, 47, 48
Gowehgyuseh, Beverley Jacobs, xiii
Grand Inquisitor, 62–63, 75
Green, Joyce, 53; *Making Space for Indigenous Feminism*, 8
Grewal, Inderpal, 170
group identity, 113

Haiti, 148
Hall, C. Michael, 181
Hall, Stuart, 60–61, 64
Hamidi, Rangina, 72–73
Hamilton, Charles, 174
Hampson, Sarah, 69
"hard" power, 74–75
Harper, Stephen, ix, 130
hate: raced and/or gendered, 29; university resistance as, 29
Haylett, Chris, 152
health, Indigenous women and, 120
hegemonic narratives, privileging of, 41
hegemonic whiteness, 37–39, 43, 49, 50, 51
hegemony, 68; Indigeneity and, 114, 115; patriarchal, deconstruction of, 121; of U.S., 141; in West Germany, 153; white, 169
Henry, Frances, 49
Heron, Barbara, 182
Hérouxville Citizens' Code, 75–76, 79
Hewitt, Sitara, 73
Higgins-Desbiolles, Freya, 180–81
Highway of Tears, 5
hijab, 59, 65, 67, 73, 75; politics of, 76. *See also* veiling

Hirji, Shemina, 76, 79
history, 121; evacuation of, 61; as meta-
narrative, 113
Hollywood films, representations of Muslims in, 64, 65
Holocaust, 62, 131
homogenization, Indigeneity and, 113,
121
homophobia, 32; class and, 152
honour killings, 75–76
hooks, bell: *Ain't I A Woman?*, 54
housing, access to, 10
human condition, universal, 133–34, 176
humanitarian organizations, 170
human rights, 91, 120, 181
human rights law, 46
human rights officers, 31
"human shield" activism. *See* witnessing
activism
Huntington, Samuel, ix, 130, 164
Hurricane Katrina, 147–48, 184
Hussein, Saddam, 141

identity construction, 117
identity politics, Indigeneity and, 114
immigrant communities, "culturalization" of, 6
immigrants: double bind of, 88; people of
colour assumed to be, 87
immigrant women, 6; academic feminism and, 52
immigration, 10; liberalization of policies
of, 6; politics of, 6
*Immigration Act* (1952), 105n12
*Immigration and Refugee Protection Act*:
(1992), 87, 93–94. *See also* Bill C-86
*Immigration Appeal Board Act* (1967),
105n12
immigration law, 91
imperialism, 92, 148, 161, 169; benefits
of, 140; reproduction of, 140–41; resistance to, xv; U.S., 135, 138
imperial precariousness, 132–37
import-substitution, 157
inclusion, in solidarity efforts in Palestine, 172–77
India: elite housing projects in, 159; fundamentalist politics in, 167n54; middle
class in, 160; Union Carbide disaster in,
168n63
Indian women, representations of, 61
Indigeneity: definitions of, 111; external
definitions of, 117, 121; gender, nationalism, and, 112–16; hegemonic defini-

tions and, 114; stories about, 114; transformation of, 112
Indigenism, 112
Indigenous children, 26
Indigenous critical praxis, 121
Indigenous feminism, 111; theoretical
and practical strategies for, 121–22;
towards, 116–21
Indigenous knowledge, 8; creation and
ownership of, 122
Indigenous men, police brutality and, 6
Indigenous peoples, xii, 43, 162; criminal
law sanctions against, 30; decline in
representation of, 51; defining, 113; discrimination against, 40; dispossession
of, ix, 5; employment equity for, 50;
empowerment of, 185n6; as fiscally irresponsible, 5; as "other Others," 37; overrepresentation of in criminal justice
system, 26, 30; physical and cultural
extinction of, 5; white citizens as colonizers of, 4
Indigenous politics, Brazilian, 112
Indigenous scholars, 26; vs. non-Indigenous, 33
"Indigenous way," 114
Indigenous women, 1, 4, 5, 9; academic
feminism and, 52; activism of, 5; agency
of, 120; as "bad mothers," 5; challenges
posed by, 127; in criminal justice system, 24–26; disappearance of, 5; disem-
powerment of, 114; diversity of lives of,
119; feminism and, 8, 9, 111–22; "hidden transcripts" of resistance of, 115;
marginalization of, 114; muting of
voices of, 116; nationalism and, 111–22;
oppression of, 111, 118; as "other Others," 38–39; as passive and subordinate,
115; as role models, 23; theorization of
experience and activism of, 8; in universities, 25–26; violence against, 3–4;
voices and knowledge of, 115
individual, survival of, 117
individualism: of liberalism, 173; self-
interested, 47
inequality, 120, 147; class, 114; gender,
114; material and social, 116; racialized,
141
instrumental rationality, 46, 47
"intellectual atrophy," 90
internationalization, 46
International Labour Organization, 113
International Monetary Fund (IMF), 153,
161

International Women's Peace Service (IWPS), 172–77, 183
internment, role of state in, 10
interracial relations, 173–74
Inuit, ix
Iran, 97, 101
Iraq: destruction of national sovereignty in, 134; invasion of, 64, 128, 185n5
Islam: alleged violence of, 7; demonization of, 139; Europe's relationship with, 67; homosexuality and, 163; as major threat, 163; media portrayal of, 60, 63; misogyny of, 132, 163; as oppressive and patriarchal, 65, 163; Orientalist framing of, 63; political, threat represented by, 63; primitivism of, 131–32; as ultrapatriarchal, 75
Islamists: Nazis and, 130; women's sexuality and, 139
"Islamofascists," 130, 163
Islamophobia, 62–63
Israel, Muslims as enemy of, 130

Jamieson, Paul, 88
JanMohamed, Abdul R., 61
Jean, Michaëlle, 148
Jewish people, hatred of, 131. *See also* anti-Semitism
Jiwani, Yasmin, xi, xiii, xv, 53
Joseph, Galen, 156
journals: academic, 31; peer-reviewed, 31, 33
*jus sanguinis*, 153
justice tourism, 177, 181

Kahf, Mohja, 67
Kamat, Sangeeta, 190n63
Kandahar, 69–73, 85n73
Kanien'kehaka, 27
Kant, Immanuel, 171
Kaplan, Caren, 170
Karim, Karim H., 64
Khadr, Omar, 89, 90, 104
Khan, Shahnaz, 65
Kincaid, Jamaica: "A Small Place," 188n36
King, Anthony, 159
King, William Lyon Mackenzie, ix
Kipling, Rudyard, 61
knowledge: experience as, 30–33; Indigenous, 8, 122; power and, 43
Kobayashi, Audrey, 49, 53
Kovasevic, Natasa, 154
Krishna, Sankaran, 160
Kuokkanen, Rauna, 119

Kurdish people, 94, 95, 97, 103

labour market, as gendered and raced, 3
labour theory, segmented, 3
La Framboise, Donna, 142n3
language, reinvention of, 117
languages, revival of Indigenous, 5
Laouni, Samira, 77–78
Larocque, Emma: "My Hometown Northern Canada South Africa," 2
Latin America, whiteness in, 156
Latin Americans, 97
Latina/o critical theory, 9
Laurence, Bonita, xiii
law: redundancy of, 94; suspension of, 132; without law, 91–92
Leeder, Jessica, 69–72
Le Pen, Jean-Marie, 164
Lerner, Paula, 69
Lévi-Strauss, Claude, 64
Lewis, Bernard, 130
Lewis, David, 105n12
liberalism, 163; constraints of, 169; contractarian, 171, 185n11; deontological, 185n11; fairness and equality and, 171; as hegemonic political outlook, 171; individualism of, 173; left-wing vs. right-wing, 171; paradoxes of, 172; racial, xv, 10, 169, 171–72; racial contract and, 171; racial subordination and, 171; social justice and, 170–72
liberation, Western, 68
Lisle, Debbie, 178, 182
*Little Mosque on the Prairie*, 73–74
Live-in Caregiver Program (LCP), 6
local: flexible conception of, 121; global vs., 112; and global responsibility, 170
Locke, John, 171
Lorde, Audre, 53; *Sister Outsider*, 54
Louw, Eric, 66
"lower races," ix

Macdonald, John A., ix
macroretribalization, 163
Mahrouse, Gada, xv
Malik, Kenan, 165n8
management: diversity, 47; diversity as, 46
managerialism, new, 46
Manji, Irshad, 143n16
Mansour, Asmahan, 75–76
Maori, 114
Marable, Manning, 150
Maracle, Lee, 2

marginalization, 30, 118, 120; of population in North, 150; socio-economic, 148; as tourist attraction, 179; underclass and, 151
market-based logic, individualized, 46
Marx, Karl, 3
Marxism, 3
materialist perspective, 142
matriarchy, 119
Mayer, Lorraine F., 116
Mazrui, Ali, 163
McBratney, John, 61
McClintock, Ann, 61
McGuire, Patricia: First Voices, 8
media, Canadian: corporate concentration and, 60; race and gender in, 59–79
mediation, 3
Meighen, Arthur, ix
men: Afghan compared with U.S., 138; women vs., 37, 115, 119. See also Muslim men
men's rights, 127
merit, in the academy, 47
Métis, ix; women, 1
Mexico, 119; tourism in, 177
Michaels, Eric, 112–13
middle class: in Argentina, 156; Black, 147; desire of to separate masses, 159; in India, 160; in Third World countries, 158; West European norms, 149
Mighty, Joy, 53
Mills, Charles W., xv, 150, 169, 170–72
Minh-ha, Trinh T., 3
"minority" scholars, 31
Mirchandani, Kiran, xiii
misogyny, 129; global, 139; of Muslim men, 7, 131–32, 139
modernity: alternative, 162; capitalist, 149; multiple, 162; telos and status of, 157–58; unconditional membership of working class in, 152
modernization theory, 154, 157; as exclusionary, 158
Mohamud, Suaad, 87–90, 104
Mohanram, Rhadika, 118
Mohanty, Chandra, 61; "Cartographies of Struggle," 118
Mohawk, 27
Monture, Patricia, xi, 3, 4; First Voices, 8
moral-cultural property, 152
morality, 181
Morrison, Toni, 90
motivated ignorance, 41–42
Mujahedin-E-Khalq (MEK), 97–99, 101

multiculturalism, ix, 6, 74, 75, 76, 118, 155, 158, 161, 173; hegemonic discourses of, 152; neo-liberal, 147
Muslim men: confinement of, 75; demonization of, 140; as "Lethal Others," 75; misogyny of, 7, 131–32, 139; racialization of, 139, 140; representations of, 64, 131; as responsible for oppression of women, 73; as terrorists, 61, 75
Muslims: as anti-Semitic, 131; citizenship rights and legal protections of, 7; as common enemy of U.S. and Israel, 130; media portrayal of, 60, 63–64; targeting of figure of, 7; white feminism's war on, 129–32
Muslim women: bodies of, 59; flashpoints about, 75–78; as gendered hypervictims, 66; gender oppression and, 140; homogenization of, 65; imperilment of, 76; oppression of, 130; "over here," 65, 66–73; "over there," 65, 73–75; representations of in Western media, 65–78; "saving" of, 8; status of, 128; tyranny of possession of bodies of, 77; veiled, 64–79; victimhood of, 67; Western feminism and, 137–40
Myrdal, Gunnar, 165n8
mysticism, marketing of, 177

Napope, Shelley, 29
Narayan, Uma, 71, 76
national identity, 75
national imaginary, 76
nationalism: cultural, 167n54; Indigenous women, feminism, and, 111–22; as relational, 111; transnational, 164; white, 164
National Organization of Women, 129
National Post, 60
national security, 91, 132
nation-building, ix
Native Women's Association of Canada (NWAC), 5–6; "Voices of Our Sisters in Spirit," 5
nativism, politics of, 167n54
naturalization, 60
natural resources, 120
Nazis, Islamists and, 130
neo-colonialism, 122; helping as vehicle for, 169
neo-conservatism, 6, 8, 130, 138, 163, 167n54
neo-liberal capitalist globalization, 147–65
neo-liberal governmentality, 47, 48

neo-liberalism, xiii, xv, 6, 138, 149, 150; poverty and, 151; violence and, 7
neo-liberal orthodoxy, 39, 46
neo-liberal restructuring, 127
Nepal, 178
New Orleans, 147–48
"new racial domain," 150
news, "hard": authenticity of, 74
New Zealand, 114
Ng, Roxana, 3, 53
non-governmental organizations (NGOs): ethical tourism, 177–82, 184; peace and development, 169–70
non-Indigenous peoples, Indigenism and, 112
non-racism, 147
non-tenured scholars, vulnerability of, 30
non-white men, 38–39
non-whites, 43; academic feminism and, 52; decline in representation of, 51; discrimination against, 40; employment equity for, 50; improving conditions for, 46; invisibilization of women, 52; as "other Others," 37–39
normativity, white, 55n5
North: global, 150; reconfiguration of, 156; relations of power with South, 170
North Atlantic Treaty Organization (NATO), 153, 161; troops in Afghanistan, 129
Norway, government of, 99
Nyasha, Jodi, xii

Obama, Barack, 147
"old (white) boys club," 31
Omar family, 101–2
oppression, 3, 4; colonial, 25; gender, 139–40; of Indigenous women, 111, 118; of racialized women, 3; university resistance as, 29; Western vs. non-Western understandings of, 121
Orient, feminization of, 64
Orientalism, 60, 63–64, 66, 83n59, 153, 161, 182; feminist perspective on, 77; nesting, 155
orthodoxy, neo-liberal, 39
"other Others," 37–55; women, whiteness, and, 53–54
Other(s): barbaric cultural practices of, ix; colonized, 61, 64; culture of as misogynist, 76; dehumanization of, 132; Eastern Europe as, 152, 154; exotic, 74; good fortune compared with, 181; inferiorization of, 61; intimacy with, 176;

Islamic, 128–29; Islamist, vs. white Western Self, 10; management of racial, 4; other, 37–55; physical exploitation of, 62; the poor as, 150; racialized, 61, 91; Self vs., 133–37; stigmatized and valorized, 60; whiteness and, 10; "wholesome amalgamation of," ix
Ouimet, Émilie, 78

pacifism, 130
Paglia, Camille, 142n3
Palestine: alliances between Jewish women and women from, 190n60; cinema in, 136–37; Israeli occupation of, xii, 185n5, 190n60; IWPS in, 169, 172–77; solidarity efforts in, 172–77; suicide bombers from, 136; women in, 172–77
Palestinian people, 97; dehumanization of, 136; media treatment of, 136; support of intellectuals for, 130
pan-Europeanism, 163
Parvez, Aqsa, 76, 79
Patai, Daphne, 142n3
patriarchy: of Afghan and U.S. men, 138; colonialism and, 119; Taliban and, 71; violence and, 138; "women's issues" and, 121
Peace Brigades International, 187n28
peacekeeping, 7; myth of, 8
Pearson, Patricia, 60
pedagogy, anti-racism, 170, 182–84
peer-review process, 32, 33
Pennee, Donna, 58n66
personhood, white men and, 171
Philippines, domestic workers from, 6
Philips, M. Nourbese, 49
philosophical approach, 134–35, 142
PKK (Partiya Karkerên Kurdistan; Kurdistan Workers' Party), 94–97, 99
"place," theorization of, 2 , 121
PLO (Palestine Liberation Organization), 96, 98–99; Fateh faction, 98
police, 92; brutality of, 6
political correctness, 130
political identity, 112; Indigenous, 113–14; as marker of inclusion and exclusion, 113
Pon, Gordon, xiii
Popular Front for the Liberation of Palestine (PFLP), 103
population, surplus, 150
populism, right-wing, 167n54
post-colonialism, 156; feminism and, 111, 118

post-9/11 environment, xii, xiii
post-socialism, Eastern Europe and, 152–55
poverty, 114, 120; culturalization and racialization of, 150; individualization and pathologization of, 151; as moral issue, 151; as tourist attraction, 179
power: colonial forms of, 4; complexity of, 34; corporate, 5; dynamics of, 10; fixed relations of, 61; Indigenous scholars and, 28; knowledge and, 43; productive and disciplinary aspects of, 45; racialized, 15, 169–70, 172, 178, 182–84; racialized representations and, 62; "soft" vs. "hard," 74–75, 85n77; technologies of, 45; of whiteness, 60, 156
power relations: asymmetrical, 112, 175, 181; in geopolitical order, 134; North-South, 181; obscuring of, 182; shifting of, 169
Prashad, Vijay, 167n54
precariousness: imperial, 132–37; of whiteness, 155
preservation, ethic and logic of, 112
prison-industrial complex, 147, 150
prison system, 5, 150; abolition of, 150; as saturating social and institutional life, 42; vs. universities, 25, 34n6
property rights, 114; white men and, 171
prostitution, 4
psychoanalysis, 37, 62, 134–35, 142
public spaces, colonization of, 158

Quebec: cultural sovereignty, 77; dual colonization of, 78; election (2007), 76
queer women, challenges posed by, 127
Quranic law, 75

race, 3, 4; as "floating signifier," 62; bureaucracy and, 87–104; class and, 148, 162; gender and, in Canadian media, 59–79; gender and, in university, 23–34; grammar of, 61, 64; language of, 7; liberalism and, 182–84; nationalist discourses and, 172; as social construction that orders and constrains, 9; spaces of exception and, 90–93
RACE (Researchers and Academics of Colour for Equality/Equity), x–xi, 3, 23; conferences, x–xvi, 169, 184, 185n5; founding of, x
Race and Gender Teaching and Advocacy Group (RAGTAG), x–xi, 23, 24
race/culture debates, xiii

race knowledge, organization of, 24
race-making, xvi, 10
"race question," 10
"Race, Racism, and Empire: Reflections on Canada," xii
racial imaginaries, xvi
racialization, 5; in academy, 26; anti-immigrant and anti-refugee animosities and, 7; citizenship and, 89; of class, 3; of gender, 3; gender equality and, 39; Germanness and, 153; of Indigenous peoples, 5; of Indigenous women, 24; of Muslim men, 139, 140; of Muslim women, 140; of prison system, 150; in setter society, 5; Third World and, 162; underclass and, 150; of women, 3, 11, 27, 173, 176–77; working class and, 150
racialized Canadians, 87
racialized groups, 60–61, 104, 147, 151–53, 170
racialized hate, 29
racialized inequality, 141
racialized injustice, 170
racialized Other, 61, 91
racialized power, 15, 170, 172, 178, 182–84; social justice and, 169
racialized privilege, 169
racialized relations, 9
racialized scholars, 29–32; communities of, 30
racialized social arrangements, 30
racialized spaces, as degenerate, 28
racialized violence, 26, 30
racial liberalism, xv, 10, 169, 171–72
racial politics, 5
racial prejudice, 89
racial profiling, 7
"racial state," xvii
racial supremacy, 162
racial thinking, xvi, 91, 162; privileging of, 60
racial violence, xii, xiii, xiv; gendered, 4
racism, xiv–xvii; in academy, 31; "active," 61; anti-Arab, 162–64; anti-Muslim, 162–64; attitude towards Eastern Europe as, 154; banality of, 50, 51; Black domestic workers and, 3; blatant, 170, 171; in Canada, xiii, xiv, 2; class and, 152; colonial, xvii; colour line and, 147–65; common sense, 50; equity policies and, 31; free rein for, 99; in Germany, 153; "homey," 52; imperialism and, xvi; inferential forms of, 61; internalized, 1; lack of social legitimacy, 147,

150; logics of, 62; media representations and, 61; new forms of, 147, 161, 162; overt, 98, 150, 152; relegation of to past, 139; reproduction of, 51; resistance to, xv; return to, 149; routinization of, 92; of security process, 100; social legitimacy of, 150; state, xvi; systemic, 1; Western historical exemplars of, 62

Rae, Robert, 95–96

Ramirez, Reyna, 115, 117

Ramos, Alcita, 112

rape, threat of, 77–78

Rawls, John: marginalization of racial inequality by, 171; *A Theory of Justice*, 171

Raymond, Eliza Marguerite, 181

"Rayyan" (*Little Mosque on the Prairie*), 73–74

Razack, Narda, xii, xiii

Razack, Sherene, xi, xii, xiii, xiv, 4, 23, 28–29, 66, 75, 170; *Casting Out*, xvii, 7

reality tourism, 177, 180–82

reciprocity, 181

refugees: asylum for, 94; Convention, 100; inadmissibility of, 93; inherent duplicity of, 88; people of colour assumed to be, 87; police and, 92; security delayed, 89–90; travel documents and, 87; as "unthinkable," 93

relocalization, 112

remilitarization, 138

re-nationalization of borders, 163

re-nativizing of citizenship, 163

resentment, 29–30

"reserve," 28

residential schools, 4, 25–26

"respectable" spaces, 28; vs. "degenerate" spaces, 29

reverse discrimination, 51

rights: discourse of, 112; international, 114; men's, 127; suspension of, 91; women's, 114, 128. See also human rights

Rio de Janeiro, *favelas* in, 178–79

Rose, Bird, 115, 117

Routledge, Paul, 112

Roy, Arundhati, 160

Royal Commission on Equity in Employment, 40

Russo, Ann, 66

Said, Edward, 184n3; *Covering Islam*, 63–64, 83n59; feminist critiques of, 64

St. Denis, Verna, 8

Sami women, 119

Saney, Isaac, xiii

Saskatoon, 29

Schick, Carol, xiv, 53

Schochet, Gordon, 113–14

Scott, James, 115

Scott, Joan, 66, 76

secessionist vs. unifying logic, 160

Secor, Anna, 91–92

security certificates, 7

"security delayed" individuals, 89–90

Security Intelligence Review Committee (SIRC), 95

segregation, Jim Crow, 150

Self, Other vs., 133–37

self-determination, Indigenous, 112, 114–17, 119, 121

self-governance, 44

self-ownership, white men and, 171

self-purification, 62

self-reflexivity, 45

self-regulation, 44

sensationalism, 72

September 11 attacks, 64, 75, 128, 162–64; as anti-Semitic, 130; injury done to U.S. by, 132–37; root causes of, 132; sexual motive for, 139; War on Terror and, 4–9

settler colonialism, 1–2, 4; resistance to, 2

sexism, 117–18, 121, 140; class and, 152; reproduction of, 51

sexual discourses, 77

sexuality, 64; control of, 138; hatred of, 139; nationalist discourses and, 172

sexual orientation, 32

sexual terrorism, 137–41

sexual(ized) violence, 2, 4, 72, 77–78

Shah, opposition to, 97

Shah, Saira: *Beneath the Veil*, 71

Shaheen, Jack, 64

sharia law, 75, 76, 78

Sharma, Nandita, 52

Sheth, Falguni, 53

Shohat, Ella, 170

Sikhs, 97

Silvera, Makeda, 49; *Silenced*, 3

Silverblatt, Irene, 91

"sincere fictions," 41

Singh, Nikhil Pal, 162

Skeggs, Beverley, 151–52

slave, construct of, 61–63

slave men, 63

slavery, American, 62, 138, 150

slave women, 63

slum tourism, 178–79

Smith, Andrea, 170, 184, 185n6
Smith, Graham Hingangaroa, xii
Smith, Linda Tuhiwai, 115
Smith, Malinda S., xvi
Smolash, Wendy Naava, 77
social collectivities, 46
social contract theory, 185n11
social death, 101
social exclusion, 44
social insurance numbers, 100–101
socialism, Eastern European, 153
*Social Justice*, xii
social justice, xiii, 38, 43, 46, 47; actors, 170; consumer-based approaches to, 169; equity as, 45; interventions, 169–84; liberalism and, 170–72; pedagogical implications, 182–84
socially responsible tourism, 169–84; paradoxes of, 177–82
social programs, 5; decimation of, 127
social relations, asymmetrical, 112
social services: access to, 6; roadblocks to, 102
social welfare, 46; exclusion from, 150
"sociogeny," 135
sociology, 27
"soft power," 74–75
solidarity: configurations of, 112; in Palestine, 172–77
Somalia, refugees from, 88
South: global, 150, 178, 180; reconfiguration of, 156; relations of power with North, 170
South Africa, 181; poverty in, 147
South America: elite in, 156; political projects in, 160
sovereignty, 4, 5; territorial, 120
Soviet Union, 153
Spivak, Gayatri, 184n3
Srivastava, Aruna, xi
Srivastava, Sarita, 53
"starlight tours," 29
state: responses of to injustices, 170; role of in internment and abandonment, 10
"state, racial," xvii
"state racism," xvi
Statistics Canada, 39
stereotypes, 74, 90, 181
stigmatization, 76, 147, 148
storytelling: disruptive, 41; about equity, 42–44, 49; hegemonic, 51; political theory of, 40–42; as profoundly political act, 43
"stroll," 28, 29

subjectification, women's, 64
subjectivity, whiteness as, 10
subordination, 62, 122, 148; cultural, 120; epistemic, 54; racial, 171
Summers, Lawrence, 145n25
surveillance, of Muslims, 7
sweatshops, 162
Switzerland, 168n64

Taliban, 65, 66, 68, 129, 141; patriarchy of, 71
Tamils, 97
Task Force on Federally Sentenced Women, 24–25; *Creating Choices*, 24
Tator, Carol, 49
tax cuts, 138
Taysup, Eva, 29
telling tales: about equity, 42–44, 49; political theory of, 40–42
tenure, 29, 32
terrorism, 93, 96–97, 128–29, 130; sexual, 137–41
Third World, 154; bourgeoisie in, 155–60; erosion of, 157, 167n54; First World vs., 156; imports and exports in, 157; middle class in, 158; poor people, drug testing and, 162; racialized and gendered construct of men in, 139; racialization and, 162; women in, 118, 140
Thobani, Sunera, xi, xii, 23, 53, 66, 170, 176, 188n34; *Exalted Subjects*, xvii, 4
*Time*, 150
Todd, Sharon, 78
Todorova, Maria, 155
tolerance, ix, 7, 76
*Toronto Star*, 88
tourism: ethical, 169, 177–82; exploitative nature of, 177, 178; socially responsible, 169–84
Tourism Concern, 178–80, 183; *Ethical Travel Guide*, 179, 180
traditional practices, Indigenous, 5, 116, 120; codification and enforcement of, 113–14; integration into politics, 113–14
transnational alliances, 7
transnational bourgeoisie, 148, 155–60
transnational solidarity activism, 169–84
Trask, Haunani Kay, 170
tribal critical theory, 9
Tsing, Anna, 114
tsunami, Asian, 178
Tunisia, Palestinian community in, 98–99
Turkey, 167n54
Turton, David, 112

ture of, 52; destabilization of, 149–60; gender and, in the academy, 37–55; hegemonic, 37–39, 43, 49, 50, 51; as "normal," 24; Other and, 10; power of, 60, 156; precariousness of, 155; privileges of, 140, 161; racialized privilege of, 169; recentring of, 184; restabilizing of, 161–65; secessionist vs. unifying logic of, 160; social justice and, 172; as subjectivity, 10; transnational, 155–60; universal, decline of, 149–52; women, other Others, and, 53

white spaces: as respectable, 28; universities as, 30

white supremacy, 149, 155, 184

white women: as imperial subjects, 137; reproduction of racial supremacy by, 140

Wieviorka, Michel, 62

Williams, Patricia J., 44, 48

Wilson, William J., 151

Wing, Adrienne, 170

witch, figure of, 62–63

witnessing activism, 172, 175

women: Afghan, 65, 66–73; bodies of, centrality of, 59; of colour, 2, 4, 5, 6, 9, 49, 111, 118, 127, 173, 175; disabled, 52, 127; discrimination against, 40; from global South, 175; immigrant, 6, 52; improving conditions for, 46; Indigenous, ix, 4, 5, 9, 23, 24–26, 111–22, 127; men vs., 37, 115, 119; Muslim, 8; as Other, 37; as perpetual victims, 127; privileging of white, 37, 49, 52; queer, 127; racialized, 15, 170, 172, 178,

182–84; representation of, 63; rights of, ix, 114, 128; sexism and, 117–18; social category of, 37, 49, 52; Third World, 118, 173; under-represented, 173, 175, 176; victimization of, 120; violence against, ix, 117, 129; visibility of, 128; Western vs. non-Western understandings of agency and oppression of, 121; whiteness, other Others, and, 53

"women first," 38; as self-fulfilling prophecy, 37

women's issues, 114, 116, 119, 120–21; vs. equity issues, 40

women's movement, 46, 138

women's studies, 127

workforce, restructuring of as low-wage economy, 6, 127

working class: racialization of, 150; in U.K., 150, 151–52; in U.S., 150; white, 151–52, 161

World Bank, 113

Wuthnow, Julie, 116

xenophobia, 155

Yeğenoğlu, Meyda, 71, 77

Young, Marion, 173

Yugoslavia, disintegration of, 155

Yuval-Davis, Nira, 64

Zapotec people, 119

"Zapatourists," 177

Zine, Jasmin, 67, 75–76

Zionism, 130–31

Žižek, Slavoj, 68